MW00586969

Building Material

Building Material

The Memoir of a Park Avenue Doorman

Stephen Bruno

HARPER

An Imprint of HarperCollins*Publishers*

HarperCollins books may be purchased for educational, business, or sales promotional use. For information, please email the Special Markets Department at SPsales@harpercollins.com.

FIRST EDITION

Designed by Bonni Leon-Berman
Illustation by Oliva McGiff

Library of Congress Cataloging-in-Publication Data

Names: Bruno, Stephen, author.
Title: Building material: the memoir of a Park Avenue doorman / Stephen Bruno.
Description: First Harper hardcover edition. | New York: Harper | HarperCollins
    Publishers, [2024]
Identifiers: LCCN 2024010571 (print) | LCCN 2024010572 (ebook) |
    ISBN 9780063347557 (print) | ISBN 9780063347571 (ebook)
Subjects: LCSH: Bruno, Stephen (New York City doorman)—Biography. |
    Doorkeepers—New York (State)—New York City.
Classification: LCC HD8039.B896 U56 2024 (print) | LCC HD8039.B896 (ebook) |
    DDC 647.9/2092 [B]—dc23/eng/20240708
LC record available at https://lccn.loc.gov/2024010571
LC ebook record available at https://lccn.loc.gov/2024010572

24 25 26 27 28 LBC 5 4 3 2 1

To Grace Isabel Bruno.
Mami.

CONTENTS

viii   Contents

Building Material

PROLOGUE

When the old lady stepped in front of the building, I knew she'd be trouble.

I wasn't afraid of her coming into the lobby: I had locked the front door the last time I stepped inside. Of course I'd locked the door. *Always keep the door locked* was the first thing I had learned at the building, just like it was the first thing I learned at the last building, the one where I'd received my start as a doorman. Once the front door of a Park Avenue building is locked, it's closed on you with conviction. You'll need a chainsaw and a clear schedule to get inside. I wasn't worried about the old lady trespassing into the building.

She wasn't impressed by the mammoth prewar residence before her anyway. She was too busy rocking back and forth and wailing beneath the front door's canopy. It was a warm summer day, and she'd gotten comfortable in the shade. A hardhat walked past, and she quieted herself. Pulling up beside him, she moaned and peered into his eyes pleadingly. Then, as if realizing she hadn't done enough, she raised the shard of cardboard up to her nose. There was a series of stringy, uneven letters scrawled on it. *Much too small,* I thought. *The sign and the words are too small!* And the way she moved, like a buoy in a storm, wasn't conducive to reading.

She couldn't speak English and hoped the sign did the talking for her, but she wasn't doing herself any favors: keeping it raised at her nose made her look like a stranger outside your window. Every pedestrian walked past the old lady without acknowledging her pleas for help. Hers was a plight for the ages.

This lady doesn't know what she's doing, I concluded. She could've learned a thing or two from Junior, a seasoned panhandler in the neighborhood. He passed by the front entrance every morning and waved at us, shouting, "Start o' my shift!" I always laughed because it was the start of my shift too, so it was like we worked together, though in different departments. While I stood on my feet inside the building, Junior sat at the corner with a giant cardboard sign that had enough space for two requests: one for money and another for a blessing. Holding that sign, Junior made himself a couple hundred dollars every shift and would later tell me about it with a smile. The operative word is "corner"—Junior panhandled at the corner, never in front of the building. The lady was doing it wrong: you can't panhandle in front of a Park Avenue building. Everybody knows that.

She'd been in front of the building for ten minutes, an eternity's worth of loitering by Park Avenue standards. Like I said: she wasn't a threat to building security, but she had to go. It wasn't *her*; it was the sight of her, her look: the pained eyes; the black headscarf knotted beneath her chin; quivering lips that plunged at the corners; the hunched resolve to stay under the canopy. I cringed at the thought of the residents seeing any of that. And that's what happens, you know? After a while, you start thinking for the residents. You consider their needs and defend their sensibilities. The old lady couldn't possibly know that, of course, but it didn't matter. Part of the job is shielding tenants from ugliness and sorrow they haven't bought into.

I turned around to see what George, my shift partner, was doing. My eyes landed on his sweeping, white mustache. George was deep in the mail room, his short arms lurching forward with every envelope and magazine that he plunged into a mail slot. It was my least favorite part of the shift, the hour I covered the passenger elevator *and* the front door while George sorted the mail. Always around eleven in the morning and right before lunch so I could earn my meal in full. Sometimes he lost himself flipping through the tenants' magazines, and that's when it would happen: the building would swamp me with deliveries, calls from residents, and rides on the elevator, and all at the same time.

The old lady in front of the building was already the biggest curveball, but then she caught sight of an oncoming businesswoman. The suit and leather briefcase must have signaled to her to work harder because she raised the sign past her nose until it covered her eyes. The businesswoman rumbled past the old lady, whose cardboard face pivoted along with her. Nothing. No dollars or cents from the businesswoman. A stampede of tourists rolled past. None of them spared any change. I heard the old lady's cries from behind the cardboard as the barrage of chunky cameras and hiking backpacks marched past her on all sides. None of them stopped to read the sign: I COME USA FROM VENEZUELA. CHILDREN IN QUEENS. PLEASE HELP!

I let out a long sigh. The old lady had become a situation. She was no Junior, whom I'd toss from the front door in a second flat. The old lady from Venezuela was different. She had come here to survive, not to live, and was barely succeeding at the former. I watched as she lowered the cardboard sign in front of a man in dark sunglasses and read her words aloud for him. He wore a fleece vest with his firm's logo embroidered on the chest. You never saw a finance bro with a faster side-step. My heart plummeted for her.

Building protocols started filing through my mind. *Wait four rings before picking up the building phone. Always say Mr. or Miss or Mrs., except with Mr. O'Leary, who says we should call him Ben, but call him Mr. O'Leary anyway because you're his doorman, not his friend. Never compliment the ladies on their appearance. Always compliment Mrs. Lottman on her appearance. She's widowed, for Chrissake. Keep the sidewalk in front of the door clear of everything and everyone.* The old lady couldn't know that the narrow strip of sidewalk extending from the door to the street, all of it shaded by the green canopy, was sacred. It's the first thing residents see when they walk through the door I open for them. It's their launching pad. I sympathized—she was an old lady crying—and it was my job to make her disappear.

Oh shit, I thought, watching the old lady get swarmed by tourists. *Ms. Hastings is out right now!* Ms. Hastings was a fifty-something real estate heiress who had bought two apartments on the thirteenth floor and connected to have ample space for herself and a female Chihuahua named Geraldo. A native New Yorker, Hastings was a tough, no-nonsense lady who was as quick to laugh as she was to snap at a doorman who let his guard down.

I glanced at my watch. Ms. Hastings had been gone for two hours. She was a homebody and would return soon. The old lady was still outside, wailing and spinning around with her cardboard face like a drunk ballerina. If Ms. Hastings saw her production, I'd get blamed for it. That's when I realized the quickest way to get rid of the old lady was to give her what she wanted, a few dollars. Hopefully, she'd take the cash and move on to the next block.

"Stepping out for some air!" I shouted over my shoulder at George. I turned the lock and shoved the door forward, allowing the sounds of car horns, jackhammers, and pedestrians to tumble over me.

Wallet in hand, I stepped onto the pavement and into the path of a stalled Jan Hastings. She had stopped in front of the building to observe the old lady.

"Hi, Ms. Hastings!" I shouted, backpedaling into the building. I offered a broad smile, but she wasn't looking. Her attention was on the panhandler. "Beautiful day, eh, Ms. Hastings?" I was prepared to go through every line in the doorman script to get her attention off the old lady.

Still glaring at the crying woman, Ms. Hastings angled her head my way. "Why do we have *that* . . ." she said, pointing at the old woman, ". . . happening . . . *here*?"

Good question, I thought. "I—I don't know, ma'am," I stammered.

I rounded myself back into form quickly. "Ms. Hastings, how was your appointment with your hairdresser?" I asked, venturing out onto the sidewalk with her. The only thing better than knowing the doorman script is knowing the residents' script: when they talk about themselves, they forget everyone else.

"Ohhh, it was fine," she cooed. She smiled. It was working! "They never get my hair exactly the way I want it, but we all need our jobs, right?" Ms. Hastings didn't have a job, at least not one I could detect, but she'd forgotten the old lady!

"You're right about that, ma'am!" She walked into the building and stopped right inside the doorway. She turned around slowly and, in a grave voice, the elderly Ms. Hastings said, "We don't need that here, Stephen." She waggled a shaky finger at the old Venezuelan woman. "Not *here*."

"Okay, Ms. Hastings," I said with a nod of my head.

She continued into the lobby where she was met by a smiling George, who had finished the mail just in time to cover me on the elevator. *I* was the shift's elevator operator, but *he* led Jan Hastings into the elevator and ran her up to the thirteenth floor. No words had to be exchanged for him to understand: when I remained at the door silent and unmoving as the crowd swelled outside, I became the doorman.

1

SUMMER GUY

I was leaving a doorman job for a *girl*. That's how Mami saw it. She'd been holding back for weeks, but with the summer nearing a close, the disgust and tired rage sealed in her face finally burst through. *"Por una muchacha!"* she shouted one evening from the kitchen. She caught me by surprise. I'd been watching sports highlights in the living room. She'd been cooking. I peeked into the kitchen. Standing rigidly at the stove, Mami seethed over a crackling pan like her eyes were heating the oil instead of the flame.

Mami broke her own spell at the pan and began shuffling around in the kitchen, from the fridge to the cabinets and back to the stove, in complete silence. I wasn't going in there. It wasn't the threat of her *chancleta* keeping me at bay. She hadn't struck me with a *chancleta* in many years. It was her time-forged disapproval, which my little Ecuadorian mother wielded like an axe, holding me back.

A good job fixes things—everybody in the Bronx knows that—and it's a doorman job we're talking about. My mother figured that I'd see its value despite it being a temporary summer gig. I'd understand that it was like making an investment in myself and that I'd simply wait until I received a call about a full-time spot. Then I'd slide in like the last six years of my life hadn't happened. I'd wear the doorman jacket and forget how my academic trajectory as a gifted student had nose-dived into obscurity.

Mami looked at life through a wide lens, the way adults often do: the doorman job was my big break, a hard shove into a second life. Reason

being, you could have flunked every test in high school and been issued a restraining order from a diploma, and it didn't matter, you *still*
received a custom-tailored uniform, full medical benefits, a 401k, and
membership into one of the most powerful unions in the nation. The
doorman job is the ultimate consolation prize, and after seeing me fail at
school the way I did, with gusto, Mami became an ardent spokeswoman
of the doorman job.

There's no online application or job fair for a position as a doorman.
Doormen aren't going to parties saying, "Hey, my building's hiring!"
It's one of those primo New York City jobs that's hard to find and rarely
discussed. When you knock into a doorman job, you hold on tight, *real*
tight.

I'd been hired as summer relief at a cooperative on Park Avenue,
which meant that some weeks I worked as a doorman and other weeks
I worked as a maintenance man. Some weeks I worked a mixed bag
of both jobs. It all depended on who was out on vacation. I hope you
appreciate these details because Mami rarely did. She was just happy
knowing I had my foot in the door: I would be the logical choice for a
future opening at the building. That's all she cared about. She expected
me to do my part too, to cozy up to full-time doormen and residents, because she was thinking about a locker and a union card with my name on
it. Summer guys are often the most ambitious, hardest workers because
they want to make an impression and prove they're building material.
They don't want to be considered "summer guys" forever; they want to
eventually become full-time guys who work all year and get envelopes
filled with money at Christmastime. In the fall, a summer guy calls the
building to say hello; his voice keeps his name alive. He knows he won't
see his name etched on a damned thing if it doesn't remain in a super's
mind first. Mami believed that if I left, I'd be forgotten at the building.

A summer guy doesn't walk away; that's not the move. Except for me.
For me, it was *absolutely* the move. Never once during that summer did I
think about a locker with my name on it. I had no aspirations of becoming a doorman with union-guaranteed job security and a great benefits

package. Instead, I envisioned reuniting with my girlfriend that fall. She was in Minnesota, where I'd lived for a year and a half before coming back home to work as a doorman. I was moving back to Minnesota, this time for good.

Look, I didn't hate the doorman job. It had its benefits. A fat check every Friday was nice, no doubt: I had previously worked as a kitchen expeditor at a restaurant and was sent home whenever the kitchen was slow, which was often; they cut me the most anemic paychecks. Doorman work was easier on the body than that of other jobs too, especially when I worked in the lobby. While some men poured cement and others welded iron forty stories high, I spent most of my time in the building doing small tasks. Stuff like bringing a newspaper to a tenant's door or calling a tenant to announce a newly arrived guest. These weren't demanding work conditions. It wasn't that kind of job.

It was the kind of job that made you wear a uniform and demanded you look presentable. A suit, a shirt, and a bow tie. It was my favorite benefit of the doorman job. I didn't appreciate it immediately. Mr. Evans, the building superintendent at 905 Park Avenue, had made it clear when we first met that I would be hired only if I made some changes. It was my first interview, and Mr. Evans sat across from me with his hair parted and his clothes fitted. He looked like a recruiting officer for Park Avenue. I'd just finished doing eighteen months in the Midwest and had no handle on presentation: I sat across from Mr. Evans with a chubby face, wildly gelled hair, and a too-big shirt. Mr. Evans motioned to my goatee and said it would have to go. That, and the long hair. I sighed and said, "Yeah, sure." Even then, at twenty-two years of age, I knew it was a reasonable demand. It was a job on Park Avenue, and Mr. Evans didn't intend to hire a kid who looked like the least important member of an irrelevant boy band. Seemingly satisfied, Mr. Evans asked if I was interested in the job. I said I was, and that was it; I became a summertime doorman in May 2004.

So I would wear crisp white shirts in the lobby. A black bow tie too. It was one of those one-second bow ties, the ones with the clasp in the back, but who cares, it was a bow tie! I started using cologne, good cologne, not just Old Spice cologne. The good stuff. I kept a bottle in my locker and sprayed myself with it even when I worked maintenance in the basement. I started getting a haircut every two weeks and a shape-up every week, just so my lines looked clean. That was the job. The job had me working hard to maintain a clean, refined appearance, and after a while, I liked looking that way, like I cared. It stuck.

The job would've been harder to leave if not for one of its core values: *Don't get close.* I learned all about it on my first day at the building, and it made me feel the chill of adulthood.

I was ridiculously early to my first shift at 905 Park Avenue. I had wanted to make a good impression on my first day, so I ironed my clothes the night before. I also set an alarm to wake up, another alarm reminding me to start getting dressed, and another to leave the apartment. I lived in Kingsbridge Heights after all, and that's not a stone's throw. I didn't expect a train to be rumbling into the train station when I arrived at the platform. It was the downtown express, and it got me to the Upper East Side an hour early.

After getting dressed, I stood in the basement's locker room with my suit jacket draped over a chair and thought, *Well damn, what do I do now?* I had more downtime than I could handle. The locker room's silence. It was a brushed, vapid sound of nothingness, and it was swirling all around me. You should've seen the lockers. They appeared to me like an assembly of coffins looking down on me. I couldn't take it anymore. I rose to my feet and walked out of the locker room. I was twenty-two years old—I was there for paychecks, not to think about my mortality.

I walked out to find someone to talk to. Luckily, a few of the building's men had gathered in the clearing where all the basement's hallways converged.

Luis wasted no time making me feel at home. "Your first shift, huh?" he asked, removing his jacket. He was a middle-aged Puerto Rican and one of those building veterans who took many liberties, like leaving his post before he was relieved from it, which was exactly what he'd just done. "You nervous?" he asked.

I was Luis's relief. He must have heard I was in the building an hour early and expected it to translate into his leaving before the official end of his shift. When it didn't happen, he'd walked off the lobby floor. It was a veteran move, one I wouldn't imagine attempting as the new guy.

Mr. Evans was in the ring. So was Luka the handyman, and two porters, more commonly known as "maintenance men" to the rest of the world. I worried the most about Mr. Evans. He'd been friendly during the interview but hadn't acknowledged me when I'd walked into their circle, not even with a nod or a hello.

It felt like a test, like I wasn't worthy of the building's clip-on bow tie yet. I got anxious, and my mind scrambled. I had to prove that I belonged there and that I was the right man for the job! I thought back to things I'd said immediately after being hired and picked a line I was certain would resonate.

"I'm a friendly guy," I started, "and I'm eager to show it!" I smiled. Showed all my teeth too.

I heard the words leave my mouth. The first thing I thought was, *That sounded really stupid.*

My response, if it could be called that, had not answered Luis's question—You nervous?—in the slightest. It had missed the mark completely. First, his question was of the yes-or-no variety; it wasn't a fill-in-the-blank question with room for self-expression. Then there's my tone: I had responded with a bluster of mistimed, uninformed eagerness. These men had families, funerals to attend, and driveways— their words carried the weight of experience, and sounded full and heavy as a result. Everything I said sounded like a pack of Skittles spilling on the floor.

I looked to the men to convince me otherwise.

At first, no one said anything. Luis took a breath through his nose and nodded his head slowly, as if trying to believe he'd heard me say something else. Luka raised his eyebrows in disbelief and shook his head as the porters shuffled uneasily.

Mr. Evans, who was leaning against the wall with his arms crossed, sighed and nodded at Luka, who stood beside him with his fists at his waist like a failed superhero. All eyes turned to Luka, and that's when I knew I was about to get schooled.

Luka took a step in my direction and into the huddle. There was no confusing who his words would address—I was standing directly across from him. "The residents are not your friends," he began, his deep, guttural voice doing nothing to soften the magnitude of truth. "They don't care about you. To them, you're just another guy working in the building. A new guy, a *summer* guy, in fact, which is worse. Don't think you were hired to be a friend. You weren't. Don't speak to them unless they speak to you, and even then, don't go thinking you're a friend. You're a doorman, nothing more. Don't get close."

I had yet to work my first shift on Park Avenue and had already heard the least motivational speech of my life, had been rejected by residents I'd never met, and had been scolded by a second-in-command I'd never spoken to before. If there's a record for Most Discouraging First Day at a New Job, send this page to Guinness.

The biggest problem was that everything Luka said was so obviously true. It was like one of those oft-overlooked items that were once considered innovative, like ziplock bags or toilet seats. They're items you use often, that you can't do without, but now you're staring at them in your hands wondering how you didn't think of them first. Somehow, as smart as you are, as creative as you've always been, you didn't think of Thousand Island dressing first. You had the ketchup, you had the mayo, but you never thought of mixing the two. That's how I felt, like a dumbass who should've arrived at Thousand Island sauce. *Of course* the residents didn't care about me! They were affluent, busy people—Mr. Evans had told me all about them at the first interview—and they didn't need me for a friend.

One reason you don't come to work an hour early is to keep the co-worker you're relieving from raising his expectations. You relieve a guy an hour early, and it's over; he expects to work seven-hour shifts for the rest of his doorman career.

Another reason? So you don't hear someone utter words that strike at your heart and nature. Don't get close to people? Park Avenue was out of its mind. I couldn't help trying to endear myself to people. I don't think I was weird about it, but I've always extended myself in the hopes of making connections with others. Did it always happen? No. It happened often enough, however, that I knew how great it felt to be close to people and hoped to experience it more and more. I was twenty-two years old when I discovered a superior class of people I wasn't allowed to get close to. The notion felt like a deep violation of *my* core values, and it dampened my spirits.

I was more embarrassed by my ignorance, however. When you get caught with your pants down like I had, you pull them up in a hurry and act like everything's gravy.

I worked the hell out of that first week at the building. Said hello and smiled and waved at residents like the giant Mickey Mouse patrolling Times Square, all the while reconciling myself with a few ice-cold realities: the building didn't want *me*; it wanted forty hours a week and if I played my cards right, there might be a locker in it for me.

2

EMPTY SPACES

As a child, I never dreamed about being a doorman. What kid does? Kids dream about being a baseball player, an astronaut, or a president. I briefly dreamed about being an archaeologist like Indiana Jones, because in his movies, he sailed high above the bad guys' reach with priceless artifacts in his arms. Sometimes he dropped the treasure in favor of a beautiful woman without the slightest dip in his flight.

I never found the time to come up with a replacement dream. There was a young life to derail and questionable choices to make. My decision to walk away from the doorman job in 2004 wasn't the first time I'd known my mother's disapproval. Mami had been angry since 1998.

That year, I started my career in romance with a record of 0 and 1. That's not an extended history, but my first foray into love was an abysmal failure, like opening a BBQ joint in Mecca during Ramadan. It was the kind of first attempt that shouldn't see a second.

My father didn't know anything about my girlfriend Camila at first. My high school was in Hell's Kitchen on Manhattan's West Side, an easy forty minutes on the train—sometimes more—from home. I was ambivalent about the school at first. Those kids looked nothing like me: they were skaters, hip-hop kids in baggy jeans, and punk kids with spiked hair and clothing pins everywhere. There were straight kids, gay kids, and kids in between. There were kids who looked clean and sleek, and other kids who looked like they slept under bridges at night. I'd never met White kids before then—in Hell's Kitchen I met a hundred of them in a week. I met a hundred Asian kids that week too. I'd previously only seen them running in and out of Chinese restaurants in my neighborhood, but we'd never talked. In Hell's Kitchen, we talked. They were fans of the Knicks and Yankees like me. The school was a steaming cauldron of personality and identity, and I became determined to attach myself to some of it, or let some attach to me. The day Camila said "Yes, I'll be your girlfriend" was the day I became someone.

It's not like I could've run to my father and said, "Hey, Pa! I'm dating the prettiest girl in school!" Those weren't the kinds of things you said in Papi's domain. He ran a Pentecostal household, which meant that when you weren't leaping around the church, you were making sure you avoided anything that could send you to hell. That second look at a woman could send you to hell. If a woman wore pants, she went to hell. If she wore a tight skirt, she went to hell too, so I rarely had the occasion to look twice, thank God. High school was far enough away that I thought I could enjoy two realities: one where I was the clean, dutiful kid my parents needed me to be, and one where I could dabble in the fascinations of my heart.

Reverend Cesar Rosado was our pastor and Papi had been a conduit for his messages: that God was always on patrol; that despite the AIDS and crack epidemics of the eighties leading to his record-breaking kill numbers, he was more than happy to make room in the Lake of Fire for another disobedient Bronx kid in the nineties. During the week, Mami and Papi refreshed my memory: "Not everyone is going to heaven. *Lots* of people are going to hell. Make sure you're not one of them." You think I was going to tell Papi that I attributed some of Camila's beauty to her body and the way she filled her jeans? Get serious.

After years of having my ears scalded by my parents' fiery messaging, I knew I couldn't tell them about Camila. She was Catholic, and a nonpracticing one at that. She said as much while we lapped at ice-cream cones in Central Park after school one day. She said, "My mom's Catholic, so I guess I'm Catholic too?" She wasn't even sure about it, which was crazy to me. How could you not know when you're going to hell?

After a decade of listening to Reverend Rosado's sermons, I came to understand that hellfire burned hotter and longer depending on the sinner. The hell hierarchy went something like this: everyone outside our church was going to hell, obviously, as entry-level sinners; gays went to extra-hot hell; Democrats went to lava-hot hell, where their thirst was quenched with gasoline. Bill Clinton? Forget it. That dude shared a private, supermax hell with Monica Lewinsky, while Hillary watched them burn from her own private hell. All the other sinners had their own cells where they passed little, burning notes to one another, but not Clinton and Lewinsky, which sounded, appropriately, like the name of a law firm, since lawyers went to hell too.

Rosado went through the entire hell lineup almost every Sunday, and Catholics were on it, though usually at the bottom, where you placed the least-threatening sinners, sinners like homeless people, lesbians, and those annoying squeegee guys at exit ramps. They were entry-level sinners and not worth spending much time talking about. So when Camila disclosed that she was *maybe* Catholic, I looked away and thought, *Okay, maybe that's information I won't share with Mami and Papi.*

My relationship with my not-Christian girlfriend was doomed to be discovered. There was no way around it. We lived in an apartment building in the Bronx, not a house in Westchester, where you could sneak in through the back door or climb up a drainpipe the way you saw in movies. There was one door, the one that said 5A on it, and it opened into the dining room; with a family as large as mine, there was always someone at the table with a clear view of the door.

You want to know what my family saw every time I came home late? They saw me walk in with hickeys on my neck. My hair gave me away too. It had been customary for me to spend ten minutes every morning styling my hair with gel, which could then maintain its hold and shine for the rest of the day. After Camila became my after-school program, however, I started coming home with the disheveled hair of forest children. Mami knew something was going on.

At some point, I asked for my own phone line, you know, so I could

stay in touch with "friends," and that was it, my parents took a stand.
Mami reminded me about hell's vacancies. Papi yelled. He yelled and he
pointed and he commanded me to stop bringing demons into his home.
Papi cocked his head at an angle and shot crazy eyes at me from behind
his thick lenses. "You're being used by the Devil!" he shouted one night.

Pastor Rosado taught his congregation how to deal with the Devil.
First, you had to identify his favorite helpers: women; women's insatia-
ble appetite for gossip; women's proclivity for showing skin; and the
television, which often depicted women.

He called the television the Devil's box. The Spanish-speaking pastor
yelled it from the pulpit: "Take *esa caja del Diablo* out of your home, or he'll
leave demons in your home with every program you watch. Then your
entire family will be possessed!" My mother normally listened to every
word of Rosado's sermons then raised her hands and said "Amen, amen,"
but when the television was mentioned, she'd go rigid and maintain a
tight gaze forward. She had her own little television in the kitchen, and
she liked that little television.

Always sitting next to her was my father, who rarely noticed the
attacks on home appliances because the only thing stronger than his
loyalty to Rosado was his inability to stay fully awake during Rosado's
sermons.

Papi wasn't napping the first time the words "Devil's box" rang out
of Rosado's mouth. I was sitting in the front with all my buddies—
Rosado had recently ordered all the church's youth to sit in the first
row where he could see them better—and turned to look for my father
in the crowd. I spotted him easily. His was the long forehead with the
rising hairline. His eyes were red and irritated, as if he'd just awakened. "Remove the Devil's box and you're removing his power from
your home!" Rosado continued. My father strained his eyes, brought his
hands together in a bouncy touch-clap, and, nodding delicately, uttered
words of praise from memory: *"Aleluya. Gloria a Dios. Santo."* Rosado
continued hammering home the Satan's box theme, and I watched in
horror as my father squinted and repeated the words, "Yes, it's Satan's

box! Be gone, Satan's box!" Papi was wide awake now, his brow tensed behind his thick glasses.

Days later, I came home to a bare wall. Our family TV was gone. "It's Satan's box," my father said with the finality of a courtroom gavel. He slurped from the coffee cup in his hand. "And we're going to obey the servant of the Lord." The servant of the Lord, Rosado, was separating me from my father.

The Devil's box had joined me to him. It had helped me imagine my father as a boy, then known as Bobby, a little Nuyorican kid who ran across Brooklyn streets during the fifties to get home to watch his favorite programs. He'd laugh at funny men like the Three Stooges and Jerry Lewis, despite knowing the dangers that awaited him at home. He'd be beaten that night. Or the next. He never knew when. His parents weren't there to protect him: his father was away on another womanizing expedition, and his mother was shoved deep in the bowels of a mental institution. The city must have determined that having two absentee parents wasn't tragic enough for little Bobby—it embedded him in his godmother's home, and she made him pay for intruding on her life.

Many times, Bobby would be tied to a radiator like a dog. "They'd leave me tied up for hours," Papi once said while turning the steering wheel. "I'd cry, and they'd tell me to shut up, so I did. I was afraid. I'd stay quiet for a long time, but they'd walk by me and leave me tied to that radiator for hours." One time, his godmother hit him over the head with a hammer. Blood streaked across the bathtub's white porcelain like red lightning. My father would tell me the stories decades later. We'd be on a car ride, just me and him, and I'd tug on the seat belt, feeling too small. That's when Papi would talk about the funny men on the black-and-white TV screens who helped him endure that Brooklyn apartment.

These stories seemed to weaken my father when he told them to me; he sounded like paper crinkling. I'd stare at my father's face from the passenger seat and absorb it all.

My father rarely talked to me about the nebulous younger version of himself named Bobby, especially about his darkest moments. But when he did, I sat in the front seat showing the same reverence I showed at church. Bobby was a boy who might have enjoyed watching Saturday-morning cartoons with me. I used to imagine him sitting on the couch next to me. He was next to me in the front seat decades later, but he was Papi by then.

I went on fewer car rides with my father when I became a teenager, but I never stopped trying to bridge the gap between us by watching what little Bobby used to watch. Lots of black-and-white shows like the *Honeymooners.* Teenage Bobby liked Westerns, so I watched those too—lots of Clint Eastwood riding into towns on a horse. The television became the best way to connect with my father.

Papi was a self-employed copier technician and the family's bread-winner. You want to know how much copier technicians made during the eighties and nineties? Not a lot, and Papi had a hard enough time stretching his dollars; with the family growing the way it was, there seemed to always be another baby on the way. He made it a point to buy the family a dessert every night, however. It didn't matter what we had had for dinner, if it was steak or a meager plate of eggs over rice—there would be cake or a box of donuts in the fridge that evening. Bobby didn't have many desserts, so Papi made sure *his* family had dessert every night. Papi stretched his dollars to the max too when they covered a Sharp TV set. We'd only owned ugly TV sets with hangers for antennas before then. The day it arrived, I drew near the big cardboard box, saw the foam corners and the sleek blackness inside, and thought it was the most beautiful thing. Our first modern television! Cartoons, movies, and Bobby's favorite TV shows were all better on the Sharp TV.

But when Rosado preached about the Devil's box again, the Sharp television went into the garbage (where the Devil belonged). Months later, my father heard some rock and roll on the radio—the music Bobby used to like—and he stopped feeling so obedient. One day the door swung open and my father rumbled in, cradling a giant Devil's box. He placed it on the dining room table and stared at it intensely as he removed his leather flatcap. "I saw it in the garbage," he explained. "People throw these things away the moment something goes wrong, and half the time it's just a blown fuse."

I didn't understand what was happening. It was Satan's box, resurrected. The next day, he pushed that TV set in front of the cleared white wall that had previously been covered by the Sharp television. It was wonderful. We all got back to watching TV shows and movies, and I got back to connecting with Bobby.

Weeks later, Rosado preached about the Devil's box again. And Papi came home and threw out the Devil's box again.

We continued this way for a decade: I'd come home to long-forgotten swaths of wall and learn the TV's brand name had gone once more from "Sony" to "Satan"; months later, he'd pull another TV from the trash pile and fix it on the dining room table, then slide it in front of the vacant space in the living room. But soon, the box would be gone, and leave me staring at an empty space in front of the wall.

Through the television, Papi had introduced me to sitcoms, classic cinema, and spaghetti Westerns. It was everything—his heart—and it had always been on full display on the face of the Devil's box. Rosado, the servant of the Lord, needed only to point and shout, and my father would make the box disappear again and again.

When Papi found out I was dating a nonbeliever, he moved quickly, taking my phone away first and then the Devil's box. He took Mami's little Devil's box too. I never watched hers—it was definitely the big one in the living room turning me into a pervert—but the possibility existed that I'd get a peek of the voluptuous weather ladies on the Spanish-speaking channels, so Mami's little TV had to go. A woman was involved in my sins, after all, and all televisions show half-naked women, especially the ones speaking Spanish.

I came home from school early a few days after the latest of Rosado's Devil's box sermons. I walked in blustery and tall. "Hey, Mami!" I yelled as I made my way into my bedroom. "What's for dinner?" There were no hickeys on my neck. No disheveled hair. Camila's mother had picked her up at school and taken her straight to Westchester for the weekend, freeing me up for a sinless afternoon. The innocence made me feel light on my feet. My only worry was homework.

Mami didn't answer, but I thought nothing of it and stepped farther into the room. I remember passing by the light switch and not flipping it on because the room was bright from all the afternoon sunlight splashing in. The sunlight sliding into my room that spring day came clean and easy.

I noticed as soon as I entered my bedroom. *Where is my red toolbox?* I thought. It was supposed to be on top of the bookshelf. Papi had given me the toolbox so I could store my favorite comic books there. It kept them safe and dry. It had been *just* the right size for my comic books too. Any narrower and it would've squeezed my comic books and put a curve in them. If you opened it looking for a screwdriver, you got a stack of Spider-Man or Superman or Batman comics instead. The red toolbox was gone, leaving a space on my bookshelf as barren and disturbing as a smile missing a front tooth.

I was ten when Papi took me to the newspaper stand to buy my first Superman comic book. He patted the comic book, still wrapped in its clear plastic cover, with all five fingertips and said, "*This* is Kal-El, the Son of Krypton," with wide-eyed sternness. "Here on earth, we know him as Superman." Apparently, he was not a superhero to be trifled with.

Comic books had been another love of Papi's, so he knew what he was doing: if his oldest son was to start a comic book collection, he should begin with Superman, the strongest superhero. If Superman is who *he* had started with, Superman is who his son would start with.

During our trips to the newspaper stand, Papi eventually swung me from DC to Marvel so that I would become acquainted with heroes and villains from both universes. The more their worlds became mine, the more they mattered to me. I learned their motives and fears, I rooted for some and wished doom on others. Sometimes, they fell in love, and when they did, it manifested from one panel to the next. I spent years wishing I could dive into every other panel in the comic books I stowed away in the red toolbox my father gave me.

That afternoon, the red toolbox wasn't where I had left it last, where I always left it: on top of the bookshelf. Seeing that empty space was unnatural, even in daylight. It was like walking toward my favorite tree and finding gutted earth. I ran out of the bedroom, shot through the hallway, and turned into the kitchen. "Mami, where is my toolbox with all my comics?"

Mami was stirring food at the stove. There was an empty space above her head too. Over her shoulder, the shelf in the window previously occupied by her small TV was empty, allowing an unusually wider block of light into the kitchen. It was an unnatural sight. Mami said one word. "Papi." She continued stirring the rice and shook her head. "The pastor said we had to take the Devil out of our homes. Papi felt the Devil was in your comic books too."

The last thing I expected when I brought my clean conscience home that spring day was for the top of the bookshelf to be as empty as the walls in the living room and the window shelf in the kitchen. The always-fascinating worlds inside the red toolbox were gone. Papi had shared his love for comics with me the way he'd shared his love for film and television, then he took it all away. The day Papi took away my comic books, he stole away my desire to be close to him too.

With the phone, the television, and now my comic books gone, there weren't any more happy things left for my dad to take from me. He couldn't take Camila away—she was at school, where he couldn't reach her—so I weathered my parents' campaign of re-spiritualization with contentment.

I still had Camila, didn't I? I'd tell her about all the empty spaces at home, and she'd say awww and hug me, and everything would immediately be okay. But then Camila's mother found the binder where Camila had been collecting my letters.

It was a binder that shouldn't have existed. I'd asked Camila to throw away my letters after reading them; I'd told her to flush them down the toilet if she had to, ensuring she got rid of every sheet. Why was I so adamant that she eliminate all traces of my writing? you ask. Because I had written about having sex with her in vibrant detail and didn't want any of that information being discovered. Camila's mother hated me. I knew if she got her hands on one of those letters and read my account of her daughter in various stages of sexual activity, she'd declare war on me.

Camila had filed away my letters like bank statements. She'd compiled them, even used a hole puncher on the plain, white pages so that she could flip through my letters like a book. No words were lost, no racy thoughts discarded. A sweet and stupid idea. One Saturday, Camila disappeared without explanation from her apartment in White Plains, neglecting to tell her mother she'd be spending the day with me in Manhattan. Her mom went looking for clues.

The best place to look for clues is a Trapper Keeper, of course. The ones with the colorful designs and the Velcro flap and the shiny plastic cover. Camila's mother ripped open the binder and read each and every letter. With just a few flips of paper, she discovered that her daughter had not only lost her virginity to me but had lost it many times over. I was sixteen years old and had now incurred the wrath of three parents. It's an impressive feat, don't get me wrong, but it was tough to celebrate with a storm approaching.

I'd met Camila's mother once, after Camila suggested I join the two of them as they shopped for clothes on Madison Avenue. It didn't go well. Camila tried syncing us in conversation, but her mother refused to make eye contact with me, opting instead to paw at clothes on the racks. As Camila seesawed between the two of us, I knew I stood no chance. And judging by the way she later scowled her way to the register, I never did.

They lived on the Upper East Side. *They* were Puerto Rican and a quarter Spanish, like from Spain, so *they* were special. Me? I'm a Latin kid from the Bronx, yo. That's just bodegas and big families.

Camila's mother was furious after reading my letters. The first thing she did was pull Camila out of our school. I used to walk the hallways with Camila, feeling like I was strolling through my kingdom. That was over. I never held Camila's hand at school again. Next, her mom went on the offensive—she sent copies of the letters to my parents. That's really bad, I know, but hold on, it gets worse. Not satisfied with the damage my letters would certainly cause me at home, she flipped through the pages in search of more useful information and stumbled upon the most jarring tonal shift in the history of sex letters: my church's address.

It was the most ridiculous thing to include in my notes, true, but while contemplating the wetness of sex with Camila and the impracticality of doing it on the floor, I reflected on playing congas at church on Sundays, and how a holy day was sandwiched between the days we fornicated. It got me thinking about possible solutions, like maybe we'd push all the sex to Monday and leave Friday for just talking. We wouldn't even hold hands because once together, our hands always got sticky and for us, any kind of stickiness, even glazed-donut stickiness, was a trigger for sex. No holding hands, just talking. And while I figured out a more sustainable solution, maybe my girlfriend should start coming to church? Here's the address.

My girlfriend never visited my church, but my letters did.

In the span of a week, my parents and my family, my pastor and *his* family, knew everything: they discovered my fondness for going down on Camila and even read my thoughts on the taste and the sticky warmth of the affair. They were informed about my plans to move in with her after graduation. They learned the range of my voice through my letters. On some pages I ached and on others I burned. Every page was branded with my conviction.

The discovery of my premarital sex life was viewed as an unpardonable assault on the church's health and God's hegemony on the Bruno household. You might not have guessed it. To be clear, my church didn't frown on sex. In fact, our pastor encouraged it and was concerned when it *didn't* happen, like the time Pastor Rosado wagged his index finger across the congregation and said, "The Lord is telling me that there's a man here who's not fulfilling his duties at home. Men must sleep with their wives!" I was fourteen years old and nodding like an amused sage who slept with his wife all the time. "And the Lord is telling me that if he doesn't come to the altar for prayer, he's going to become a faggot!" It took Miguel, the church's janitor, a while to reach the pulpit—senior citizens tend to move slower than younger, more virile folks—but he eventually did and repented of his sin, subsequently avoiding his assigned homosexuality from God.

Sex was a God-approved, God-sanctioned act. I learned that at a young age. Here's another thing I learned at a young age: sex is for married folks, not a teenager itching to skip the line.

Rosado didn't receive a sudden alert from God in my case. He found out all about me through my letters, and since he couldn't read, write, or speak English, which was an accomplishment after living in the States for three decades, his sons translated and read the letters to him. I was sixteen and suddenly in print, in audiobook, and widely distributed in two languages.

Rosado wasn't a literary critic. He didn't waste time unspooling his thoughts, then knitting elaborate responses with them. No. Rosado was raised chopping sugar cane in Puerto Rico. When he met with me and my father, he delivered his feedback raw and straight up. Sitting behind his desk in his dimly lit, low-ceilinged office, he said I would be punished for my sins. He was blunt and precise, like a weather report.

He sentenced me to a year of *disciplina*. That may not sound so bad to you, but to a kid whose entire life was defined by the church, a year of *disciplina* was a death sentence: I couldn't participate in church activities, I was ousted from the band—no congas for me—and I couldn't sit in the front row with my buddies anymore; I had to sit in the back with other convicted sinners, most of whom were in their twenties!

Everyone notices. Everyone talks. It's a stain that remains beyond a year and sticks, so you start running in your mind first. You imagine yourself running as fast as you can, as far as you can, until no one can see you anymore, and maybe someday, if you get lucky, you eventually run away for real.

My profoundly sinful relationship with Camila represented a star-tling failure on my father's record. His job had been to protect our home from dangers both foreign and domestic, but when considering the contents of my letters, and the nights I'd arrived home late with the hickeys on my neck, it was clear he'd lost control of the home front a long time ago. There was yelling. I didn't listen. I was too busy brac-ing for his choice of punishment. What would he take away now? He'd become unpredictable when doling out punishments and had learned to strike where it hurt the most, the way only the most renowned strong-men do. You see him holding pliers and you think, *Oh, the home repairs he promised.* But he's staring at your fingernails.

When he was done yelling, he issued his most successful, ingenious, and painful punishment: he quarantined me in the living room; I was banned from sleeping in the same bedroom with my brothers. Con-demning me to the living room was punishment for me and protection for them. It was a stunningly brilliant move. With nothing material left to take from me, he ripped away my status as beloved, heroic big brother to the little ones and replaced it with the thorny crown of stigma. I don't remember how many months I slept alone in the living room, looking at a painting of a Victorian woman Papi had found in the trash and hung on the wall. I can tell you that the blur of nights I spent as the monster in the living room, all under the wordless gaze of the pasty Victorian woman, while the wooden floors creaked and the garbage trucks made their rounds through the neighborhood, changed me.

One night during my first week of quarantine, Mami stopped at the wide entrance overlooking the living room, as I lay staring at the woman on the wall. "How could you write those things?" she shrieked at me. I hated seeing Mami in that state, vacillating between breathless shock and disbelief. I had put her there, helplessly seeking answers at the top step of the sunken living room. My eyes remained on the Vic-torian lady on the wall. When Mami realized that I had no answers to offer, she stormed off. It was the first time my mother had ever asked about my love life. It was the last time too.

My school life did little to provide relief from the onslaught at home. Before leaving, Camila had fostered a strange symbiotic relationship with the gang members at school. Her beauty, curves, and sweet, bubbly personality had earned her their reverence and shielded me behind a stalemate I was unaware of: she allowed them to watch her frolicking through the hallways, and they refrained from pounding me into the concrete.

The gangbangers at school were already on edge when Camila was pulled out of school. The Bloods had recently arrived from California and were slashing faces like they were being paid commission. It was in the papers and everything. The streets were electric with fear. Members of Zulu Nation, the Ñetas, and the Latin Kings begrudgingly agreed to a truce and together guarded against the Bloods. With Camila gone, and the specter of the Bloods lurking around the corner, I must have looked like target practice.

They slammed me against the hallway lockers one day and rummaged through my pockets as I remained pressed against the wall like a picture frame. Dissatisfied with my pen and a wilted pack of Winterfresh gum, one of the boys wound up to take a swing. I prepared for the end. That's when a security guard rushed in and shouted, "Hey, get off him!" and made the boys scatter. I'd been left alone and unaffiliated, with only a hefty bookbag covering my back. To them, I was light work.

The walk from my school to the train station usually took seven minutes. It was a little less than a half-mile walk. But when the Gangbanger Alliance started meeting at every corner along my path, I had to come up with new routes to the train station. I'd do figure eights around the neighborhood or duck my way into stores before running into Central Park and continuing to the East Side. It was all so exhausting. All of it. I had hoped to remain in the crawl space of grief over losing my girlfriend and stay there awhile, never being bothered by anything else, but was instead being chased by a swirl of menacing faces at church, at home, and now at school. The threat of physical harm in Hell's Kitchen overwhelmed me, and after a month of devising creative, elaborate ways to survive the .3-mile walk to the train station, I dejectedly asked my father to transfer me to another school. I knew exactly what I was doing: I'd been attending a magnet school with students coming from all over the city, not just the surrounding neighborhood. I didn't care. Nothing mattered enough for me to continue fighting.

With no one else to write to, I began writing letters to myself. My journal earned its creases during this time, when it spent hours splayed open as my pen roped words describing my young, plundered life.

My first shot at love was an unmitigated disaster. My mother had seen her firstborn go from a highly favored boy who sat with the pastor's sons in the church's front row to sitting in the back with Lazy Eye Benny, who carried a knife, and Chino, who wore driving gloves indoors despite not owning a car. For me, there was a noticeable drop in the quality of banter, but not just in the back row with Lazy Eye Benny. At home too. Mami lowered her eyes around me for years.

Mami didn't raise her eyes to see me in the light of hope until years later, when the doorman job rolled around. She wasn't looking for a devout son or a promising gifted student anymore. She just wanted me to have a consistent paycheck, medical benefits, and a locker with my name on it. There was hope in all that. I saw it too. But then she heard me talking about giving up that job, a *good* job, over *another* girl. She wasn't about to let me throw my life away again, not without a fight.

Mami got to stalking the apartment's hallways muttering prayers under her breath. It was her modus operandi: when things weren't going her way, she called the Big Guy, the El Shaddai Abba Father, to intercede and make things right. She knew she needed all the help she could get. The back-row banishment and the surrender of my magnet school enrollment hadn't been the end of it. There had been another catastrophe after the Sex Letters of 1998. It came three years later, in 2001, and it was the disaster that closed the book on me. After that one, Mami knew only a doorman job could save me.

3

MARTIN LUTHER KING, *GOOD*; MALCOLM X, *BAD*

Mami never saw my collapse coming. The only thing I did better than church was school, and it made sense. I was a child of God, and children of God excelled at whatever they put their minds to. You never met a student with more promise.

Our dining room was the apartment's Grand Central; we couldn't get to another room without passing through it. When it wasn't hosting meals, it served as a study hall where I did homework under my father's supervision. With the conviction of a tenured professor, Papi looked over my shoulders as I wrote sentences and pored over textbooks. He was invested in every sense: Papi had enrolled me in Christian private schools since kindergarten; he paid for the schools to maintain their workload and high standards. I responded by maintaining high marks. I was always on the high honor roll, not just the honor roll where all the average kids went. Papi beamed when he read my report cards. Teachers constantly praised me over my classroom behavior, my classwork, and the way I aced pop quizzes. Papi read their comments the same way he read the Sunday newspaper, with pleasure and coffee. He'd hold my report card up to his face, and I'd see his eyes get even smaller behind the thick lens of his glasses. His mustache crinkled as he said, "Oh wow." Back then, laying As and Bs at my father's feet was a delight and easy to accomplish. I simply stayed planted at the dinner table doing homework and the high marks kept rolling in. I could never have imagined my collapse either.

Papi had always worked hard to cover private school tuition on his income, but when his family became a *really* big one, having four boys enrolled in private school proved a bridge too far. I was in the sixth grade when Papi was forced to do the unimaginable: enroll me and my little brothers in the local public school.

The day Papi walked us to P.S. 246, he made sure the school knew I was special. He hadn't worked as hard as he had, spent as much money as he had, for a bunch of administrative assistants not to know that. I stood beside him as he told the lady behind the tall counter, "My son doesn't belong in a regular class with regular kids. He has received a high-quality, private-school education. He should be in a class with gifted students like him." Standing next to him, I watched as Papi showed them my report card and waited. I was ushered into an exclusive class for gifted students moments later.

My father began fading away after my transfer to P.S. 246 and gradually stopped showing interest in my studies. It was not immediate. He initially asked how I was doing at school, I'd say I was doing okay, and he'd nod and say good. By the time I'd earned a spot in a middle school for gifted Bronx students, however, he'd checked out. He wasn't impressed when I brought home copies of the *New York Times* to read. Reading the *Times* felt like the most adult thing to do—I'd even learned to fold it, then fold it again, in such a way that only the article I was reading showed—and I read it at the dinner table so Papi could see, but he didn't care. One time, Papi took me to the emergency room for an ingrown toenail that got infected. I brought a book to read. Alex Haley's *Autobiography of Malcolm X*. I knew what I was doing. He'd taught me "Martin Luther King, *good*; Malcolm X, *bad*"—and I sat in the emergency room holding the book to my face so that the giant white X on the book's black cover was as conspicuous as possible. There was no reaction from Papi, not a word or a slap. He didn't care anymore. Papi worked hard to keep the lights on, the fridge full, and the demons at bay, but when he waved goodbye in the principal's office on my first day at P.S. 246, he checked out of his role in my schooling. It seemed that at eleven years of age, I had grown old enough to look after it myself.

Papi could always be counted on for a ride. He drove me to DeWitt Clinton High School, the school I'd transferred to after my stint at the Hell's Kitchen high school where I'd met Camila. Within walking distance of our apartment, the school was far removed from its glory days as a prestigious all-boys school, but just like P.S. 246, it dedicated a floor to a selective honors program. After a conversation and a look at my school records, the school's honors program accepted me on the spot. Despite being exposed as a fornicator, a double banishment to my church's back row and my apartment's living room, and placement at the top of the Gangbanger Hit List in Hell's Kitchen, I could still move the needle in any academic setting. Seeing I had made inroads in the latest honors program, Papi waved and said goodbye again.

I eventually spoke to a guidance counselor at Clinton. He was old, balding, and the only guidance counselor in a giant room filled with empty desks. He expressed awe at the number of credits I'd accumulated in my two and a half years of high school thus far. "They were running you into the ground with all those classes!" he said while rubbing his temple. He said that after the spring semester, I'd be within three credits of graduating. Why not take a math class during the summer session and be done with it? He tossed his glasses on the manila folder holding my entire academic life. "Who could say they finished high school in three years?" He was the only guidance counselor in the room, so I couldn't ask for a second opinion. The old man sat behind his desk smiling broadly.

I ventured a smile. It was a wildly unexpected opportunity—going to college a year earlier than planned—and it was a shot to exchange the narrative I saw being rolled out about me for one I liked, the one with the crown of accomplishment being returned to my head. Announcing the leap to college is universally accepted as a win. It was also an escape. Camila, my love, was long gone. Her mother had enrolled her in a boarding school far upstate where she'd embraced her fate and forgotten about me. I had seemingly become a prisoner myself, in Papi's living room, or in the back row at Rosado's church. I convinced myself

I should go to college right after the summer math class. In a matter of months, I would escape my wretched life in the Bronx, where I had a bed and never paid rent and always ate my mother's savory cooking. I was closing in on my seventeenth year of life without knowing how good I had it.

I eventually chose a private college in Nyack, a town a short ride north of the city. I figured it would help matters if the college was Christian. It didn't. My parents immediately said no. It wasn't even a discussion. Straight up *no*. Papi said no because—well, who knows—maybe there were demons on the bus that took people there from the city. Or maybe there were demons on the Major Deegan Expressway. The bus made a stop in Hunts Point, where the prostitutes stood around all day, after all. Mami said no too, but she seemed more thoughtful. Maybe she saw it in my eyes, that I had gone full kamikaze, that my reasons for going to Nyack weren't to change my life, but to change my feelings. I had no plan by then, no idea of a life trajectory, and no outlet to a dream. All I wanted was to feel better. I wanted to be far from Rosado shouting about hell, far from my parents' disapproval, and far from a life where things kept getting taken from me, and I was willing to load up on loans and credit cards to do it. The college asked me to declare a major. I couldn't think of one. Then I chose Business Management because businesses made money, and making money sounded like fun.

I went on a campaign of behavioral terror at home. I yelled, bullied my little brothers, and said curse words. Mami waved her hand at me one day and told my father, "Just let him go." When my father signed the papers allowing me to attend college as a seventeen-year-old, I calmed down. I assured him that I'd get better, that I'd change. I'd go from a spiritual delinquent to a well-behaved Christian again, don't worry. I was so certain I'd get good grades since I was a smart kid and school was easy for smart kids. Papi gave me his boar-bristle hairbrush (he said it was a good brush) and his Seiko watch (he said I should have a watch) and said goodbye again.

I was on Nyack College's campus by August of that year. I felt like a lion unleashed, and without purpose or direction, that's exactly how I behaved, like a wild animal. I was a blip on Nyack College's radar two years later after starting a fraternity, which was itself a violation: the college had a no-fraternities-allowed policy.

I had named the fraternity the Shepherdhood as a mocking tribute to the often-unnamed but dependable transients who make appearances in the Bible. I called myself Oracle Shepherd since I was consulted before any moves were made. I approved only those actions that broke rules. We stood for all things culturally backward, sideways, and taboo: we skipped chapel, were openly and gratuitously profane, and snuck girls into our rooms at all times of the night. Eventually, I wanted more. I wanted the Shepherdhood to be the top power on campus. The best way to accomplish that was to unseat the group holding all the power and celebrity, the elite upperclassmen living in Griswold Cottage, the little white house on campus.

When considering a strategy for the Siege of Griswold Cottage, I landed on the Plagues of Egypt, God's campaign of natural disasters rolled out upon Egypt. The problem with the Plagues of Egypt is that they're nearly impossible to duplicate when you're not a deity. We could donate blood for years and still never accumulate enough to turn the Hudson River red. And none of my guys had any special weather-modifying abilities, so deadly hailstorms were out of the question. The Plagues of Egypt were not a sound military strategy, not en masse, but one or two could be managed. I started with the plagues of locusts.

Hours before the Siege of Griswold Cottage began, I drove to the nearby pet shop and purchased a thousand crickets. That night, the most agile and hostile of the guys—the appropriately named Violent

Shepherd—climbed through an unlocked window at Griswold and released the crickets into the darkness. He ran back to our waiting car shouting, "That's it! War has begun!" The next day we attacked with everything we had. As the upperclassmen frantically cupped handfuls of crickets out their cottage windows, water balloons filled with hot sauce began flying in. Water guns shooting mustard-infused water soon followed. I really hoped the hot sauce and mustard might re-create the plague of boils on the upperclassmen's skin, but I never received a confirmation. I didn't have time to stop and ask.

Griswold Cottage was surrounded by freshmen and me, their sophomore leader. Girls from nearby Christie Hall were perched at their windows and, oohing and ahhing, pointing incredulously at the mayhem we had created. I opened the last remaining window as another guy, Chico Shepherd, threw a small, shiny bag into the room. It exploded, releasing thick smoke that set off the fire alarm. Several fire trucks soon arrived. It was a beautiful sight. The resulting chaos led to multiple classes being canceled that day. It should've caused me to reflect, maybe put the brakes on myself, but that was maturity for another day, for another person. I was in a wondrous free fall by then.

A week after the siege, a friend walked into my dorm room to inform me that the police were investigating the cause of the fire alarms and had been looking for me for days.

Ten minutes later, I walked through the security office's door, to everyone's surprise. The head of campus security, a security guard, and a Nyack police officer stared at me with their mouths open as I stood at the door. Behind them on a cork board were student photos—presumably fellow delinquents—arranged in the shape of a triangle. It was their watch list. Way at the top of the triangle, above every other problem student, sat my photo. I almost cried. I hadn't accomplished anything in a long time. Your boy was at the top of the mountain!

I was handcuffed and arrested. I know how it sounds, like a dip in the story, but I was having the time of my life! Hours later, I sat cuffed to a bench in the South Nyack Police Station, basking in dissident glory. When my frat buddies brought me food from McDonald's, I reached through the jail cell's bars to grab hold of the bag and said nothing; my martyrdom spoke for itself. I was eventually charged with disorderly conduct after one of the upperclassmen had identified me as the one who'd tossed the smoke bomb into the cottage. I was annoyed. They had the wrong guy! I almost said it too, almost said, "Hey, Officer, it wasn't me; it was Chico." Then I remembered I wasn't exactly an innocent bystander myself. I kept my mouth shut. I was rewarded for my devotion to the Shepherdhood: my accuser failed to appear in court months later, and all charges were dismissed. My ascension as a revolutionary continued.

The guys from Griswold Cottage were vacuuming crickets out of their little house for a month, and the Shepherdhood became legendary.

Though the Siege of Griswold Cottage hadn't gotten me expelled, the administration had heard I'd orchestrated it and issued me a warning. "That was strike two, Stephen," the dean of students told me in his office soon after.

"What was strike one?" I asked him with a mock look of disbelief on my face.

"Everything else," he said. He was one of those old school Puerto Rican cats who grew up in that *other* New York City, the mean one at the tail end of the eighties.

I didn't bother protesting; I knew I had gotten off light. My frat had been getting blamed for every prank on campus, even the ones we weren't involved in. The time the library's bell was painted orange? Word around campus was that we were responsible. We weren't, but I laughingly said, "Hell yeah, you know that was us." Another time, a friend pointed outside the cafeteria window and asked, "Is that your doing?" My jaw dropped. A smiley face had been burned into the soccer field. It was one of the most beautiful things I'd ever seen. Scorched earth and joy. "Oh yes, it was absolutely us," I said. And there was the time someone unscrewed all the chairs in the chapel and piled them into a gnarled mess of steel legs, then yanked an electric part from the organ and threw it into the Hudson River. They watched in silence as bubbles gathered at the surface the farther it sank. It was a sacred moment to them, a ceremony marking the day they'd done something truly wrong.

Okay, that one was definitely us too. I instructed the guys to avoid taking any credit or even speaking about it. We could've all been kicked out for that one. And we could've been brought up on charges for trespassing, destruction of private property, vandalism—you name it. I let everyone on campus enjoy the cancelation of chapel services for one week and silently said, You're welcome. I got off easy my entire sophomore year. When the dean of students told me I had two strikes on me, I took it and ran, resolving to stay out of trouble during my junior year and raise my grades, which were embarrassingly low—a 1.8 GPA. After the years of hearing my father correlate my grades with salvation, my failings seemed like sacrilege, and I was awakened to it.

The first semester of my third year, I changed my major to Computer Science. I thought it would make my mom happy. Inner-city Latinos want their kids to make money, forget all that painting and poetry shit. Mami wanted me to have money, and I'd heard computers and the internet were going to make everyone involved rich. I signed on. Lots of ones and zeros, lots of math. I held on for dear life. Late one night in the fall of 2001, my buddies walked into my room and asked if I wanted to join in sneaking into the cafeteria for food. I'd been staring at a blank screen. I said I felt like I could use a snack.

The cafeteria was managed by an outside company, rendering students' after-hours presence there trespassing. It didn't matter that the cafeteria was due to open soon for breakfast, and that my loans covered my room and board at the campus; I was prohibited from being there at the time. The locked doors should've clued me in, but they didn't.

The next morning, the dean was waiting for me in my dorm's parking lot. With a smug look on his face, he passed me an envelope and said, "I warned you. Three strikes." I was stunned.

He had seen my name on the security report that morning and likely spilled his coffee, realizing the gift that had fallen in his lap. It was the opportunity he'd been waiting for. He expelled me from Nyack College.

Had I known the college would Al Capone me over a bowl of cereal, I would've poured myself a barbaric portion of Cocoa Pebbles. That's cereal that didn't reach our Bronx cabinets in the nineties without government assistance. My mother might have understood.

Look, I was devastated; I had nothing else. In the three years since the circulation of my sex letters, my girlfriend was taken away, my church made me a pariah, and I was being treated like a pervert at home. I had felt exiled from the entire world until I arrived at Nyack College, where I found meaning for myself through the Shepherdhood. Now all of that was over. No college and no fraternity. I was again displaced and alone.

When I called home to break the news, I hoped Papi would be the one to pick up the phone. I knew if he picked up the phone, I could count on that stout apathy of his to cushion the blow of my disclosure. I'd say the words "Hey, I got kicked out of college," and he'd say "Well, okay," and boom, that would be it, we could talk about where I'd sleep in the apartment.

That's not the way things went, however, because Mami picked up the phone. The anxious smile on my face disappeared. "Ma, the college . . . they kicked me out."

Mami said nothing. Seconds later, she was still silent. The electric buzz coming from the phone's speaker continued for a few more moments before she drew a breath and, in a faint voice, said, "Oh, God."

She sounded tired, as if her tank of disappointment had finally emptied and she was trying to conjure some up for old time's sake. Desperate for a different response, I considered asking her to put Papi on the phone. My parents were wildly different. Mami was the more outgoing, emotive parent, and my father was asleep at the wheel by then. I nixed the idea.

I said, "Goodbye, Mami," and hung up the phone.

You think I went home after that phone call? That's something you *don't* do. My expulsion came two months after the Twin Towers went down. There were men inhaling cancerous plumes of asbestos just to pull bone fragments from the rubble, and here I was breaking into a cafeteria in a pretty town for a bowl of Kix. There was not enough sympathy to spare.

For Kix! It was Nyack. Rolling hills and hippy cafés. They even had an ice-cream parlor, I shit you not. I could've had Post's Banana Nut Crunch! It was still around back then. Had I said, "Banana Nut Crunch," you might have said, "Well, I kinda get it." Instead, I went for welfare cereal.

There was no way I'd pack my bags and run home anyway, not with my personal record. Now I was tossing "Christian college cast-out" into the mix. Listen, even *I* didn't want to see me anymore, so you know what I did? I began running away by staying put: I settled in Nyack. There was a shitty house at the bottom of the hill where the college sat. A bunch of the college's undesirables lived there. There was a gay Black guy—I didn't know they came in Black when I met him—who sang R & B with a blunt in one hand and a glass of vodka in the other. There was a short Puerto Rican kid who had been kicked out after one semester for not doing anything right, not paying tuition or going to classes; and an overweight White girl who hated herself, first and chiefly, then everyone else on Earth for being more attractive and desirable than she was. I thought I'd fit in nicely in this little colony of scoundrels, so I rented a room in that shitty house and nestled in.

I believed I was too deep in the hole to pull myself out, so I dug deeper. There were always others in that darkness looking to share their sensibilities. There was the shitty house, and there was Don Pablo's, a Tex-Mex restaurant in the mall nearby, where I started picking up shifts. I took sensibilities from my coworkers—from the cook who snorted coke, from the server who sold him the coke, and from the married manager who was sleeping with the hostess—and draped myself with them like articles of clothing. With every shadowy pull of the Don Pablo's T-shirt over my head, I burrowed deeper into obscurity and thought it good.

In early 2003, my buddy Brian invited me to go home with him for the summer. Then he said "home" was Minnesota. I had to go look it up on a map. I opened an encyclopedia and ran the tip of my finger around and across the map of the United States until it eventually stopped underneath the word Minnesota. I had never cared to remember its location on a map, even when I was acing school and knew the capital was Saint Paul.

Minnesota was far, of that I was certain. It sounded *extra* far, the way Kentucky and Nebraska sounded far and foreign and transformative. It sounded far enough to be another country offering the opportunity of a lifetime: I would live well beyond the scope of relatives and friends in the Bronx and escape headlong into a blissful ambiguity where I would never see the trail of broken things behind me.

I discovered there was a Don Pablo's in Saint Paul too. I treated it like a sign from God, which was ridiculous since He probably had a palm to his aggravated face by then. A few weeks later, I was wearing a Don Pablo's T-shirt in Minnesota. I thought things were looking up, like *really* looking up.

Brian's family asked me to go with them on a canoe trip shortly after my move there. I could tell that canoeing was a big deal in Minnesota by the way the men slapped me on the back as they talked about all the fun I'd have. I shrugged and said "Yeah, sure" like I was a professional canoe person, and I could be indifferent about another outing, but I had only been in a canoe once in my life, when I was fourteen. New York City's Summer Youth Program, hoping to change the scenery for at least one day, took me and a bunch of kids from the hypodermic needles and used condoms of Fort Tryon Park to the shit-brown waters of the Harlem River. We spent a couple of hours canoeing past bloated diapers and more-bloated dead cats on a day we called a getaway.

I met Sally, Brian's cousin, on that canoe trip. She blew me away. I want to say it was the blond hair or her crystalline blue eyes or her figure. There was plenty to look at, plenty to like, but I was mostly attracted to her sorrow. She spent most of the afternoon at the end of the canoe silently gazing at the lake's shoreline, a belly bulging through her U of M hoodie. She didn't do any rowing, and after her two teenage cousins saw five minutes of my rowing technique, neither did I. One of the cousins grabbed my oar and rowed the rest of the way. I was left with nothing to do but stare the length of the canoe at the very pregnant Sally. Autumn winds were glancing off the lake and tussling her hair, but she remained quiet. Her eyes had softened and radiated the sweetest melancholy.

I called Brian after the canoe outing and asked for details on his cousin. He was thrilled. One of his college buddies falling for his pregnant cousin? What's not to love? He was happy to share information: Sally's boyfriend had ghosted her the minute she became pregnant; she'd been avoiding family gatherings as a preemptive defensive measure. It excited me. I'd been to my share of family gatherings since my church blacklisting. I knew all about the hushed conversations, lingering stares, and the plans excluding me. Her end of the canoe carried as much weight as mine.

When I returned to New York City that summer, I told Mami not to get used to my being around, that I was there to work the job at 905 Park Avenue, and that I'd be gone after a few months; I had a girlfriend and a son to return to. Their names were Sally and Jake, and they were my family. I really thought she'd handle it better.

4

DIY HERO

Quitting a doorman job three years after getting expelled from college is *one* thing, a very stupid thing, but quitting for a girl? The men in Mami's soap operas were derailed by women, not the men in her apartment. I was her oldest too, the one she'd spent the most time on. I'd learned her system so well that I became her assistant at twelve years of age: I watched the kids while she cooked; I changed the occasional diaper despite it being my least favorite Mami thing to do; I made the task of buying groceries with five boys easier. Sure, the supermarket was only two blocks away, but try being the little Ecuadorian lady taking five young boys with crackling personalities along the Kingsbridge Road storefronts. Nothing about the Bronx was easy. You look away for a moment—to ask the Korean owner at the fish market if he'll convert your food stamps to cash just one more time—and you'll lose a kid, maybe two. But I was there. It was me with two boys pulling at my hands so that her only concerns were the two other boys and getting the Korean guy to hand her some cash.

I was on call even when Papi was home. He didn't iron clothes or mop floors or wash dishes, so I was often summoned for spot duty. I'd say, "Okay Mami," scurry off to complete a task, and run back to my homework. Ten years later, it was *me* being upended by a girl. Her firstborn. Mami shook her head and sneered when talking about it. *A girl.*

I had a different take on things. One evening during that summer of 2004, I tried to break through her defenses. "Ma, this isn't about having a girlfriend in Minnesota," I started as I stood at the kitchen entrance. I perked up. "I have a job there, Ma. Two of them, actually."

Mami kept stirring the rice.

I stretched, then wondered aloud about the few people who could say they were escaping the Bronx's hardness, the barbed wire, and the nighttime merengue that shook the walls. "Ma, how many people could say they're leaving this mess to live in a state with lakes and trees and . . . quiet?"

Her brow plummeted, and she stirred the rice. I hadn't made a dent. I knew why. Mom didn't care about love or multiple jobs waiting for me in Minnesota, she cared about the one great job staring me in the face here in New York City.

"Ma . . . I don't like that job anyway," I said. I raised an elbow against the doorway and pushed my forehead into my hand in exasperation. I could hear myself. I was having a conversation alone, and pleading. I went on the offensive. "Doorman? Wear a monkey suit and kiss rich-people *culo* all day? Come on, Ma, it's not for me." She pulled the lid off the beans, inspected them, went back to stirring the rice. Her eyes darkened. She was rarely a fan of my word choices.

That was the worst, when she tuned me out. It was strategic, especially when I was younger. She'd go silent and lull me into a false sense of security. I'd eventually let my guard down and that's when it would come, when I lowered my shield: she'd be upon me in an instant, a *chancleta* in one hand, and an impressive close-range attack would ensue.

She was a master of the *chancleta* beating. Some mothers shout and make a show of removing their slippers, then throw them wildly. They usually miss their targets. Not Mami. After blanketing a conversation with her silence, she'd wash a dish, move on to another activity—like watering her plants—and she'd attack at arm's length, converting the *chancleta* from a projectile to the perfect melee weapon.

I later shared with my mother how I'd fallen into good graces with my boss. It was meant to be small talk for the sake of reminding her I was in the room. I was merely describing a moment from my day. My mother heard the news and snapped out of her apathy. "So there's a chance he'll call you back for a permanent position!" she said excitedly. We were midway through the summer of 2004 by then, but she had leapt into the future, one where I was a middle-aged doorman with kids and the family dental package. Sensing the bloom of expectations, I haphazardly said, "Yeah, I guess," but I didn't mean it. I had already decided I was leaving New York City at the end of that summer.

My younger brother Jason is the only reason I had a doorman job to abandon. I'd been gone for a summer and a fall when, in late 2003, my mother pleaded with him to talk to his boss. She'd seen Jason go from young and broke to young with money in his pockets and structure in his life. She wanted the same for her oldest, who suffered from crippling immaturity and an aptitude for self-sabotage.

Jason agreed and delivered a good word about me to Mr. Evans, the superintendent at 905 Park Avenue, who was looking for summer help at the building. Thankfully, the good word was *brother*, and not about the last few years of my life, or I might still be fat and depressed in Minnesota. Evans granted me an interview. Elated, Mami called me to share the news.

She breathed easy when I told her, "Okay, I'll come back home and talk to this Mr. Evans." I told her I'd come with a caveat: if I got the job, I'd return to Minnesota after my summer term at the building ended. "No ifs, ands, or buts, Mami. It isn't even a discussion, Mami. I have a life back in Minnesota, Mami. I'm only working that job for the extra cash, Mami." She said, "Yeah, okay, no problem!" She said it too enthusiastically, too absentmindedly. I said "Okay, Ma" but knew better. She never thought I'd work a doorman job for six months and go back to Minnesota just like *that*.

Judging by the way she looked into the boiling pots at the end of the summer, it was clear she'd expected me to stay in New York, no matter what I'd told her on the phone months earlier. She'd probably prayed about it too, and considering her faith's high success rate, she had every reason to believe I'd stay in New York City.

Hearing cicadas signal autumn's descent had always brought me dread—who wants to trade basketball shorts and ice pops for dark days and cold streets?—but not in 2004. I was going back to Minnesota for love, and I chose to see it that way, as a quest to reunite with my girl-friend. Mami was ruining everything with her tombstone silence. My flight back to Minnesota was only days away, and if I didn't do some-thing quickly, the lasting image of my mother would be of her mouth beaked over the stove, her hand stirring a pot of simmering rice as the cicadas outside rattled louder.

5

THE NEIGHBORHOOD WATCH

One afternoon in August, Mr. Evans walked out of his office, locked it behind him, and called out to me on his way to the service gate. I'd been daydreaming over the basement's logbook in my porter blues. Startled, I caught my breath. "Hey, Mr. Evans! What's going on?"

"Going outside for a minute," he said. "Come with me."

I was surprised. A building superintendent can leave the premises whenever he wants, for coffee or to pick up supplies at the hardware store, but he never asks any of the doormen or porters to tag along; they're held captive there every day for eight hours. Mr. Evans had offered to take me outside of the building and get paid for it. I couldn't pass up the rare opportunity.

"Yeah, sure!" I said, and with great enthusiasm.

Mrs. Hoyt from 5B had looked outside her window and reported spotting someone taking photos of the building from the other side of the avenue. She'd called it a "photo shoot" and said it looked suspicious. Mrs. Hoyt called the management office often for any little thing, like too many taxicabs honking or a bad smell near the garbage compactor chute (imagine that). That day, however, I cut her some slack. She was doing her civic duty: the Twin Towers had fallen three years earlier, and it became culture to report anything out of the ordinary.

"So you wanna take the lead, Mr. Evans?" I asked, not thinking at all about terrorists. I was outside the building! "I could rough him up a little, push him against a wall, and you get in his face, show 'im what we're about." It would've been difficult to set up an interrogation room on the street. We'd have to wing it. A cop car would roll by and I'd nod at it while pinning the terrorist photographer up against the wall. The cop in the passenger seat would nod back and look away. We Americans were more united back then, when terrorists holding AK-47s stood at the end of our collective gaze.

Mr. Evans clenched his lips and fought back a smile. I saw it in the corners of his lips; it was looking for an opening. The average person has an assortment of teeth, molars and incisors, but Evans had teeth like a shark, long and twisted and crammed together. I used to stare at his smile-bared teeth with wonder and fright, like the first time I saw a girl naked.

He kept his lips tightened until we reached the corner of Park and Eightieth, where he finally spoke: "Let's see what we find. It's probably nothing."

We reached the other side of Park and didn't find anyone in the middle of an unsolicited photo shoot. I looked for clues because that's what a self-certified detective does. I found nothing.

"I wonder what they were looking at," Mr. Evans said moments later. We had begun our walk back to the service entrance on East Eightieth when he stopped at the Park Avenue median to look up at the building.

Nine Oh Five Park Avenue sat on a corner and showed off two impressively clean red facades, but besides the sturdy look it shared with other prewar buildings, it had no flair. Other prewar condominiums are more elaborately designed and included a spire or two, but our building was a giant red block with a green canopy like a spigot pouring humanity onto the sidewalk.

Standing at the median splitting Park Avenue between east and west sides, I saw only red bricks and windows, but I was determined to prove my worth.

Without thinking, I said, "Well, it wasn't Mrs. Hoyt naked at the window, that's for sure." When I tried imagining a withered, wrinkled old woman standing at a window overlooking Park Avenue, I grimaced.

"It woulda been one picture and that's it. Photo shoot over. Terrorist attack over too."

Mr. Evans didn't fight it. He opened his mouth, showed his teeth, and had himself a good laugh. Then he swiped playfully at the top of my head, stirring something inside of me I hadn't felt since I was very young.

It was the kind of gesture usually derived from fathers to their children. I was freaked out, but not because the entire thing felt inappropriate. I was freaked out because it *didn't* feel inappropriate. Imagine me telling my Bronx friends that I was okay with a man patting my head and I was fine with him doing it a second time if he wanted to. There's no way to keep it real and say, "Shoot, he coulda put his arm around me and went for the full father-son bonding experience." That story doesn't fly anywhere in the Bronx. No man is allowed to replace your pops, not even a *blanquito*. Your pops could be a deadbeat dad or the kind of father who beats you to a pulp or a father who doesn't notice when you've grown seven inches. Your father could be dead inside like mine was, but it doesn't matter. No man can take his place. That's how it is.

Mr. Evans and I weren't in the Bronx, however. We were standing on Park Avenue. It wasn't my hood. I could allow myself to feel like a son sharing a moment with a happy father.

Mr. Evans had done something similar after I offered an equally unhelpful statement weeks earlier. He shook his head in amusement and tussled my hair before walking away. I was angry at first—it took lots of time and gel to style my hair.

"You can stay with us past the summer if you want," he said that afternoon on Park Avenue. His eyes remained locked on the building. "I like you with us. You're a good kid."

I kept my stare on the building too. It was still only bricks and windows. I was still uncharacteristically mute.

"Just throwing it out there," he continued. He lowered his chin and turned to me. "I'll find the hours for you. I'll get you to forty hours every week. There's always a man calling out, and even when there isn't, I'll bring you in to do side work."

Imagine a whale swimming past you at a red light. That's what Mr. Evans had done by offering to keep me, a summer employee, at the building past the summer: he'd gone into the business of miracles.

The summer guy rarely loses the distinction of being the summer guy. He's the summer guy because at the start of the fall, he pulls his belongings out of the locker he'd been sharing with an impatient permanent worker, and that's it—he's back in the jobless pool. Mr. Evans had offered me full-time hours beyond the summer with the implicit goal of giving me a permanent position when it opened up. I'd almost certainly see envelopes filled with cash at Christmastime too. Summer guys don't normally have that kind of luck. Mr. Evans had offered me the golden ticket.

I declined his offer and made it official: I'd be moving away in a few weeks; I even said something about my girlfriend and the baby, all the while knowing it sounded bizarre to Mr. Evans. Who gives up a doorman job for a girl in Minnesota and a baby that's not his? Me, that's who. I stayed true to form and squandered my latest opportunity, but at least I added a word of thanks and one of clarification: it wasn't a move to a state within the tristate area; it was a move to *Minnesota*.

New Jersey is in the tristate area. So is Connecticut. There are plenty of doormen commuting every day from those states to work their doorman shifts in New York City. But from Minnesota? When you tell a building superintendent that you're moving to a state that's so far away the printer needs extra paper to print the MapQuest directions, you're also saying you're unavailable for a doorman job on Park Avenue.

During my last weeks of the summer, Mr. Evans often shook his head when he saw me. One time, he blew air through his pursed lips as I walked by him in the basement. I knew he was disappointed. And in disbelief. I'd turned down a job on Park Avenue.

I'd been treating my first job in Minnesota like a highly coveted position, like I'd been recruited all the way from the Bronx because of my
specialized background.

I was a kitchen worker at Buffalo Wild Wings.

No one in New York had heard about Buffalo Wild Wings as the
franchise had yet to arrive in the city. During those first phone calls
from Minnesota, I spoke syrupy about it, like I was a vital member of
a cutting-edge, progressive company leading the charge to transform
culinary traditions. It was just chicken wings. Chicken wings and wing
sauces, and while done well, a revolution it was not.

Then I mentioned a second job to my mother, and for a moment, I
thought I'd swung her over to my side. For Mami, there was nothing
better than a job, but *two*? My mother migrated here from Ecuador and
worked as a seamstress, then bought a car, then bought nice clothes, and
paid rent, all things she couldn't do in Latin America. To her, a job fixed
everything, and she'd made it clear I needed fixing in the worst way.

One evening, I tried convincing my mother to ease up on her campaign of disapproval and maybe feel some optimism. She was at the
stove again and stirring rice with her mouth wrung forward and her
brow dipped low. That wasn't a good sign, but I held out hope for one
reason: Papi was at the table. He could back me. Yes, Papi had seen
me get blacklisted at Rosado's church and kicked out of college, and
while those were good enough reasons to withhold any support for any
pitch coming from me, Papi was no longer the 1996 version of himself,
remember? He'd stopped supporting Rosado and wasn't spitting fire
about hell and sex demons anymore. He'd stopped sneaking around for
clues into my personal life, and as long as I didn't allude to having one, he
didn't ask questions. Papi went to work every day, came home for dinner,
went to bed, then did it again. He walked through life the way he'd sat
at Rosado's church, in a slumber, which meant I could count on him for
several agreeable nods and sleepy okays, no matter what I said. Papi was
the perfect wingman. I'd tell him the story, loudly, and it would go over
his nodding head and right into Mami's ears.

"So yeah, it's the Don Pablo's in Roseville. That's a town in Saint Paul," I said, my voice booming. You use names and people feel things, is what I've heard. Mami kept stirring the rice.

"You won't believe this, Pa. I make a phone call and boom, just like that I'm transferred from the Don Pablo's in Nyack to the one in Minnesota. They're waiting for me as we speak!"

Papi's eyes had rounded. He lowered his cup of water. "Oh wow," he said. "So they can just fax your paperwork; you don't have to fill out any new paperwork!"

One thing about Papi hadn't changed: he appreciated any maneuver that vaulted you ahead of the opposition. That evening, my father beamed knowing I'd made the phone call that transferred me from one state to another and likely took a job from a Minnesotan. Adding to my coup, I wouldn't spend any time filling out an application because my file was in the GM's office already, the ink still warm, the paper freshly out of the fax machine. I'd made out like a bandit, and, just like when I brought him report cards as a young boy, my father beamed with pride.

I had indeed made the phone call—that's not a lie—but the manager at Don Pablo's had sleepily told me to pass by the restaurant when I got back in town. They had enough servers and they were all set at the bar, but maybe they could find a spot for me in the kitchen? No promises either way.

Here's the truth: there was no job at Buffalo Wild Wings. It was gone when I left for New York City for the summer job at 905 back in June. And the job at Don Pablo's would be part-time at best. I was returning to Minnesota with few options outside of winning the state lottery.

I said, "Yeah, Pa, no paperwork for me!"

My father nodded happily and said, "Okay. Okay." Then he nodded some more.

Mami took a few steps from the stove, pointed at me with that big spoon, the one with the holes in it. "That's it!" she yelled. "I don't want to hear any more about chicken wings and enchiladas!" Her brow had dropped and her lips had beaked together yet again, making her look like an eagle in flight. *"Este sin verguenza,"* she added. "Throwing it all away for a girl." From that point forward, all mention of chicken wings and enchiladas was banned at home.

Mami didn't resemble the Black, Puerto Rican, or Dominican mothers in our Bronx neighborhood. She had the straight, black hair and the wide, wind-swept face of her Incan ancestors, the ones who conjured up a fight against the Spanish only to later stand on hills watching their cities burn. It's in her blood to express displeasure through her face, in case all else is lost in translation.

Things changed after enchiladas and chicken wings were stricken from the family vocabulary. Only days away from my return to Minnesota, my mother began poking at steaks so they cooked evenly and stirred rice so it wouldn't stick. None of it was about me. With all talk of my job security prohibited, she went back to taking easy steps around the apartment, where she looked more like a thinker at a monastery than a small Ecuadorian lady keeping a big family together.

When I said goodbye on my last day before returning to Minnesota at the end of the summer, I said goodbye and nothing else. I didn't communicate it with my eyes. I couldn't. I had to avoid reading her face, which most assuredly spelled *You are a dumbass.* I pulled in for a hug, said "Goodbye, Mami," then peeled away quickly.

If you walk away from a doorman job, you better have something lined up because you can't return with talk of Hey, I'm back. The moment you quit, a new application is pulled off the pile at the management office and a call is made. And that's if the super doesn't already have someone in mind, because in that case, he calls management and says "I got a guy." If you're that guy, all you do is take the urine test and you're in. Trust: if you walk away from a building, your spot disappears with the quickness, and no one ever remembers you were ever there.

I didn't walk away from New York in the fall of 2004, I ran away, *again.* The cicadas outside rattled louder, and the boiler room at 905 Park Avenue continued churning just the same.

6

THREE PHONE CALLS

The first call comes as I shower before my shift at the restaurant. My cell phone is on the couch, and I'm under the showerhead still panting loudly from my midafternoon jog. I'm terribly out of shape, but I figure the occasional jog will negate the multiple servings of food I'll enjoy at the restaurant. I sweat a little, gorge a lot, and call it a strategy.

Sally is at work, and the baby is with his grandmother. I'm alone in the apartment and can use my cell phone with no trouble, but I duck into my bedroom anyway. I close the door too. The screen says there's a missed call from 905 Park Avenue. And there's a voicemail; I can see the tape recorder symbol. I don't even flip the light on. I stand in the dark bedroom watching the stifled afternoon sunlight collect behind the drawn window blinds. I'm there, but I feel as inconsequential as the hamper or the coat hanging in the closet. That's what I want, to be a block of lifelessness and not be obligated to acknowledge the phone call's significance.

I coach myself into proceeding. *Let's do this*, I tell myself. I press Play as I reach for a Don Pablo's T-shirt. The speaker crackles while I pull the black shirt over my head.

Mr. Evans has called to say that Carlos is set to retire at the end of the year; he could offer me a permanent job at the building when that happens, none of that on-call, cobble-forty-hours-together business. It's the most grown-up thing I've ever heard: a full-time doorman gig with benefits, sick days, and vacation time. I don't even know what to think when I hear that. Mr. Evans says I wouldn't be offered Carlos's shift, obviously—he's the senior man on staff, so the next guy on the ladder would have first dibs. Still, it means a spot on the roster will open up in a few months, and that spot could be mine. All I have to do is say the word.

Carlos. His retirement is a long time coming. The oldest man on the staff, he's a short Puerto Rican who had a thing for stashing knives throughout the lobby. You'd find one in the back of a drawer and think, *Where does he find time to buy so many knives?* During the summer, I heard a few doormen whisper, "When the fuck is Carlos gonna retire?" Most of the men wanted him gone, and if you got him when he was distracted— like when he'd huff and puff through a set of dips on the lobby bench when he wasn't supposed to—I think he'd say it too. "I'm tired, *compai*," he'd say. "I wanna retire so I can retire the knives too."

I can't lie. Walking into the building to replace a hated man appeals to me. When that happens, you're greeted with enthusiasm and happy sighs of relief. Right now, I could use some of that treatment. Sally has been having doubts about us ever since we were kicked out of that basement apartment we moved into. The Mexican homeowners explained that a cousin would be crossing the border soon and would need the apartment when he arrived. I thought we could get more time: unless that cousin was an Olympic long-distance runner, there was no way he'd arrive from Texas anytime soon, not with the assembly of heartland states he'd be journeying through. While my girlfriend and I scrambled to find housing, I silently grumbled about being ousted by members of my assigned ethnicity: the locals constantly referred to me as Mexican because, in Minnesota, speaking Spanish means you're from Mexico; you can't even be from Spain because that's a stretch, apparently; you can only be from Mexico if you speak Spanish. I was kicked to the curb by my border-crossing countryman.

Mr. Evans knows why I'm here. It's not the first time someone makes a move for love, so I don't know why I'm being tested on it, why it's being overlooked. I've told everyone—I'm here for my girlfriend—why can't everyone leave me alone?

I convince myself that since I missed the call, I am freed of the obligation to return it. I erase Evans's message, and just like that, the call never happened. I decide to add Mr. Evans to the list of people I'll prove wrong about me. I don't need any of them doing me any favors and certainly not Carlos. Fuck Carlos and his cache of Park Avenue knives. I'll make love work. I'll get a win.

I go for a jog a few days later. It's an easy pace I jog at; it's not aggressive, but you can still hear me huffing. You can hear my sneakers grinding the pavement with each step. There's a little sweat and a show of effort, and for me, that's enough. I slow my jog to a walk when I see the trees. Strong winds are thrashing the trees on both sides of the street, causing their leaves to rustle into a chorus of small terrors. I'd stopped hearing the leaves as much when Papi moved me from private school in Yonkers to public school in the Bronx, and by the time I moved on to middle school, I didn't hear them at all. I was too busy watching my six and listening for huffing, puffing, and the grind of sneakers. I didn't want to get jumped on the way to school. The neighborhood around Middle School 118 was one of the roughest in the Bronx. Kids got jumped on the regular, for their Jordans or their bookbags or sometimes just for sport. It was all noise to me, like the trees. I braved those streets to reach my English teacher Mrs. Piotrowski, whose voice rang louder than the leaves.

Mrs. Anne Piotrowski shot to the front of the class from the back of the room, where she'd sit after every episode of *Eyes on the Prize*, and slashed words onto the blackboard like an angry butcher. When she was done hacking the blackboard, she whirled around, her puffy hair whipping forward, and stuffed a hand in her pocket. Then she pointed the chalk at us with her free hand. With menace in her brow, she demanded that we contribute to classroom discussion and expected us to scrape our ideas from the innermost parts of ourselves. An Italian, Piotrowski was as physically emotive as it gets. "What do you guys think about *that*?" she asked, hammering chalk into the blackboard with every syllable of her words. Listening to pieces of Piotrowski's chalk fall to the floor and scatter around my sneakers are for me as Bronx a sound as the *poppoppop* of guns I often heard at nighttime.

One day, Mrs. Piotrowski pinched her chalky fingertips and pointed a new stick of chalk at me. She wanted my thoughts on the O. J. Simpson trial. I offered a squirm at first. It was uncharted territory for me: Pastor Rosado had never asked for my opinion, and Papi sometimes slapped me in the face when I offered one. I believed Mrs. Piotrowski really wanted my thoughts, however, so I proclaimed the obvious, that O. J. was guilty. My classmates immediately went into an uproar, some shouting of, "Oh, hell no . . . Yo, this kid's buggin'!"

Mrs. Piotrowski hushed them and began gesturing at me with the doomed piece of chalk. "Tell me more, Stephen," she demanded, her hair swirling around her face like sea plants around coral. "I want *more!*" I continued, of course. Piotrowski was bent at the knees like she was ready to tackle someone. I didn't want it to be me.

I had never been urged to unveil my mind. I felt dangerous, and dangerous felt good. I faced the other side of the classroom, where my pro-Simpson classmates sat, and continued. I said the evidence was there and that evidence meant O. J. Simpson was guilty, despite his celebrity and being funny in the *Naked Gun* movies and despite Mark Fuhrman's blatant racism. O. J. Simpson was guilty despite Rodney King.

Mrs. Piotrowski stood in front of the row of classmates across from me. I didn't sense her siding with them or siding with me—I sensed *her*.

I've caught my breath. I've cooled down actually, and that's not such a great thing, especially on these cool fall days when it takes me a while to warm up. I start my jog again, but I'm still gripped by Mrs. Piotrowski.

I realize now that she confronted me to sharpen my mind and took great pleasure in it. She used to return my essays and ask questions that demanded pointed answers. Then she'd invite another classmate to follow with a contrasting opinion, then another, and before I knew what was going on, the classroom had become an arena pitting teenagers against one another in a battle of intellects.

I realize, too, that Mrs. Piotrowski, Tormenter of Blackboards and Chalk Sticks, had gone further than my pastor—she had liberated my mind.

I'm on a half-hearted jog through rural Saint Paul. I'm far from Sally, for whom my love has waned. No matter how sweet she is and how good she sounds saying the word *papi*—and let me tell you, homegirl says it with an accent so sexy that sometimes I look at her all mystified and shit, like maybe she isn't entirely Viking, like maybe she has some blue-eyed Rican in her too—I can't help it, my heart isn't with her because it's elsewhere. It's in the classroom. It's been there, quietly and without effect, since my expulsion from Nyack College. It's been there long before that.

The second call comes while I'm driving to the restaurant. I see *905 Park Avenue* on the screen and press End, sending the caller to voicemail. I know it's Mr. Evans. No one else at the building would call me because buildings forget summer guys the moment they leave. The only person from 905 Park Avenue dialing my number would be him, to talk about my replacing Carlos in January.

I drive for a while longer before feeling the building's tug on my thoughts. Mr. Evans had been good to me. We clashed only once, when I interviewed with him in May, and it was mild. He looked at my goatee and said it would have to go. That, and the long hair. I sighed, said, "Yeah, sure," and that was it. I shaved my goatee and cut my hair. He had given me a chance without once asking about my past.

Two times I sent Evans's message to voicemail, where he was wedged between calls from a creditor and a mechanic reminding me about my next oil change. Evans deserves better. I pull off to the shoulder and dial the building.

"Hello. This is Arthur Evans. How may I help you?" He has a way of making his greeting sound new every time, as if he really wants to help and knows he's the man for the job.

"Mr. Evans, it's Stephen."

"Oh hi, Stephen. Just called you. Left a message."

"Yeah, I saw. I was putting gas in the car."

"Ah, okay."

"How could I help you, Mr. Evans?" The things we say. How could I have helped him from I-90 in Minnesota? My journal is in my backpack on the passenger seat. Parceled among its pages of rap and sad poetry are my observations on life in my adopted town. Perhaps a short reading from my dossier on Minnesotan life:

People from the Midwest use their hands and stain their clothes. They fix their trucks and Harley-Davidsons in their driveways and often stop to wipe sweat from their brows. They hold beers at their waists. Tall and rosy-cheeked, the men hunt and return from the woods with deer the sturdy, course-skinned women convert to venison chili. If you ever see a Vogue magazine in their hands, it's in the toss to a hungry bonfire.

Mr. Evans hasn't called to ask for my notes on Midwest culture.

"It's a sure thing," he says. "Carlos is gone in January." He doesn't waste any time. "A spot will be opening up in the building. I want you to take it."

"Oh . . . right."

"Stephen, it's October, and I have to find a guy soon or they're going to send me someone from Management, someone I don't know. I know *you*. Take the job." No more tender, father-son bonding experiences with Mr. Evans. He's all business now.

A tightness grips me in the car, and it's like all of Minnesota is looking down on me from a perched seat and waiting for my response.

The call's electric hum continues as Mr. Evans waits for my answer. The cars shooting past me on I-90, however, are not so patient. Their continued procession looks like the shiny blur of a New York City train roaring by just inches from my face. The traffic blows gusts of wind that rock my car back and forth. Even Minnesota traffic is trying to knock some sense into me.

Mr. Evans has succeeded in making me feel exceptional despite the offer to replace a doorman who does push-ups in the back of the lobby, regularly curses out his coworkers, and ignores residents. Anyone with a heartbeat is an ideal replacement for Carlos, honestly, but Evans makes it seem like I'm uniquely qualified for the position. It has been a long time since I've felt unique or qualified. I am quieted.

"Mr. Evans," I begin finally, "thanks, but no. I'm out here with my girlfriend. I appreciate it, but I can't take the job." I'm trying to convince us both.

I can't take any more losses, and that's what leaving Minnesota would be—a big fat L. I've taken too many losses. I'm angling for a win, and I'll take one in any form. I can't leave Minnesota. I want to be able to say I have a job. I want to be able to say that I have a girlfriend, that my relationship is working. I can't accept another loss.

The third call comes in late November 2004, after the last game of the ALCS. The Yankees had taken a 3 to 0 lead early in the series, and I was euphoric. It was the closest I'd felt to a winner in a long time. But then the Red Sox won the next three games to even things up.

I'm at work when they drop the final game of the series. Standing at the mouth of the kitchen, I see a crowd at the bar. It's a slow Wednesday at the restaurant, but the dining room is empty. All of the guests have left their tables to crowd the TVs in the bar. Something is wrong, I know it: they're buzzing even though their hometown team, the Minnesota Twins, which was bounced from the playoffs by the Yankees a few weeks ago, isn't playing. I need to know what the Twins fans are enjoying so much, so I walk over to the bar.

It's difficult for me to blend in: I'm wearing an apron smeared with so much red salsa I look like a Civil War surgeon, and because of all the guacamole I've been slinging at the restaurant, my boots have transitioned from gray to Vietcong green. I'm the only one in the crowd who looks and smells like the menu, but it doesn't matter; I must see for myself: it's early in the game and the Yanks are getting blown out. It's embarrassing. Moments later, I toss my apron at the bin for soiled linens, and it catches the bin's mouth. The red salsa on the apron has dried and crusted the way blood might. The Yankees can't rally. Their season is over. Mine doesn't have to be.

I finally get home. I walk past the living room, where my girlfriend is watching a movie. She looks up, says, "Oh, hey, baby," and I say, "Oh, hey, baby" back. She won't ask about the Yanks giving up a 3 to 0 series lead to lose a seven-game series, something that's never been done in the history of sports. She certainly hates me enough by now to ask. But her hate has cooled the way lava hardens, and cannot be bothered to change back. She doesn't show her contempt; she'd rather ignore me and spend the night watching a movie with commercials. I don't fight it. Most of them look like she wants to look: happy. All I bring home is the promise of weight gain and the smell of a Tex-Mex restaurant. I get it, I understand. I can't make her happy. I add her to the list of people I've disappointed and go to my bedroom to fetch some clean clothes.

I find the two envelopes I need and bend the clothes around them, then walk into the bathroom. Sitting on the lid of the toilet moments later, I open one of the envelopes and pull out a drawing made by my baby sister Rachel.

It's ghastly, an affront to the arts. In plain blue crayon, Rachel has translated the two of us into a wild mess of lines. She scribbles my name over the scrawled mess that represents me and scribbles her name over the smaller, scrawled mess that represents her. A shoot of blue extends from each bundle of lines so that she and I could hold hands. Her drawing never saw the refrigerator door, and it should have—the lines make me look thinner—but I know it's a ploy. Mami sent the drawing to me three months after I moved to Minnesota last year, before she called about the doorman job. I knew it was her way of saying, "If you won't listen to me or care about me, maybe you'll care about your sister. She misses you. Come back home for *her*."

Rachel is the youngest of the brood. As a toddler, she often ran to me begging to be carried. Family friends have called us twins since then, but when I look at her I see a pretty face and smooth, fair skin. It's our Spanish ancestors' far-flung echo that never reached me. We both have light eyes, but I'm brown with thick lips and a large head, and still people remark on an uncanny resemblance, so I say, "Yeah, but *she's* pretty" and laugh them off. Sitting in the bathroom tonight, my head hangs low and well beneath the mirror, but that's when I see it, the resemblance. It's in the drawing, where my eight-year-old sister has dumbed it down for me; it's in each slash of blue jutting wildly this way and the next; it's in the absence of any discernible symmetry or meaning in the lines' paths; it's in the two bundles of blue gashes on the page joined at the center by a desperate stretch of blue. I didn't see it last year when I received this drawing in the mail, but I see it now: my history with love is worse than I thought.

The third call comes after I open the second envelope. Inside the second envelope is a short story I wrote for Mrs. Piotrowski. I flip the packet so I can see the last page, and it's still there, the rarest of grades: the letter A followed by a tail of plus symbols. It's an A++++++. An A with vertebrae. Underneath the A and the many pluses are the words "I'm speechless," just so I know all the pluses aren't a mistake, that she hadn't caught a seizure while attempting to write a lone A+, then got stuck slashing pluses on the page. It's certainly a possibility, judging by the way she treats blackboards. It's the worst writing of my life, but it's also my first attempt at writing a story, and it has Mrs. Piotrowski claiming to have reached for words and pulled back a line of pluses instead. Her inscription on my pages, the "A++++++ . . . Speechless," are written in bright red ink.

I was in kindergarten when my mother taught me one of the most enduring lessons on how to deal with conflict.

One morning she was helping me get myself together. A stickler for appearance, she combed my hair to the side, tucked my shirt securely into my pants, and made sure I'd tied my shoes correctly (she'd taught me how to tie them a few months earlier). When she was satisfied that I'd passed inspection, she hunched over me, swiped away a few wayward folds in my shirt over my shoulder, and showed me her fist. "If a kid ever hits you," she said, pumping it rhythmically, "you hit him back and you hit him back harder." I was stunned. I didn't have the mental dexterity to make a leap from crayons to the art of war. I slowly recited the kindergarten rules of engagement: "I can't punch kids, but if kids punch me, I punch kids . . ." It was a lot. Mami tightened her fist until her knuckles shone white. She brought it near my face like it was a crystal ball showing me a future.

"You hit back harder, okay?" she repeated. I said okay. I stopped trying to make sense of it all and accepted it: if I ever got hit, I hit back.

The third call comes after I ball my fist the way Mami taught me to. I'd taken two classes at Metro State University before flying to New York City to work as a summertime doorman. I'd enjoyed the writing assignments and the instruction. Adding my voice to classroom discussions gave me a thrill, and I thought I'd come back to Minnesota and do it again, take a class or two as a side hobby or something like that. I want back in a classroom, but not as a hobby, not anymore. I want to respond, to take control of my story, and I know the best way to do so is to find my way back into a classroom in New York. I'd need to pay for the classes and my outstanding balances at Nyack College and Metro State University—the doorman job would help with that. The doorman job would put me back in a classroom. It wouldn't be a hobby; it would be a position. A fighting stance.

When I see my phone flash *905 Park Avenue* again, I drop deep into the couch. It's not the greatest timing: I just finished getting dressed for another jog that I believe will prepare my body for that night's enchilada intake at the restaurant. The jog can wait. I need to answer this call.

I don't give Mr. Evans a chance to finish his thought. He's done and said enough. It's my turn. He says, "Stephen, I really need to know—"

"I'll take the job, Mr. Evans," I say.

7

FIRST THINGS FIRST

I landed in LaGuardia and went straight to my parents' apartment, where they invited me to stay with them under strict terms, all of which were different variations of *No sex in the apartment.* At the end of his speech, my father, sounding exhausted, said, "Listen, just don't bring that stuff in here." He pointed to the window to help me understand where "that stuff" came from and where it should stay. After agreeing, I went back to bunking with my little brothers. I was twenty-three and waiting on my mother for dinner again.

The doorman job isn't as physically demanding as construction or sanitation. Those guys lift heavy objects, grunt, and sweat a lot. Doormen stand around wearing tailored suits waiting for something to happen. Sometimes we complained about it. "This shift is so dead; I wish something would happen." Then things happened. On Sunday evenings, Mrs. Weiss used to roll up to the front door in her SUV. By August, I knew to take a breath whenever I saw her truck pull in. It would slow down to a crawl, and I'd see her turned around, yelling at one of her annoying sons in the back seat. I'd close my eyes and say a short prayer. Releasing my breath, I often heard the other doorman on duty add a well-timed groan or a "Goddamn it, it's the Bitch." He'd seen her too.

Mrs. Weiss wasn't good at being wealthy. Instead of sending her understandably morose housekeeper to buy the family's groceries at Eli's or Gristedes, or ordering via Fresh Direct and having food delivered, Weiss shopped at Costco. It was a fact that wouldn't raise the average middle-class eyebrow—a deal is a deal, after all—but she was a resident of a Park Avenue building where her husband paid maintenance fees, which included a service entrance for deliveries and a staff waiting to deliver them to each residence. None of that appealed to Mrs. Weiss. She traveled far and wide for value, then purchased in bulk, and because shopping at Costco means packing groceries into discarded, topless cartons, all her items arrived strewn about the truck's floor. The service entrance was never open on Sunday nights. There was only me and another doorman, and both of us rolled up our sleeves with disgust on our faces whenever Weiss's SUV showed in front of the building; it wasn't even a new SUV. She drove a shitty, fifteen-year-old Lexus that whined as it rolled to a stop. Mrs. Weiss was still a Crown Heights girl who didn't know how to be wealthy on Park Avenue. Doormen worked harder as a consequence.

I once opened the rear hatch and caught a jar of pickles in midair. The following week I missed the jar of pickles, and it exploded on the pavement right next to my shoes. Another time, her fruit popped out and scattered across two of Park Avenue's lanes. Bent at the waist, I shot this way, then darted that way, chasing after oranges and apples and kiwis like they were scrambling chicks. After collecting all the fallen items, I packed the lobby's cart until groceries hung from the sides. When they didn't fit on the cart, I tucked them into the crook of my arms and arrived at the Weiss apartment looking like an aid worker with food for a dusty village.

Did Mr. Weiss ever join her on her disastrous Sunday grocery trips? No. He went on long rides in his Porsche. You see, *he* was good at being wealthy.

I clocked into my first shift as a permanent doorman almost as slim as I had been when I left—I had been working out and had lost ten pounds since my return, with more weight dropping as the weeks went by. I would soon handle Mrs. Weiss's Costco runs with vim and vigor while keeping fat jokes far from my coworkers' reach.

I moved into a small studio apartment the following year. A nice development, but I didn't stop there. After a few months without crisis or catastrophe, I approached the City University of New York, a school system comprising twenty-five colleges, with my 1.87 GPA from Nyack College. It was too low a GPA for most CUNY schools, apparently. Even Lehman College, once notorious for hiring bogus professors, turned me down. After only one college on the list accepted me, it became easy to choose a college to attend. John Jay College was in familiar territory too, just a block away from my first high school in Hell's Kitchen.

That's how you do it: step by step, slowly leveling up. Each move I made was reinforced by the last, compelled by the last; I was building. I knew I'd find my way into a classroom eventually, but I wanted to structure my life first, find some order.

Then I caught another big break. My mother's neighbor, a manager at a small Bronx real estate company, shared that a homeowner was looking for a live-in super who would pay discounted rent so long as he maintained the house. I took the job—and the giant basement apartment in Throggs Neck, a suburban neighborhood in the Bronx I'd never heard of. Throggs Neck didn't even have an exit ramp on the highway inviting the rest of the city inside, but there I was, moving into an apartment with a private entrance and a big backyard for $500 a month. It was my own nook in the Bronx, and I called it home.

I was grounded, finally. The last eight years had seen a medley of failures, false starts, and sudden moves. I'd never truly unpacked, never felt anchored anywhere, and never knew how much I needed to. Two years after becoming a full-time doorman, I had my own mailbox, a couch, and a bookcase—the kinds of things meant for people who stick around. Feeling stable allowed me to better assess myself: I'd gone a long time without cultivating my gifts and abilities, and I became keenly aware of their dullness. During a quiet moment in the lobby at work one day, a reckoning washed over me: I was ready to return to school.

In late 2006, I registered for classes at John Jay College determined to show that the college had chosen wisely and that the other schools missed out. I felt unsheathed and menacing, like a sword, and determined never to go dull or dry again.

8

TECATO

My coworker Lenny was in the middle of another impression during our shift. It was a slow summer afternoon, and on days like those, we'd give ourselves things to do. Today, my job was to guess who Lenny was impersonating. "Hello, Stephen," he said slowly, his back hunched and his feet close together. I immediately knew who it was: Mr. Fletcher from 3F. It was one of Lenny's best impersonations, one I'd sometimes catch him doing by himself when I came back from the restroom. I hated how good he was at doing a Fletcher, but with my competitive edge always cutting into me, I hated more how much I enjoyed it.

Anybody could take on the lurched posture of a tacky, old banker, but not everyone could do the face. Lenny could do the face. He opened his mouth, covered his bottom teeth with his lower lip, showing his upper teeth only, then raised his cheeks until they pressed his eyes into tight slits. "I need a taxi," Lenny said through a creaky, pained voice. Fletcher would walk through the lobby and meet us in the vestibule wearing the most unfashionable brown suits and open-mouthed looks of silent pain. Lenny had him down to a T. "Actually . . . cancel the taxi . . . Stephen, please cancel it." Lenny did the most obnoxious U-turn in the lobby and trudged toward the back of the lobby. "I left my cell phone upstairs, that stupid thing." It was another one of Fletcher's slow, torturous walks through the lobby, and Lenny had nailed it. Coming to a rigid halt, Lenny straightened out of his stoop and smiled confidently. Even his physique made him naturally capable of impressions: Lenny had one of those average, compact frames that wouldn't be categorized as thin or wide, tall or short, and he could project it however he wanted. "Who was I?" he asked, sighing with the satisfaction of someone who'd just done push-ups for cancer awareness.

Shaking my head begrudgingly, I said, "Fletcher."

Lenny's impersonations of tenants were better than mine. He knew it, and I knew it. That didn't mean I had to admit it, you kidding me? I never gave him the satisfaction. It was my first summer at the building as a full-time doorman, and Lenny had delivered several Oscar-worthy impersonations of tenants in that time. I'd always laughed along, then looked away, stifling the rest of my laughter. It wasn't that I hated him for being that much better than me at impressions; it was that I hated *myself* for being that much worse.

There was only one way to close the gap between Lenny and me in the impression games: I could do an impression of Jose Ruiz, our senior coworker. It was a cop-out, the path of least resistance: Lenny was a Puerto Rican; I was half Puerto Rican and all Latino; and Jose, an old man, was another Puerto Rican! I'd been around Puerto Ricans all my life; I wasn't breaking new ground—but you do what you must to compete.

"It's my turn," I said and rubbed my hands together in anticipation. Lenny leaned against the far wall with a smile on his face. One thing about Lenny: he enjoyed watching me try impressions, and when I nailed one, he'd affirm it, he'd say, "Oh shit, there you go!" Smiles and laughter flew easily between us: Lenny was uncommonly close to me in age when compared to the other men at the building, who were in their fifties and sixties; Lenny was in his mid-thirties, making him only a decade older than me at the time.

I was about to get into it. I was about to say, "Hellooo, Meeses Co-heng," and squint my eyes and, in the case of *this* old man, show *all* my teeth in a reenactment of Jose's open, breathy smile. I was about to say, "Lemme tell ju: ju daughter Marissa is getting veddy big. Veddy big. Looking maw like her lovely mather evry day!" I would've thrown my hands behind my back and walked around the lobby with my head lowered, my back bent at the waist, and my hands clasped together. Unlike Fletcher, who bent at the waist because he couldn't help it, Jose did it from time to time because he had this thing with projecting a layered persona; as if being an old Puerto Rican with an irrevocably thick accent wasn't good enough, he had to relate to the planet and the whales and specific icicles on Mount Everest too. My favorite was when Jose tapped into his inner-poet persona. I loved every attempt: "But I tell ju, Meeses Coheng," I was about to say. "It's not only the physico resemblance I see—it's here." That's when I would've tapped my chest softly with my fingertips. It would've made Lenny laugh, I know it would have, because he would've had to imagine Jose talking to Mrs. Cohen, and she never stopped to chat in the lobby. It was hello and goodbye, and with a distant look on her face; we never knew what she was thinking. "It's the heart too, Meeses Coheng. Shees got ju *corazón.*" I was prepared to give it my all. Sure, it would be an impression of another Latino, but yo, I would pull from my *corazón* on this one. I bowed my head and closed my eyes.

"What the f—" Lenny interrupted, his voice whipping away from me.

I raised my eyes, following Lenny's gaze through the glass in the front door.

A thin, hunched figure had edged into our view of the sidewalk. He moved like he was walking along the ocean floor, all slow and flowy. He came to a full stop underneath the canopy, but his legs must not have updated his torso because it swayed forward, as if trying to abandon his lower half. In response, his legs sank toward the ground, causing his torso to sway backward. As if attempting to reconcile both sides of a war in his body, he shot his hands forward and settled himself. His knees bent and his arms drooped, pulling his torso along so that his head fell too. His knuckles reached the sidewalk, and that was it; with his sorcery activated, he lowered himself, impossibly, into a sitting position. The man had sat in an invisible chair in front of the giant Park Avenue cooperative as I was about to deliver the performance of a lifetime.

I drew closer to the front door's glass pane and said, "Aww shit, here we go." The young man was making himself *real* comfortable, like he was sitting in a love seat in the middle of my living room. I didn't know the man, but I knew all about him. The way he was bent at the knees, moaning, with a line of saliva hanging at the corner of his lips? Undoubtedly addicted to heroin. I'd seen his type before.

"Fucking *tecato*," Lenny said.

He was the tall, stringy type of addict, the type that can't hide his affliction. Short ones can, sometimes. They can wear baggy clothes and curl up into balls of battered flesh and bones at the end of a train car, but not the tall, skinny *tecato*. He stops and hangs over a sidewalk like a tattered flag because, even in his heroin-induced trance, maybe he can claim a slice of New York City for himself too.

The *tecato* lifted himself out of his magic loveseat and started shuffling downtown again, his untied sneakers dragging beneath him like roadkill. Our noses only inches away from the door's glass, Lenny and I watched him make his unsteady trek down Park Avenue.

"Dude looks like a Spanish Harlem special," I said. "Like he shot up on One Hundred Sixteenth, jumped on the six train, and . . ."

"Went downtown instead of uptown," Lenny said, laughing.

"Riiiiight," I said, appreciating his contribution. "Now he's trying to find his way back to the train while high, but he's been walking in the wrong direction and just figured it out, so he's stopping for a power nap—while sitting on the breeze." It's magic, the things heroin addicts can do with their bodies while high.

"Dat's one determined *tecato*."

Tecato stopped beside the tree bed and lowered his emaciated body into his magic loveseat again. The impression game was over. Lenny leaned against the front door's glass pane and said, "He's gotta get moving soon, or we're gonna have to do something about him. We don't need any residents calling Management about an addict lounging in front of the building."

I shook my head and said, "I mean, the sidewalk *is* public property. But yeah, you're right."

Some residents treat the sidewalk outside their cooperative like a front lawn, like pedestrians are guilty of trespassing every time they walk down the street. Trust me when I tell you that if Mrs. Werner had walked out of the building and seen Tecato dragging himself over the sidewalk in front of the building, she would've blamed me and not Tecato for making bad life choices. I hadn't worked a full year as a permanent doorman at the building and was already used to the heavy burden that came with the position. I knew that a doorman's name was rarely mentioned for anything good; "He opens the doors so well" was praise I never heard, but "he takes too long to reach the door" I'd heard before.

I was the doorman on duty that day, so it was my job to greet tenants at the door. It was also my job to deal with all conditions *outside* the door. It was on *me* to deal with Tecato.

"Let's get a closer look," I said and reached for the door handle. I'd learned plenty by then: sometimes the job is to make problems disappear, so that no one ever knows they existed.

The building's front door was a cast-iron gate with glass panes behind the iron bars. There was a door handle, and you pressed the thumb latch before pulling it, but that didn't mean the door would cooperate by opening. You had to put your back into pulling that door or you were going to make a fool of yourself. You don't know how many times a child or small woman beat me to the door and tried letting themselves out— some residents believe it's their duty to prove doormen aren't needed at buildings—only to pull on the handle and not make a difference. They'd press on the thumb latch a few times, then pull again, using arm strength only; the door would remain closed. That's when I'd approach, motion for them to clear the way, and do exactly as I did the afternoon Lenny and I were visited by Tecato: pull at the handle out of a crouch and tilt the rest of my body toward the back of the lobby so that all my weight went into the haul. Most of the building's residents had lived there for many years and in some cases, decades, but didn't know how to work the front door. Enter doorman.

Lenny and I were standing on the building's front step moments later. Tecato didn't even notice us. He was just standing there, plugged into the sidewalk like an urban mushroom. Pedestrians walked by, looked at him, glared at us, and I shrugged. Lenny smiled blankly.

There's no section in the doorman manual that addresses heroin addicts. During my two-week training, the topic of *tecatos* never came up. Eight months working as a fulltime doorman on Park Avenue, and I'd never dealt with one. I'd seen hundreds of them living in the Bronx, however, and I knew they'd done so much harm to themselves already that they were too far gone to do any harm to anyone else. I endured a wide array of impulses around *tecatos*. Sometimes I wanted to help, but was immediately hit with the sense that their bodies would issue a defensive response, something like protracted spines made of hypodermic needles. Other times, I wanted to touch and comfort them, but I worried that their bodies would crack and flake away and the Good Samaritan law wouldn't cover me. I felt no such impulses that summer afternoon with Lenny. I simply didn't want to deal with getting *tecato* grit on my doorman uniform.

"What you thinkin' of doing?" Lenny asked, smiling. Motherfucker. He was enjoying my lack of answers here too.

"Man, I don't know." I had to figure something out soon. Tecato's moans were getting more consistent and melodic, like a Gregorian chant. Also, a line of saliva had dropped near his chest. It would eventually reach his bent knees and make contact with the pavement. The entire thing would look like a crime, *my* crime, something like negligence.

The moment I wished that he'd start moving, Tecato jolted forward. Lenny stepped onto the sidewalk to get a better look and shouted, "Oh shit, he's moving!"

Then Tecato stopped again and lowered himself into his magic love seat. "Fuck," I said. "Not this again." His chest lurched forward, giving his torso the temporary victory, and he started moving downtown again. "Okay, here we go."

"Keep going man," Lenny said. He crossed his fingers. "Keep go-iiiinng!"

It was happening. "Yup, he's moving. He's moving!"

Then he did it. Tecato crossed over the line in the pavement separating 905 Park Avenue's sidewalk from 903 Park Avenue's sidewalk. Tecato had crossed the border!

Lenny and I slapped each other high fives and celebrated. At that moment, 903's doorman shot out of its front door with a suspicious look on his face. After zeroing in on our sidewalk celebration, his eyes narrowed in disapproval.

"Hey, Jerry!" I shouted, coming out of a smile.

"What's up!" he snarled. He knew something was coming.

I pointed at the sidewalk just beyond 903's entrance. "He's *your* problem now!" I yelled. Lenny burst into laughter. Tecato had gone full-recline mode in his magic loveseat and wasn't moving. Homeboy had a rope of saliva pooling on the sidewalk and his knuckles pooling there too. He was *knocked* out.

"Aww, you motherfuckers!" Jerry wailed. He threw his head back and clenched his eyes shut. "Goddamn it!"

"Everything okay?" someone said from behind me. Mr. Evans was standing on 905's front step. He had walked the length of the lobby from the back hallway leading to his apartment.

"Hey, Mr. Evans," I said through a smile. "Yeah, everything is okay."

Mr. Evans looked down the block. I don't know if he saw Tecato or not, but he turned around and stepped into the lobby's vestibule. If he didn't have a problem, we certainly didn't. Lenny and I joined him in the vestibule and closed the door behind us.

"So there was a heroin addict and he stayed in front of our building like *this*," I said, and bent my knees, closed my eyes, and warped my lips. Then I lowered myself as far as I could go without falling. I spun my head a few times. "He had saliva comin' out his mouth too, like *this*." I pinched at the corner of my lips and brought my hand down to the floor like I was pulling at melted cheese.

Laughter erupted out of Lenny's mouth and Evans smiled, displaying all his teeth. Tecato was gone and unavailable for demonstrations. I'd been trying to show Evans what he looked like and, indirectly, the complaints we'd avoided. Why were they laughing?

"What?" I asked, still in my magic loveseat.

"That's a fuckin' great impression, bro!" Lenny said, doubling over in laughter and holding his stomach. Evans chuckled quietly.

Lenny was right. It *was* a great impression. It was an impromptu impression of a stranger, making it all the more impressive. Mr. Evans had seen it too, so I had witnesses. I took a moment and wondered if I, like Tecato, had planted a flag, and begun claiming a slice of New York City for myself too.

9

THE IVY CLEAVER

I could hear Professor Harrison, a lanky man in his thirties, shuffling between my classmates as he handed back our essays. Nearing my desk, he pinched the top of my essay and spun his wrist as he placed mine in front of me. He'd slipped it in between my hands and inches from my vital organs, then walked away like a stone-cold killer. My name was at the top left, the date was at the top right, but none of that was as prominent as that C at the top center. It was the first time I'd ever received a C for something I'd written. Sure, I'd just returned to college after a six-year hiatus that saw me booted from a Christian college, self-exiled in Minnesota, and back in New York City for a doorman job, but I hadn't lost my swing. We're talking about writing here. Putting words together. I'd been taught by erudite Christian academy teachers and instructors at programs for gifted students. I'd been mentored by the best and, knowing it, allowed it to shape how I saw myself. It was the first time I'd ever seen that letter attached to my writing.

English class has always been a religious experience for me. I wasn't the only one getting As, but I believed my As were different. They even *looked* different to me because they were above *my* writing. I believed my words were better. I had cause: in middle school, I was the boy the other boys came to for the love poems that kept their girlfriends swooning for at least another week. You think you're hot? I was running a business in the seventh grade: five chocolate milks for every love poem. I've been doing this at a high level for a long time, okay?

There was a C atop an essay written by *me*. George W. Bush started a war on lesser intelligence. It was my turn at some shock and awe.

I shot up to my feet, my essay raised in my hand. "Nah, man. Nah! You're not giving me a C! You're gonna give me an A, maybe a B, but you're not giving me a C!"

Nobody moved. Absolute silence. Then someone shifted in their chair. Harrison's hands dropped, the pages rustling against his hip. Stares from every student scattered throughout the classroom extended in my direction while the gaunt professor stood wearing a sadistic smile and a horrifying sweater-vest.

Harrison didn't seem shocked in the least by my outburst. Shit, even *I* had been startled by it. But not *that* motherfucker. He was standing there like he'd expected it, was enjoying it, and was ready to negotiate.

"I'll allow you to rewrite the essay and give you a second chance at a B," he said with shocking calm. He had the faint wisp of a smile on his face, like he'd just finished stashing a body in his commercial freezer and knew he could squeeze me in with a little elbow grease.

In my classroom daydreams, I'd imagined a *New York Post* article about an elusive serial killer nicknamed "The Ivy Cleaver" because of his clean-cut, preppy appearance. The article featured blocks of sensationalized reporting under the Ivy Cleaver's police sketch, which failed to lead to his capture. The murders continued because the police sketch artist hadn't gotten the Ivy Cleaver's eyes right.

The real story was in Harrison's eyes, which screamed tension from behind his glasses every day. When looking over his students, his eyes beaded and probed, and when he was asked a question, they went wide as saucers. His eyes seemed to emit a silent alarm as he discussed thinkers as independent as Emerson.

He was an awkward man who had always projected frailty, but not on that day. On that day, Harrison was in control, finally, and enjoying it.

He and I were both standing on our own two feet at that moment, but he was the weakling-turned-tormentor.

"Why would I write a B essay to replace an A essay?" I asked. I knew what this was all about. I took a step forward so that he and I faced each other in the center of the classroom. I gestured to my classmates. "You're just angry that the girls laugh at my jokes and not yours."

"Excuse me?" he shouted, his grip tightening around the pages at his hip. "You're out of line!" Harrison yelled. I'd breached his cool demeanor and exposed him: it was clear that if Harrison had ever earned a girl's laugh, it had been during a moment of ridicule many years ago. I imagine a girl laughed at the creases that his mom had ironed into his jeans; that was it, murderous tendencies activated; the next stop for the girl was the freezer in his basement. His first kill.

I glared at the C hanging at the top of the page like spoiled fruit and sensed the tide of support from my classmates, who really just wanted the show to continue. "You're also pissed cuz I'm smarter than you!" It was by no means a transcendent addition to my previous line of dialogue, one that was already juvenile at best, but the professor had gone silent and fire-truck red. "And what the fuck is up with these ugly-ass sweater vests!" The class laughed, which meant girls laughed too. That's when I walked out.

I sat with him a week later in the office of the chairman of the English department. I hadn't let it go. There was no way I'd accept a C, so I'd reached out to the professor's boss for a second opinion, one I had no doubt would mirror mine. I knew his invitation to mediate was a good sign. That afternoon, the department chair arranged three seats in front of his desk and sat in the middle. I wasted no time. Pointing at my essay, I said, "Read that and tell me it's not an A." He took a long breath and sighed. I think he was expecting a more diplomatic opening.

Word came a week later. The chairman changed my essay's grade to a B. My communication with Professor Harrison was icy for the rest of the semester, but I didn't mind—I had triumphed on the battlefield: I hadn't rewritten the essay; I had stopped Harrison from giving me a C; I never saw the slim professor at the college after that semester.

10

PURGE

Evans announced his retirement as the superintendent of 905 Park Avenue in 2007, two years after he'd hired me as a permanent worker at the building. His moving truck was still idling near the service entrance when I heard the whispers that the building was already looking to hire his replacement. Luka wasn't at the building when I returned to New York City in 2005. He'd left to manage a side-street walk-up, but his wife still worked at the building as a housekeeper for one of the residents, so when she informed him that the super's job was available, it was obvious what he'd do. Why not take a shot at becoming the building manager of a luxury cooperative on Park Avenue? The benefits went beyond medical and dental: he'd be given a rent-free apartment in the building; mail addressed to him would show his name sitting high over "Park Avenue" instead of it squatting over a numbered street; his children would be walking in and out of the same entrance as prep-school kids and their parents who got featured in *Forbes*. Luka decided he'd apply for a job that would move his family into a doorman building on Park Avenue for free. It was an easy decision to make.

I was working the afternoon Luka came for his interview. He walked into the lobby, working as clean a smile as his shockingly stained teeth would allow. He said hello and even kept his eyes on mine as we exchanged pleasantries. He was the super a month later, but no longer smiling or looking me in the eyes when he spoke to me. That's when I knew something was brewing.

It's wise to avoid starting trouble during a time of uncertainty, especially at work. There's no need to make yourself a target. So guess what I did two years into Luka's tenure as superintendent at 905 Park Avenue?

It's because I run hot. Really hot. (My parents didn't sleep much the summer I was born until my father, in a fit of frustration, took us for a late-night drive in the car. He turned on the AC, I fell asleep instantly, and an AC was hoisted into the bedroom window soon after.) In 2009, I found myself standing inside 905 Park Avenue's vestibule, which was far from the lobby's antiquated air conditioners, in a wool doorman suit for eight hours during a heat wave. I was obligated to wear a wool duty cap, which worsened my torment. After a few hours into a shift, sweat was running down my face and my buttoned shirts were drenched and sticking to my skin underneath my suit jacket. During one particularly humid night, I looked over at Jose Ruiz, who was wiping sweat off his brow with a handkerchief, and said, "I'm sick of this, man." He didn't say anything. Just smiled. That ticked me off even more, that he dismissed my words as so meaningless they didn't merit a response. I decided to make my words mean something.

I began writing a petition that demanded the building allow the doormen to remove our jackets and wear short-sleeved shirts on hot summer days. It didn't stop there. It included the big one, the most important stipulation: that we be allowed to remove our doorman hats during heat waves too. It was a point of contention. For many residents, a doorman without a hat was the same as a building without a doorman. If we didn't wear hats at the lobby door, what would tenants show their guests to prove we were in fact doormen at the building? "There's always one of them standing there," a resident once said over her shoulder as she walked past me. The lady tailing her looked at my face, then the hat, and blew past me in a hurry to catch up with her friend. Apparently, she wouldn't have believed I was the doorman if I had merely been a well-dressed, impeccably groomed man idling by the door. The duty cap had been my doorman badge.

Without a duty cap, there was no doorman present at the door. The

905 petition was an ambitious one. Probably an unrealistic one too, since I'd dared to imagine us with some say.

I secured every doorman's signature, even Jose's. I passed by the job on my day off, texted him, and he shot out of the building after announcing a bathroom break. Seconds later, he was in my passenger seat with the petition in his hand. While signing, he yammered away about *revolushong revolushong revolushong.* I glared at him and his signature in shock. "Thanks, Jose!" I said, my voice lifting. Listen, Jose was the type to throw on an extra jacket on the hottest day if he thought it would please the residents. Jose Ruiz was a company man, but he was a senior man and his signature was on that sheet of paper. The petition had a shot at succeeding!

I sat at my desk that night with my 2009 planner spread open at that week's pages. There were notes detailing my work and class schedules, but none revealing my plan to deliver a petition at work. I looked for the little square housing that day and wrote, in capitalized letters, "REVOLUTION BEGINS."

Luka may as well have been reading from an almanac during our subsequent meeting to discuss the petition. He said that doormen at the building had been wearing a full uniform with the hat, even on hot days, since the building hired its first doormen during the 1930s. I almost said it—"You mean, during the Great Depression?"—and with some bite, but I didn't. I kept it in my head, where I could soften it. "That also includes the gloves," Luka said. "You guys don't think I notice you taking them off, but I do." Of course he noticed. Dude had cameras all over the place.

Luka said that the uniform rules had always been that way, so why change them now? I remember putting up a mock fight. I remember smiling as I spoke. The aforementioned line had softened—I said, "Well, Luka, I'm thinkin' maybe we don't have to do what the building did during the *Great Depression.*" I may have cocked my head and held my stare. I failed at softening the mention of the Great Depression, I admit. "It's 2009 and maybe we could do things a little different." He didn't budge on my jacket proposal, but he agreed to let us remove our hats once the temperature reached ninety degrees Fahrenheit. I hadn't considered a compromise. I'd been gunning for a total victory. The men at work began celebrating the concession—*We don't have to wear hats on ninety-degree days anymore! Woo-hoo!*—but I viewed it as a defeat and stopped negotiating. On ninety-degree days, I tossed my duty cap to the side, let my scalp breathe, and thought about what could've been.

A year later, I figured out that Luka was firing young Latinos at the building. I was more than a bit concerned. Two young Latinos remained: me and a younger man named Joaquin.

He was a nice guy, one I could rely on for authentic conversation, but he stopped all that when Luka began his purge of young Latin men. He'd see me and look the other way. One day I asked him what he thought about the firings, and he said, "Nah, man. Not doing this." And that was it, our rapport went from thin to emaciated from that day forward. Joaquin was Ecuadorian. He knew I was half Ecuadorian, but his wife was pregnant; with a baby on the way, he wasn't about to risk losing his job just because our ancestry tests looked similar. And especially not for *me*. I'd caused problems with the petition. I had it coming. Joaquin agreed with Luka often during the Purge. He said, "Yeah, Luka . . . okay, Luka," and avoided me at all costs.

I was the obvious choice for Next.

Luka wasn't going to touch the legacy doormen. The Irish guys were old, moved slowly, and were cranky. There had been more of them on Park Avenue a century ago. It had been a job for Irishmen, just like the police and fire departments, and that's why they were safe for as long as they stuck around. The next tide of immigrants was Brown, and it flooded lobbies with Latin men, lots of *español*, and more Vitalis than was necessary. They were old too, and though not as cranky, they were safe because they were legacy doormen.

There was a tense harmony between the Latinos and the Irish doormen at the building. Mutual curiosity between both sides led to a vigorous exchange of culture via the why-the-fuck question: *Why the fuck is your beer*

black, you mick? Why don't you give one of your twenty kids back, you spic?
After many years, the Latin and Irish doormen realized the racially in-
sensitive rhetoric laid down neatly into couplets. They shrugged, shared
a laugh, and mused about their wild-caught synergy.

There was a Polish American doorman, Bill. He was the senior man,
the number one. He usually stood at the door chuckling alone and using
the n-word.

The building was behind the times. Albanians had been popping up
in buildings all over Park Avenue for many years. An Albanian himself,
Luka would bring the building up to speed.

First he made some room.

Kenny was half Ecuadorian like me. He was also half Dominican,
making him fully Latin, an unfortunate situation at the building. Kenny
was the first young Latino to go. He was fired after he stayed too long
in the bathroom one night. He caught a stomach bug at two in the morning, and that's when the old man in 3A called the lobby for assistance.
The missus had a headache and he wanted the shift's doorman to call an
ambulance for her, but no one answered the phone. Kenny's diarrhea was
the kind that exits with your soul, so he wasn't in the lobby to call 911
for an ambulance. The building phone rang and rang, but Kenny was in
the basement bathroom with the window raised a few inches to let hope
in. He was away from the lobby a total of twenty minutes, a mortal sin
on Park Avenue. Kenny was young. Kenny was Latino. Kenny got fired.

Julian gave Luka a good reason. He had abandoned his post too, but
with a greater sense of urgency. One of his side chicks sent him nudes
during his overnight shift. He looked at his watch. Four in the morning.
At that hour, Astoria was an easy twenty minutes away with no traffic.
It was time to *go*. He jumped in his Acura Integra, the Official Car of the
Young Dominicano of the 2000s, and drove out to check on the girl's
personal welfare.

The morning newspapers arrived at the front gate when they were
supposed to arrive, at five a.m. The African guy drops his bundle first,

then the Asian lady drops hers. But Julian wasn't there. He was in Astoria, plowing the *mamacita* who'd sent him photos, while the newspapers stacked up outside the building's front door.

Julian buzzed himself into the lobby two hours later, a bundle of newspapers tucked in each arm, and walked up to a ringing phone. *Have the papers arrived?* I'm sure Julian smiled and said, "Yeah, definitely, coming right up." Julian was a good guy, if a bit impetuous. The awning's cameras caught him leaving the building, then taking a high step over the newspapers when he returned two hours later. Julian was Dominican. Julian was young. Julian was gone from the lobby for two hours—his firing was easy.

For a short time, there was another Jose at the building. Jose Lopez. I didn't mind his firing, if even so that the rest of us could stop using full names—"Jose Ruiz? Oh, the *other* Jose." Jose Lopez had walked in as a doorman two years earlier and received my enthusiasm because *Hey, another Puerto Rican? That's great. The more Latinos, the better.* But for things to work out like that, you need everyone to be on the same page. You couldn't find Jose Lopez near the book. He was the kind of Latino that strove to show other Latinos he was top dog. It got worse when he was promoted from doorman to handyman. The promotion netted him an extra two dollars on the hour, so he started walking around the building bow-armed and with a stiff torso, like he was a half-wink away from drawing a pair of six-shooters on us.

When you stalk the workplace like Jose Lopez did, turning at the waist and not at the neck, scanning over things like a cyborg, you're stepping in line for the next reckoning. Guys like me, full-time workers with no delusions of doorman grandeur, stopped talking to him, at least honestly. And that's just the staff; it's lateral conflict, it happens. Luka couldn't have enjoyed spotting Jose Lopez in the camera feed walking through the lobby. He didn't belong in the lobby—he and his handyman uniform were meant for clogged toilets and the underneath of sinks, not the lobby's marble floors. I'm sure Luka saw a handyman hoping to duplicate the same upward career path at the building, and he wouldn't let it happen. Jose Lopez was immediately placed on Luka's Latinos to Fire list.

I was used to having the basement to myself by five p.m. By that time, Jose Lopez had usually hung up his spurs and gone home. Luka too. He was usually in the service elevator every day at four thirty waiting for me to take him upstairs to his apartment in the back of the lobby. Having the basement to myself at five p.m. was the only plus to working the swing shift, a day killer that started at noon, ended at eight, and saw me leaving the job too late to make any meaningful plans. I was always too tired after work to attempt having fun anyway. The swing shift had me running around the entire eight hours. It wasn't like the other shifts, where you could sit on a chair or lean against a heater when residents aren't around. There's a lot of downtime for men working in the lobby, but there's no downtime for the guy on the swing shift. He cleans and mops and escorts housekeepers around the building for hours before changing uniforms to relieve the lobby guys for dinner.

I was in the throes of another swing shift one evening when someone slid beside me as I rang a mop over the slop sink. I couldn't figure out who it was at first. He was stooping over me, his block head so high it eclipsed the hallway's light and kept his face netted in shadows. It was Jose Lopez. Had to be. No one else would stand that long with their hands on their hips in complete silence. I was aggravated. Jose's antics weren't welcome.

"What you got there, buddy?" he asked, his voice arcing over my head. He crossed his arms and looked down his cheek and into the sink like it was a thirty-story fall.

"I've got a mop, Jose." I pulled the wet mop out of the sink and squeezed past him.

"Oh, sorry," he said, sidestepping as I leaned the mop's head against the wall where it never fully dried. "Gotta relieve the fellas upstairs soon, eh?"

"Yeah, man. Just like every other shift I work."

"Swing shift sucks, right?"

"Yeah, man." Then I realized *my* hands were on *my* hips. A real motherfucker Jose was. He knew what he was doing. We were stuck in the same space, but *he* was the one allowed to be comfortable. I still couldn't see him and that ridiculous pencil mustache of his because he continued blocking the hallway's light. I'd had enough. "What can I do for you, Jose?"

"Well, I've got some news for you, man. It's kinda good and bad, but mostly good."

"Alright, well . . . shoot."

"Luka is gonna fire me."

"Well shit, that's definitely bad," I said and immediately registered it as good news. Jose Lopez getting fired? A cause for celebration. I smothered my joy behind the most stoic of looks and imagined later conversations with the guys upstairs. Jose Ruiz would say, "Maybe dis will lid to his evolushung as a mang," and clasp his hands behind his back, and Neftali would say, "Oh really? Damn. We're gonna be down one Puerto Rican."

I couldn't show my excitement yet. I was still at the slop sink, and that's no place for joy.

"Yeah, man," Jose continued. "Luka's framing me. Said I lost Mrs. Wankel's dry cleaning, but I didn't. I never saw it and don't even know what it looks like. And *of course* it's Wankel's clothes that gets lost . . . right?"

"Right."

"A fuckin' board member's laundry?"

"Yeah."

"It's bullshit. I didn't do it."

"Well, alright then."

"Uh-huh."

A few long seconds passed. He took a step closer to me. His hands remained on his hips, but at least I could see the pencil mustache then.

Jose Lopez's closely cropped hair plateaued at the top of his head, and

I knew, just knew, that he was the type of guy who stood at the mirror and patted his angled head after brushing his hair, then combed and patted his head again.

"It doesn't matter though," he said, a sly look cutting into his eyes.

"How's that, Jose?"

"Soon as he told me the clothes went missing and asked me about it, I knew something was up. He was trying something."

"He was building a case," I said matter-of-factly.

"Exactly."

If Jose Lopez hadn't still—while discussing his looming termination—been trying to hump my leg, I might have felt sorry for him. I didn't like anyone getting fired because it removed faces I'd grown accustomed to. Even if I hated an old face, I hated new faces more. In any other case of a man being set up for dismissal, I say something. I might argue on their behalf. But not in this case.

I was stuck at the end of the dark and dusty supply room with the Puerto Rican Patton blocking my way and keeping me in the tent of his shadow.

After four years at the building, I understood the games played by old men. They can't refuse the temptation to topple a man just to spend a few quiet moments standing over him. The impulse to find a cheap victory is as distinct as a dog's growl, and I was listening.

"Yup. So I went to a building on the West Side. Fifty-Seventh Street. Hell's Kitchen. You used to go to high school there, right?"

"Uhhh, yeah," I said, unsure of where he was going with the question.

"I'm gonna be one of the handymen at the big building complex over there. There's something like a thousand units."

"Oh wow, cool."

"Yeah, they're just waiting on my piss to come back clean."

"Ahh, gotcha. So you're basically packed and ready to go."

"Hells fuckin' yeah, man."

"Well . . . cool," I said, hoping the conversation had come to an end.

"There's something else."

"What's that, Jose?"

"You're on Luka's radar. He's lookin' to fire you next."

I had been in denial about it, but the signs that I was on the chopping block were loud and clear. Young Latinos at the building had been disappearing, and I was the oldest of the young guys. I'd also worked there longer than any of them. And let's not forget the petition. Luka had certainly not forgotten. He'd have to be careful firing me, however, because I'd garnered some goodwill among the residents and staff by then. He'd have to engineer my termination.

Jose Lopez's firing was the only one that didn't fit Luka's pattern. Luka had been firing young Latinos, and Jose's age should've saved him. He was in his early fifties. Jose Lopez was young in building years, however—he'd worked at the building for two years, fewer years than I had—and was universally scorned. Luka made an exception; Jose Lopez was gone the following week. Like him, I took his firing in stride.

The Latinos who remained were the building's old guard, and they weren't going anywhere. Jose Ruiz had worked at the building for more than a decade and was like a second grandfather to many. He said hello to the residents with arms spread wide and the most cheerful expression on his face. He referenced philosophy when he spoke and dropped in the names of revolutionaries like Pedro Albizu Campos, whom I had never heard mentioned in school before.

Jose Ruiz was the ideal doorman. Always smiling, always willing, never disagreeing. He loved baseball, so I took to calling him El Veterano because that's what you call the guy who finds his name on the lineup card every day even though the fastball is beyond him. The team owner says he embodies the organization's spirit, the players respect him, and the fans have seen their kids grow up with him in their periphery. You don't get rid of a guy like that.

Buildings love old guys who can't see the fastball.

Lenny was in his late thirties by then and fast on his way to being the building's next veterano. Unwavering in his pursuit of his next lay, he routinely arrived late to his shifts; when he convinced himself the girl was something special, he disappeared for days at a time to ride romance's crescendo. He had been hired and rehired at the building twice by the time I started there. The third installment in the Lenny series came with a simple warning: shape up or get shipped out. The president of the board liked Lenny, had seen him grow up at the building, and approved his termination both times with much reluctance.

Buildings love guys who grow old with them.

Lenny called me the morning after Bill the Polish doorman died of a massive heart attack. It turns out that neglecting physical exams for twenty years just because you're thin isn't a health plan. "That makes Luis the senior man on staff," Lenny said as I wrapped my mind around the sudden news. I'd seen Bill just a few days ago. He'd been tossing the n-word around like an extra on *Mississippi Burning*.

Luis was a young draft dodger when he started at the building, but had ironed the wrinkles out of his life since then. He had maintained an average build all those years, and without any compulsion for diet or exercise; when considering the Puerto Rican culinary practice of frying everything, it's quite a feat. His inability to gain weight with age did come with one complication: he looked like a child when standing next to his wife, who outweighed him two to one. I'd heard him speak about his type, and she didn't resemble his type in the slightest. Luis liked his women petite, like the little housekeepers in the building who he constantly flirted with, so I attributed the ring on his finger to his wife's job. She was a telecom executive, making her a great haul for a doorman with a cocaine addiction. He wasn't leaving her anytime soon. He wasn't leaving the job anytime soon either. His dealer was a doorman at a building around the corner.

Luis was Luka's Minister of Information. I knew to keep my shoelaces tied around him. Buildings love guys who do whatever it takes to serve.

Jose, Lenny, and Luis were safe. The building wanted them there, and Luka wouldn't defy the building's wishes. I was young, Latino, and not averse to conflict, unlike Joaquin. I wasn't safe.

11

RUSH HOUR

Doorman shifts have rush hours too. One cold afternoon in early 2010, I experienced the most pivotal rush hour in my time as a doorman. It all started with a guest for Mrs. Burton.

For a short time, I thought Mrs. Burton had turned a corner and joined the list of Easy Residents. "Oh, you guys don't have to ring me every time someone comes to see me," she once told me, shaking her head as she laughed. I laughed along like a fool, like I didn't know her any better.

The following week, she caught sight of my coworker Henry in the lobby and tore into him for not announcing her guest. "Why didn't you call upstairs? That was my great-aunt! She's family! How can I be ready for my great-aunt if I don't know she's on the way up?" I could always count on Mrs. Burton's manic inconsistency.

The most interesting thing about Henry was what made him un-interesting: he wasn't a drinking Irishman. A short, withered old man, Henry had only the Mets and a wife who endured the Mets more than he did, which is to say he suffered from great anxiety. The day Mrs. Burton scolded him, I spent ten minutes assuring him that he wouldn't get fired. He didn't need any assurances, though. Henry was a senior man, had worked at the building fifteen years. He was White and not on Luka's radar. He was safe.

Henry wouldn't get fired, but Burton did call management about the incident. A memo was circulated among the staff soon after announcing that Burton's great-aunt was banned from visiting her at her apartment and therefore not allowed entry into the building. No reason was given and no explanation offered. I was baffled. Burton's aunt was one of those graying, pillar-of-the-widows-community types who lingered to talk longer with her driver about his family. She was so kind that I couldn't call her "Mrs. Burton's great-aunt" in conversation anymore. I used her name—Mrs. Miley—because she was so different from Mrs. Burton, I believed I should do my best to differentiate her in name too. Mrs. Miley always entered the building waving and saying my name. *Hey, Stephen!* She'd smile and slip me twenties. This was someone I had to bar from the building? It was a shame.

Worse still, any persistence on the aunt's part could be met with a call to the police. The desk had a memo taped near the phone lest a doorman forget: *No unauthorized, unannounced persons are allowed into the building.* That's immediate termination and your name written underneath Burton's aunt's name on the list of people banned from the building. Former employees of the building aren't allowed in the building. Retired or fired, doesn't matter; if you don't live or work in the building after having once done so, you go on the list.

On that cold afternoon, a woman walked into the lobby and said the words, "I'm here to see Mrs. Burton." She wasn't Burton's aunt; she was a woman I knew had clearance to go upstairs and hadn't been banned from the building. I wasn't required to call upstairs for her. I walked over to the intercom and called anyway. Fuck Burton. If she would ban a woman I liked and respected, who liked and respected me, then I'd inconvenience her by making her hear the buzz of the building's intercom. Burton hated hearing the intercom's buzz, hated the mundane act of lifting the receiver and being forced to yell *Let her up!* every time, and I loved that I would be the one directing her actions, if even for five seconds.

You will never lose your doorman job for pushing up against the exception to the rule with the rule. Every building has ALL VISITORS MUST BE ANNOUNCED posted somewhere near the door, and a doorman can always make the call and play dumb. "Well hey, I was just doing my job. All visitors must be announced, right?" Can't get fired. I received clearance for Burton's guest to go upstairs and directed her to the rear elevator.

I turned and saw a bike messenger waiting patiently at the door. It was a delivery for 5E. Mr. Kendrick, the tenant at 5E, didn't want calls to his apartment under any circumstances. He was a trader who worked at home in front of a mosaic of monitors. I discovered his unique situation when I knocked on his door one day. He hadn't picked up his phone when we'd called moments earlier and the messenger was persistent, said he needed a signature. Mr. Kendrick was unmoved. "My wife deals with this shit!" Kendrick shouted from behind the door. I told him the messenger needed a signature, needed it because he said it was his job and wouldn't leave without it.

The closing bell. That's when you can start calling or bringing deliveries to the Kendricks' apartment. Traders don't want to hear about messengers with revolutionary aspirations. He opened the door after some time. Kendrick gave me his wife's number and told me to call her about "this shit." That's not the situation for me, calling a gorgeous young wife I had already been trying to avoid. Hers was an unblinking, girlish beauty that invited the world into its embrace. Remembering how often I spoke in uneven tones and syllables around her, I embraced the facts—she is married; I'm her doorman—and left her number at the front desk for one of the other fellas to handle it.

It's one building, but in it are many apartments inhabited by wealthy folks with different needs, and you have to learn how to juggle quickly.

I signed for the delivery and turned to bring Kendrick's package to the mail room when I heard a knock on the front door's glass pane. Another bike messenger. Another delivery. I signed for it and returned to my earlier trip to the mail room, this time with the extra package.

Another knock on the front door. A middle-aged Asian man wearing a bike helmet had a white bag raised high like it was the password. "Chahnee foo!" he shouted and returned a cigarette to his lips.

It's one of my favorite things, seeing delivery people take drags from their cigarettes while pedaling. From lunchtime until Conan O'Brien's opening monologue on *Late Night*, these guys rubbed elbows with cyclists of all kinds. Students wearing rolled-up jeans and white tees, businesspeople stretching their savvy, and the occasional zealot clad in a skin-tight cycling onesie showing off a bullshit brand's logo—none of these are smoking. The Chinese delivery guy? He'd hold two cigarettes if one hand wasn't obligated to hold the bag of food.

They come to the States with luggage and a nicotine habit they can't enjoy with the average cigarette-averse American. Migrating was their end of the bargain—the family's situation needed to improve—but each puckered blow of smoke is another kiss to the homeland.

I knew what was happening. The guest for Burton. The package for Kendrick. A Chinese food delivery. It was that pocket of time that lands in every shift. Hellfire and brimstone crammed into a tight window. I used to spend hours of each shift pacing around the vestibule waiting for it to arrive, and when it did, it felt new, like the building had raised all the windows into the courtyard and poured medieval buckets of the day's waste onto me in a slow cascade of sadism.

The delivery guy had already chained his bike to the awning's brass rail and was enjoying a still moment on the top step with his cigarette.

Chinese delivery guys often arrive at the door already grumbling. Some of it is the language barrier. They point to the spot on the receipt disclosing the apartment number and then utter a few of the words in their arsenal—"Dey pay cash; I wait"—and stand outside taking repeated glances at the front entrance like there's a score to settle. They stare and look away, stare and look away, take drags from their cigarettes, look away. Then they take a good, long look through the door's glass in hopes of spotting the other doorman returning with their money.

Chinese delivery guys often count the money at the building's doorstep and mutter under their breath. They think we steal their tips since they're foreign and speak English poorly.

I was determined to show the deliveryman that we weren't all the same. He could trust me to do right by him.

I opened the gate to grab ahold of the bag, but leaned into the door, opening it wide and with intent. "Hey, come inside, bro," I said, waving him in hurriedly. "It's cold outside." I was working with Henry that day. If it didn't stick to the wall like paint, he'd treat it like crime punishable by death. I didn't care. I knew that there were doormen stealing tips at that very moment.

The delivery guy raised his fist, showing his cigarette, and shrugged. The man wanted to smoke his cigarette.

"Well, put it out and come inside," I said, laughing and waving him in.

He shook his head no and skipped off the doorstep and onto the sidewalk. After the short walk to the far end of the awning where his bike was chained, he turned to look at the front door at a distance. He wanted no part of my olive branch.

I still had to deal with Henry.

"Hey, Henry, can you take this upstairs?" I waved the bag in his direction.

Henry took an anxious step toward me like I was handing him someone else's baby. His head jerked slightly to one side, then the next, but his eyes remained locked on the bag. Henry took another step and reached for the bag. Then he stopped himself. Henry said, "Stephen, you know we're not supposed to—"

"Henry, come on. It's not a big deal, okay? It breaks the monotony, right? And don't worry, Luka's not watching."

I didn't know that. In fact, it was safe to assume the opposite, that Luka *was* watching Henry take the bag that very moment. I'd walked into his office several times to find him relaxing in his chair, a Thermos's cap filled with steaming coffee in his hand as he watched the monitors. For Luka, watching the security feed wasn't work. For him, it was entertainment.

I went through all my lines: I told Henry the guys in the basement were busy, that they'd appreciate him helping out, that the deliveryman had said it was a rush order, that they had fucked up at the restaurant and forgotten the egg rolls—he'd been called back to the restaurant halfway into his ride—and the resident was beyond hungry. He didn't wanna piss off an irritated resident, right?

Henry grabbed the bag and hurried away, his face in full bloom.

The rush went on for a while longer: another knock on the building door; one of the kids from 10C, the oldest, returning from lacrosse practice. A few more packages. The Wall Street folks pulling up in their private cars. The UPS guy and his daily payload. I got into a rhythm that afternoon. During a rush, it's best that way.

Open the door with a smile, say "Hello, how are you," and stand aside as the resident walks by.

Open the door with a grin and dap the UPS guy, and say, "Wassup, bro." Reach for a package.

Draw close to the door but avoid the handle. Instead, motion with my thumb *Take that shit around the corner*, where Luis is ready and waiting to steal more tips.

Two more figures at the door. I pulled and said, "Hola, Maria." Another of 10C's children blew past my knees, his backpack bobbing up and down behind his head as he ran the length of the lobby corridor. "Hola, Bruno," responded Maria, who had remained at the door watching the child beat her at another of his impromptu races. She was one of the South American ladies on 10C's squad of babysitters.

Maria had started a month earlier and was already exhausted, already displaying the look of angst I'd seen on the faces of seasoned babysitters and housekeepers. Maria wouldn't last. Too many kids, two unavailable parents, but I offered a soft smile anyway. Maria began a slow, tired walk toward the lobby's rear, where the little boy was bouncing impatiently, when Henry entered the vestibule. He said, "Hey, Stephen, there's a package in the mail room with no name on it. No name anywhere, I checked. It's next to the package for Kendrick. Know who's it fuh?"

I went through the memory of the last half hour. It was a sloppy mess. "Nah, man," I said. "I don't."

Henry scratched his forehead with his gloved fingertips. "Stephen, um, well, how are we gonna figure out who's it fuh? You dunno if someone's expectin' it right now. What if it's urgent?"

If I had been tested for doorman efficiency during shifts with Henry, my scores would've set records and changed the game. My motivation for finding quick and easy solutions was often to alleviate Henry's worries and ease him back into a calm state.

"Chill out, Henry," I said, lifting my walkie-talkie to my grinning lips. "I got this."

The face on Henry said *Oh, no* in varying shades of red.

"Hey, Luka," I said, affecting nonchalance for Henry's sake. "Luka, come in," I spoke into the two-way.

"Yes, Stephen," returned Luka in his gravely drawl. Henry lowered the volume on his walkie-talkie as if reminding himself he wasn't part of the conversation.

"Hey, Luka, do me a favor and rewind the footage for the last half hour. Got a garment bag up here with no name on it. I'm thinkin' if I see myself receiving it, see the face of the guy who gave it to me, I'll remember where it's supposed to go."

I waited for a response.

Henry's face had softened, revealing a glint of mischief. He walked over to the monitor beside the door and waited. I released a long, deep sigh. Henry was impressed and ready for a show, giving me only a partial win.

It was a good idea, but I needed it to work. It was the delivery after the package for Kendrick and before the Chinese food. I had forgotten to label it. Doorman basics: *Always label the package.* If I couldn't remember which resident it was meant for, the package would stay in the mail room without a destination. It might be tied to a business deal of some kind. It may be a toner cartridge for a fax machine or printer; the lawyers working from home go through several in a month. It might be special medicine from a pharmaceutical company, which is often the case. Those items need to move.

I'd be responsible. There might be consequences.

I rushed the walkie-talkie back to my lips and pressed the transmitter button. "Hey, Luka, you there?" I asked, by that point annoyed.

"Yeah, I'm here," crowed Luka. "Looking for the remote."

"Great, thanks."

"Okay, have it."

The screen blinked and wiped away the grid showing the real-time feed from the building's cameras. Then the screen went completely gray. I walked closer to the monitor and stood beside Henry, who had removed both gloves and his glasses. Henry was no longer worried about getting in trouble and was eager to enjoy the moment. It was good to see.

The screen flickered, indicating the system's transition from its real-time feed to its memory playback. Almost there. I had it all mapped out. I'd see the face of the delivery guy, and the information I needed—the sender and the resident meant to receive the box—would rush into my mind immediately. I never forget a face, even an obscure one.

"Okay, here we go," Luka said through the walkie-talkie.

A white line appeared and sprang open, filling the screen. It was me on-screen, but something was wrong. Everything was wrong.

It looked like a still photo. The footage wasn't moving. The screen showed me wearing the black ski hat I had worn on frigid nights from months ago. I hadn't worn it that shift.

The screen showed me wearing black winter gloves, but those gloves were with my hat in my locker. It was a cold afternoon, but not cold enough for me to wear my winter gloves and a hat.

I leaned in closer, leaving Henry a step behind me. The footage was dark, too many shadows. It didn't show any sunlight coming into the lobby from the street because it was nighttime when the footage was recorded. Henry and I stood watching the screen while the daylight outside watched us. It was nowhere near dinnertime yet.

The monitor showed my gloved hand holding a paper cup to my mouth and staring at the screen just as I was at that very moment alongside Henry. Henry wasn't present in the footage, however. It was just me on the screen, from months earlier, when more Latin men worked at the building.

The nighttime image of me drinking coffee disappeared from the screen.

Brighter footage splashed into the monitor, this time moving. It was from a half hour earlier, the footage I requested. My mind remained on the still image of me holding a cup of coffee.

On the screen that afternoon was the paused video from Luka's last session with the system's playback. Switching from real-time footage to memory revealed the last file he had accessed. He had been watching archived footage of me, paused it, and forgotten to end the feed.

Henry opened his mouth, and his tongue sounded sticky, like it was being ripped from the top of his mouth. "Hey, Stephen," he said. He sounded nervous.

"Yeah, Henry."

"When did you order coffee?"

I walked back to the other side of the vestibule and leaned against the heater, which I normally didn't do until after five p.m., when I knew Luka had separated from the monitor in his office. Doormen at that building aren't allowed to lean against the vestibule's heaters. I leaned against the vestibule's heaters.

"I didn't, Henry."

"Oh, there goes the guy!" he shouted, pointing at the screen. He was right. It was the deliveryman from before. I would have to contemplate the images of myself later. "The guy . . . he's giving you the box . . . yeah, you take it . . . sign for it . . . recognize him?"

Luka had been silent on the two-way since switching to playback.

"Yeah . . . I got him."

I remembered everything. The box was meant for the lady in 14C. Probably another dress from one of her favorite Fifth Avenue boutiques.

The rush eventually subsided, and the monitor returned to its normal feed. Sixteen black lines intersecting to form a tight grid of real-time footage coming from cameras located in the basement, lobby, and the perimeter of the building.

Luka had crossed Julian, Kenny, and Jose Lopez off his list, but if he was building a case against me using coffee footage, he was desperate. He had no smoking gun on me. I had never stolen anything from a tenant or coworker, never left the lobby unmanned for too long during an overnight shift, and never had any issues with a resident in the building. He'd never find a smoking gun.

Luka had me on minor infractions. In the paused footage, I was wearing a ski cap instead of the doorman service cap—this was a violation of doorman rules. He also had me drinking coffee at the front desk, which we were prohibited from doing. It looked unprofessional, he had said, and when coffee spilled, which happened sometimes, it made the front desk sticky.

Except for Henry, every other doorman at the building worked with a cup of coffee at the front desk, but Luka didn't care about firing them; he cared about firing *me*. The ski cap. The cup of coffee. He was building a case. When it was complete, he'd get in front of the residential board and press Play on the DVD player. The screen would flicker, and the board would see grainy footage of me drinking coffee in the lobby while wearing a beanie instead of a service cap. It would make for a boring film, but that's what you get when the remaining young Latino neglects to prove his incompetence. To terminate him, you compile all the footage of him committing petty offenses like drinking coffee at the front desk. You make a DVD, then take it to the next board meeting and press Play.

I had to play it straight while I figured out my next step. I knew I couldn't offer Luka any substantial reasons to fire me, but weeks later, that's exactly what I did.

12

CYRUS VON BRUNO

S hortly after my move to Throggs Neck, I watched *I Am Legend* and
thought, I want that for myself; I want to look worthy of a dog's
loyalty like Will Smith's character, Dr. Robert Neville, the lone survi-
vor of a virus that decimates New York City's population. That's where I
should've stopped to think: aside from the millions of people sharing the
city with me, I had two cats at home. They'd been hiding under my bed
for weeks while coping with the move into the new apartment. I wasn't
used to all that space: growing up pressed on all sides by six siblings,
two parents, and the walls of a two-bedroom apartment doesn't leave
you enough space or time to curl up in the fetal position when you want
to, so you view space as a bad thing. Rather than see the bare walls
and floors and opting for a few prints, a rug, and two accent tables, I
thought, *Yes, a German shepherd just like Will Smith's.*

I named him Cyrus after the highly respected gang leader in the film
The Warriors. My cats had already been named after characters in the
film and I believed, romantically, that Cyrus would tie us all together.
I had failed to consider the ancient ruler by the same name, a king who
gobbled up so much territory that he could add "empire" to his portfolio.
Cyrus was a fitting name.

He was two weeks old when I first laid eyes on him at the breeder's
home. He had a little orange collar around his neck and looked like a
dark mitten with eyes. At two weeks of age, Cyrus fearlessly rolled up
to me like he was wondering where the fuck I'd been. "I'll take the one
with the orange collar," I said to the breeder.

Cyrus was three years old when I decided to go to the Macy's Thanksgiving Day Parade for the first time. I got some friends together and we drove down to Manhattan from the Bronx. I brought Cyrus along too. When we arrived, I parked two blocks from the building and walked to Central Park with my friends. In the park is when I realized that bringing Cyrus around a parade's crowd was a bad idea. He'd once leaped at an old lady's throat because she came too close to me on the sidewalk. That day, I yanked back on the leash as Cyrus was in midleap—imagine the kind of "protecting" he'd do at a parade. I told my friends to enjoy the parade: I'd bring Cyrus to the building so the guys could meet him.

I didn't see the failed rationale: How did pulling Cyrus from a parade make it okay to bring him to a cooperative on Park Avenue? On the list of foolish decisions I've made, bringing Cyrus to the job sits near the top, somewhere near breaking into a school cafeteria for a bowl of Kix instead of Cocoa Pebbles.

I walked him before the drive into Manhattan. That's where it should've happened, during the walk; great ideas often came to me during our walks, but not on that day. Over the course of one hour, Cyrus went from rows of houses in the North Bronx to dozens of tethered dogs and their humans along Central Park's winding paths. I should've considered his reaction to all those stimuli. It should've dawned on me in Central Park to go back home, as Cyrus pulled one way and the other, when he yelped and whimpered. Those were signs of classic anxious behavior in dogs.

No lightbulbs came on, none even flickered, as I approached 905 Park Avenue's service entrance with Cyrus.

I didn't want to walk him through the front door. That was my only clear thought. An off-duty doorman walking his German shepherd into a Park Avenue building through the front door? Come on, that's stupid.

The building's basement was a world unto itself. Lots of hard surfaces with disdain for comfort and exposed brick that indicated unfinished work instead of charm. The walls were painted battleship gray. It was battleship gray over everything, which made it hard to miss the building's orange tabby cat, who saw Cyrus that Thanksgiving Day and slinked around a corner to safety.

When Joaquin looked over from the basement's logbook and saw Cyrus, he froze and drew silent. It wasn't because of Cyrus, I knew. Cyrus isn't as scary after you hear that he hides under my desk during fireworks, or that my male cat routinely hits him with three-scratch combinations, or that despite his appearance, he loves being around children. It wasn't Cyrus that Joaquin was uncomfortable with; it was the sight of me and my dog walking down the basement ramp on *his* shift. He didn't want any part of that. Elmo the cat was the only wildlife in the basement and he belonged to the building, had been there for years, and that was it. Just Elmo. No other employee-owned animals, and especially none owned by me, the only other young Latino left at the job.

"Nice dog, man," said Joaquin, friendliest guy in the world, torn between petting a handsome dog and turning his back so that he could establish some plausible deniability.

His dread was endearing. "Thanks, man," I said, chuckling. "I'm gonna bring him upstairs. I wanna introduce Cyrus to the guys. Been talking about him for months and he's here."

It was true, Cyrus was there, but he was there panting with a frothy tongue. And the edges of his mouth were pinched forward tightly. Those were more classic signs of dog anxiety, but for a kid predisposed to sensationalism (me), they constituted the face of a dog waiting to be shown off.

It was the elevator. Cyrus had never been in an elevator before. It was the shortest ride, from the basement to the lobby, but for a dog never stuffed into a magic closet that closed and reopened to show a different room, it was an eternity.

It was the marble floor. Cyrus had never stepped on a marble floor. He knew wooden floors, grass, and concrete—they all provided the traction he needed to chase cats and squirrels. Cyrus didn't know marble floors.

Fight *and* flight. He shot out of the elevator onto the lobby's floor with confidence, trust, and a whole lot of ignorance. All four of Cyrus's paws slipped away from him and he dropped, his belly plunking onto the floor. I knelt down to comfort him, got him back on his paws, which were quivering by then, and pulled him forward a few careful paces. I glanced through the front end of the lobby at the entrance. The guys at the front door stood on the top step, the door opened behind them, and stared at something down the block. A nice car? A nice ass? Semantics. Whatever it was saved me. They had propped the door open to watch it go by, causing the street noise to drown out the sounds of the commotion in the back of the lobby.

It was at that moment that I realized, Well shit, bringing Cyrus to the building wasn't a good idea either.

Cyrus shouldn't have been there. He'd had enough new experiences for one day; a walk over a glassy marble floor was the breaking point. There was a tug on the leash. I turned around. Cyrus squatted.

Cyrus took a shit.

It landed a few feet from the mouth of the C line's elevator. It landed in front of the couch where Jose took his naps.

Yo, Cyrus took a shit on the building's marble floor.

And it was on camera too. Cyrus's shit occupied disc space on Luka's computer.

What happened next was one of the greatest feats of human ingenuity that you never heard about.

I shot another look at the front door. The fellas were still standing at the front step, by then staring up the block at something else.

I looked down at Cyrus. My once-formidable dog was jelly-legged and examining the lobby walls with the most pained eyes. He appeared to be making peace with the end of all things, an end which would surely come right there and then over a floor he had never known.

I had to move quickly.

I flew him into the magic closet and pressed B. When the doors opened again, I yelled for Joaquin and marched into the heart of the basement. Making my way to the mop room, I put Cyrus's leash in Joaquin's shaky hand and said, "Gimme five minutes." I knew Joaquin had the same perplexed look as before, but I didn't acknowledge it. I had no time to do so. I had to make moves.

Two minutes later, I was back in the lobby with the *New York Times* and a mop bucket.

If it had been solid poop, I would've simply scooped it up with a baggy and discarded it in the basement. It would've taken thirty seconds and I would've returned to the lobby like it was scene 1, take 2. I would've even nonchalantly commented on Cyrus having just "gone." That wasn't the case, however. Cyrus had left a puddle on the marble floor, and that's what the *Times'* Metro Section was for. The pages of the *Times* are wide and expansive and cover lots of ground—I wiped away the entire mess with three pages. While the guys commented and gestured excitedly up the block—it must have been an all-world ass, let me tell you—I worked an ultra-saturated mop over the lobby floor until it was glossy again. I was back down in the basement in five minutes. Joaquin's paper-white face found me at the slop sink moments later. The leash's handle appeared at my side as I stood at the sink rinsing the mop and I took it. Joaquin walked away without saying a word. It was an even trade. He didn't want to know what happened in the lobby and I didn't want to tell him.

Cyrus looked calm again, even confident in the new surroundings, but I didn't take any more chances. I was back on the street minutes later and walking toward the car with my dog. The guys working the front door that Thanksgiving Day never met Cyrus.

There were other things to worry about. Cyrus had pooped on the building's lobby floor, and it happened on camera. There was footage, footage Luka went through daily, and he had me dead to rights. It would've been the easiest termination you ever saw, possibly easier than Julian being fired for leaving his shift to get some ass in Queens. I had no defense. There were no rules I could throw back at him if he approached me, no legitimacy I could pull over myself like a shield, nothing like, "Hey, I was doing a routine patrol of the building . . . with a German shepherd." I couldn't play that card because common sense dictates: *Employees should never visit the building on their days off and bring their hundred-pound dogs when they do.* I had brought my dog to work and turned the lobby's marble floor into a pet relief area.

My anxiety was off the charts the next day at work. I walked into the building expecting one of the guys to shake his head in disapproval the moment he saw me in the lobby. I expected one or two jokes about Cyrus taking a shit in the lobby and feigned concern over my continued employment at the building. "I wonder what Luka's gonna say on Monday" is what I expected to hear. I waited but I heard nothing. There wasn't the slightest reference the entire weekend to Cyrus having been at the building. In addition to Joaquin staying quiet about seeing me that Thursday, it was clear that the two doormen who had worked the Thanksgiving shift hadn't seen anything. I was shocked. Trust me, there is nothing that a doorman enjoys more than having dirt on another doorman. Our building manager loved it that way. Luka was the J. Edgar Hoover of building supers and had a stable of doormen peeking around corners in the hopes of catching each other doing anything irregular. Seeing me at the building on my day off would've been irregular. Seeing me clean up dog poop off the lobby floor would've set off alarms.

When Monday came and went without Luka pulling me into his office to hand me a termination letter, I realized three more things. First, Joaquin hadn't told Luka anything. Second, Joaquin would probably never talk to me again. (And I was right, he never did. He knew Luka was gunning for me and didn't want to be associated with me, but then I bring a leaky dog to the building and he poops in the lobby? Joaquin would not stand close to a sinking ship.)

Lastly, and most significantly, Luka hadn't seen the footage. If he had seen it, I would've been the first doorman in Park Avenue history to be fired for bringing a dog to work and letting him defecate on the lobby floor. It would've been the easiest termination ever. I would've accepted that pink slip and signed it with gusto.

A few days later, I was standing quietly in the lobby vestibule across from Luis when a thought occurred to me. "You know what we should do?" I asked. "We should all put thirty dollars together and buy the Weisses a cologne and perfume set. Cuz they smell terrible. It's like when someone scratches a blackboard: you can *feel* that smell."

"Yeeeeah, those motherfuckers smell like shit!" Luis said. One thing about me and Luis: we knew how to get on the same page quickly.

"Especially Sarah," I said of the youngest of the Weiss clan. "How is she the youngest, smelling the worst? Little girl smells like clothes in the hamper!"

"Bro, you wanna talk about smelling the worst," Luis said through a laugh. "You shoulda been here last week. I was standing right there on the top step with Lenny the one day and we're checking out this nice ass walking by. Then we come back inside, close the door, and we're hanging out—and bro, the lobby smelled like shit."

Oh no.

"Fucking Weisses?" I asked. I was scrambling.

"No, I mean it smelled like *shit*. Like somebody had popped a squat in the lobby and taken a dump right on the floor."

"Whaaat?" I said, acting bewildered. I felt like I was being unraveled, as if my end was beginning with Luis having turned the tables on me, like the wily veteran he was.

"Yeah, I mentioned it to Luka and he laughed it off. Told me to close my mouth when the doors weren't open. But I'm telling you: I smelled shit . . . poop . . . fucking feces."

"Alright, alright, I get it." I sensed a good ending nearby. "But, um, that was it? Nothing happened?"

"Course nothing happened! What do you think I'm gonna do, go investigating the smell of shit? You want me to pull out pen and paper and write notes when I smell it real bad and when I don't smell it at all? Then maybe we'll find out who took a dump in the lobby?"

"I mean . . . no . . ."

"Of course *no*. I didn't see shit on the floor when I went on my break and that was good enough for me."

"Alright, man," I said, scratching my head.

There was a lot to process. To fire a popular doorman, you need to find irrefutable evidence of his insubordination or incompetence. I'd provided Luka with a mountain of evidence. My dog pooping inside the lobby had been captured by the building's cameras from different angles. The footage was waiting in the security system's hard drive for Luka to stumble upon and utilize in the easiest termination of all time. Somewhere in the dark of a long ride home to Throggs Neck, I arrived at the difficult realization that I had to find a new job and fast. Luka might never see the video and I'd be lucky, but if he did and fired me, I might go weeks or months without a paycheck. I had tuition, rent, and car insurance to pay for. I didn't want to play fast and loose with my life anymore, not after finding so much stability. If I was to conserve my life, I needed a new job. My time at 905 Park Avenue would come to a necessary end.

13

THE SPORTS

Jose Ruiz was like me with the newspaper: he'd slide his hand into the thick of its pages and toss it over. If he guessed right, he arrived at the first page of the sports section, which is just a hidden, better front page. He described how he would sit at the kitchen table every morning, sip on his cup of Bustelo, and read all the stories. None of that is remarkable—plenty of folks do that—but this is where he was different: he didn't stop at the articles covering the previous night's games. He'd read each player's stats and analyze their season's averages. That's fanhood from another era.

Jose would go line by line, making sure to get a sense of which way players were trending. He did the same with the *caballitos* too; he'd research the jockeys and then run to an OTB to place bets. Standing across from me in the lobby one day, he interrupted the description of his morning routine to say, "Is no an addiction. I jus' like to see if I still goddet, the nose for a weener. I bet only a few dohlas anyway."

Jose was only an inch taller than I was, but his broad shoulders and erect posture made him seem a lot taller, more commanding. And he was never at a loss for words. He'd routinely show off his conversational range by swinging from poetry to sports to Puerto Rico with ease. And that was my problem with him: he was all story, no strength. He'd talk for an hour about baseball, but never convey a bold, critical statement. It was always love and poetry, always agreeable, and always maddening. "Baseball is so beautiful, like poetry, and boxing, ahhh, a sweet science," he once said, his English grated by his thick Puerto Rican accent. I almost punched the wall. I couldn't get a pernicious thought out of the old man.

Jose Ruiz had been young at a time when civil rights wasn't just a hot-button topic; it was fire on the nightly news. I envied him as I listened to his stories, like the one about Lolita Lebrón and her friends shooting at San Juan's Capitol.

"Hey, Jose, what were you doing when this stuff was going on?" I asked him one shift. "What did *you* think?"

A resident stepped up to the entrance, interrupting our conversation momentarily. "Awwww, Hellohhh, Mrs. Wankel! Howar juuuu?" Jose cooed, clasping his hands for added effect and disappearing into the elevator with her. A smile lingered on his face when he returned to the lobby. I returned to our conversation. "So Campos received radiation poisoning in jail? From our government?" Then his elevator rang. A resident on one of the floors needed a pickup. Jose hummed a song all the way into the elevator. The conversation was over, and I knew it. We let Lebrón and Campos rest in peace.

Maybe you think I'm being hard on him. He was an old man after all; why couldn't I let him be? *He was tired. He had lost a step. He had paid his dues and deserved to be made comfortable.* I thought about the politicians on Capitol Hill, in Congress, the Senate, and the House. They bloviate about issues and make decisions over the populace in a flurry of rhetoric, their dentures flapping around their flaccid faces as they speak, all while collecting Social Security. Jose was just as smart as every one of their old asses, and he was Puerto Rican—the Brown skin stays tight. Was it too much to ask for the old man to have an opinion?

Jose was never more alive and enthusiastic than when he stalked after residents for friendly banter. I used to get embarrassed for him. It aggravated me seeing a man fully capable of commanding respect groveling for validation. You give me Jose's high shoulders, the stately way he carried himself, and his insight, and I'll stamp *myself* with validation.

Jose passed away a few years ago. Luka had forced him out of the building; he told Jose he was too old; he told Jose he should take his pension and retire. Jose put so much effort into avoiding conflict with Luka and the building's residents, and they had forced him out anyway. He found a job at a smaller, less-demanding building a block away and died while working as a doorman.

Had I been more like Jose, I might not have confronted Luka about the target on my back. It was a foolish move: you really shouldn't confront the person engineering your termination, especially when you don't have another job lined up. One evening, Luka walked into the lobby wearing a Members Only jacket just like Jose's, however, and it set me off.

It was similar to Jose's jacket, but Luka wore a size small. I cringe seeing a Members Only jacket on a thin man. They belong on stocky old men, men who have lived and earned the right to be indifferent to carbs and food scales because they've made it that long without dying. Seeing forty-something Luka in a Members Only jacket, seeing him channeling old age and a secure, all-Albanian future, sickened me.

And he was in the lobby. He normally used the side service entrance to get in and out of the building. I'd see him on the security monitor. He'd return from his walk-and-smoke through the neighborhood with his jacket zipped up halfway. He'd ascend the staircase to his apartment's rear entrance taking two steps at a time, but slowly. And laboriously. It was as if each high lift of his skinny leg might be the gulp to finally swallow the entire staircase.

He would not relent, not even for himself. He was the type who poked at cheese cubes with a toothpick when no one was home. Luka could have gone for leisurely walks through the tree-lined neighborhood with the aim of decompressing. Park Avenue folks go for strolls all the time. Instead, he kept himself in a constant state of conflict. As he was never truly at rest, I could not trust him.

Luka offered Lenny a dry greeting at the door and began a relaxed walk through the lobby. He'd pass me soon. I stood at the mouth of the AB elevator and faced the front entrance.

Is he gonna say hi to me? How's he gonna do it?

What do I say? Respond the same way?

Saying "Hi . . . Hello . . . How are you today," that's all part of the job. During shifts, the words exited my lips repeatedly, and even when it wasn't easy, I made sure my lips curved into something like a smile. Greeting residents is at the top of the job description. It's discussed with the super at the interview, and it's part of Day One's training. *Doormen must always greet residents.*

Luka stuffed his hands in his pockets and lowered his head as he neared me. I'd have to greet him when he passed me and not because he was my boss and technically a resident of the building, but because it was the decent thing to do. You say hello to people you know. I had no desire to greet motherfuckin' Luka.

Luka lifted his chin, tossed a "Hello, Stephen" my way, and kept walking. I was in a difficult spot. I wanted him to know I wasn't afraid of him, but I wanted to avoid an argument in the lobby and let *that* be his smoking gun.

I arrived at an inner compromise. I said, "Ey." It's hey without the H, delivered in a low grunt, like a Neanderthal.

I said this without turning my head in his direction. I would not look at him; it was part of the compromise. Still facing the front entrance, I heard a "Hello, Jose" in the back of the lobby, followed by an "Ahhhh, hiiii, Luka!" and the thud of the hallway door being pushed open. Just inside the door was a short staircase Luka was sure to scale with two high steps. At the top of the steps was a long gray hallway that reached the fire stairs, but Luka wouldn't be walking that far. His apartment door was a few paces from the top of the staircase. He'd be home in moments.

I swung around and ran to the back of the lobby where Jose was stationed. "Hey, flip my elevator," I blurted at Jose while pushing up against the side door. Jose's eyes widened in shock. I belonged in the vicinity of the AB elevator, not the C elevator he was operating. I worked the AB car on Monday evenings, but I was nowhere near my post at the moment; I was trying to beat Luka to his apartment and Jose knew it wasn't to compliment him on his jacket.

Doorman rule: *You should always be near the elevator you're assigned to.* That way, you're a step or two away when it rings. Residents don't enjoy pushing the button for the elevator and checking the display in their hallway to see it still showing "L" because the elevator is still in the lobby. On the rare occasions when a guy (me) goes to the bathroom and forgets to flip the elevator to automatic, or he goes outside to help a coworker with luggage and doesn't hear the elevator's chime, the residents will return to their apartments and call the lobby. I've answered these calls. Residents ask, "Why is the elevator still in the lobby?" I've always remained calm and blamed it on the elevator. That's a pro tip: blame it on the elevator. It didn't ring; maybe the super needs to call the elevator company, but Oh look, I see the light flashing, I'll be right up.

Holding the side door open, I stopped and faced Jose, who had not moved. "Hey, Jose," I implored again. "I need you to flip my elevator, okay?" I said it loudly this time in the hopes my voice would carry into the hallway and alert Luka to my presence, maybe hold him there. Jose nodded, dug into his pocket for the key, and began walking to the front of the lobby where the AB car was located. I shot through the side door into the hallway's battleship gray.

Luka was standing at the top of the steps in wait for me. He'd stopped when he heard me telling Jose to flip the elevator. "Everything okay, Stephen?" he asked. His hand was hanging by his side, the keys to his apartment pinched at his fingertips like a baby knife.

"Luka," I said. "The other day. On the screen. What was that?"

"What was *what*?" he asked, his eyebrows raised.

"Luka," I said, sighing. I was annoyed. He was working me. Feigning ignorance would buy him some time while I revealed what I knew.

I was aggravated but settled in. "That was me on the screen, from months ago, drinking coffee. The footage is old. Why were you watching it?"

"Stephen, don't worry about that. It's nothing. You've got nothing to worry about."

Neither of us moved. I waited. In moments like these, I hope for the best, and the best looks like my opponent huffing and puffing and letting his shoulders go lax. He's given up the fight, which means I can too. Then we have a good laugh, slap each other on the back, and run to the nearest cantina for margaritas. But Luka wasn't about margaritas.

I leaned in. "I know what you're doing," I told him. Albanians and Latinos are warring, if quietly, for the jobs at many buildings on Park Avenue. I had become the latest target by the Albanian side.

Luka's face didn't give. "What are you talking about?"

"You're firing all the young Latin guys so you can bring in your own guys." I waited again. "Other Albanians."

Luka's thin frame clenched. He was unsettled. "Stephen, Julian had it coming, Jose lost dry cleaning, and—"

"You set Jose up . . . and Kenny?" There was no denying that Kenny's firing had been unjust and, for me, personal. I was fond of Kenny. "Luka, Kenny was one of the best guys here. Never caused problems, always in a good mood, and he switched shifts with everyone so we could put a few days together and enjoy some time off. He was one of the best guys here, and you let him go cuz he had the runs at three in the morning."

"You can't abandon your post," Luka said.

"So take a sloppy shit at the front door?"

"Look—"

"Nah, Luka. *You* look: we go years without anybody getting fired, then *you* become the super and people start getting fired. Three Latin guys get fired, three Albanian guys get hired, all in one year. Julian had it coming to him? Julian was never gonna be voted shop steward, but you could've talked to him. Jose didn't lose any dry cleaning. You set him up, don't deny it."

The difference between myself and the guys Luka had fired was that they never saw it coming. They had arrived at work every day as employees of the building and nothing more, nothing cluing them in to Luka's plans. But standing across from him in the hallway, I was more than a doorman at the building; I had made myself an enemy of the building. That's the way it works. The building is made of residents who want a super to give them everything they want when they call. If the super knocks on a board member's door and says, "I've got a guy down here that I don't like because he gets in the way of making you happy," then voilà, he's gone.

I was raising my fist at a tank. Luka was a resident manager with an agenda I couldn't prove on paper. I was an unambitious doorman who Luka could prove didn't always follow building rules to the letter.

Luka and I stood across from each other for several moments saying nothing. The magnitude of the situation, what it had become and what we knew had to happen, was clearer than ever. The light fixture buzzed loudly in the hallway's stillness. Luka had collected himself. His face was like stone, giving nothing.

"Just remember," I said, tearing into the calm between us. My mind had grabbed onto the only words that felt solid. "I know what you're doing."

I turned, plunged down the steps, and banged open the door separating me from the lobby. Behind me, a key rumbled into a lock. I had challenged Luka at his front door, a realization that added to my feelings of aberrance. I pulled the side door's knob and swooped into the lobby, hoping its soft light and marble floors might emanate the meaning I needed—that matters hadn't worsened, that my firing wasn't at the top of Luka's to-do list. They didn't.

The conflict at the building fueled me at school. In my fourth semester at John Jay College, Professor Matt Stockwell of my seventeenth- and eighteenth-century literature class nominated one of my essays for Best 300-Level Essay of the semester. Using text from de Las Casas's *A Short Account of the Destruction of the Indies*, I'd written on the irony of the "noble savage," the native held in the gaze of the Spanish colonizer guilty of his own savagery. I won.

Another time, I received an email from a professor asking if I minded reading a portion of my essay in class the next day. I figured it would be me and a handful of other students reading from their essays. I said, Yes, of course. It was an honor I didn't mind sharing with my classmates.

The following day, she pointed at me and asked me to read. I began. "Please stand as you read," she interrupted. I rose to my feet and read and read and read. I read an entire page. It became clear that I would be the only student reading. As I read, a friend of mine sucked her teeth and rolled her eyes. I smiled and pressed on. As I neared the end of the second page, I dramatically slowed my cadence. I was leaning in. I was performing. My professor shouted, *"That's* how you write an essay!" She could've let me finish.

Did I mention I had slimmed down again? When I read my essay, I stood at a cool two hundred pounds, the lightest I'd been in years and, for my build, the leanest I'd looked too. A few months ago, I had seen a picture of myself wearing a shirt with buttons being pulled so tightly at the middle, they looked ready to launch. You could see flashes of my stomach between the buttons. *When did* that *happen?* I thought to myself. So I went on an extreme diet. For two months, I ate nothing but green beans and brown rice and did a lot of jogging.

I had the looks and, now, the grades too. I'd mastered myself, something I'd never done before.

I was twenty-nine years old, had no passport, was paying back debt to a college that had expelled me, and owned a four-cylinder car the color of vomit green, but I didn't feel silly. None of it defined me. I could step into any arena and win. I had fought hard to get out of a deep hole, and that was all I saw, darkness pining for my return.

14

McCARTHY

I walked up to Charles H. Greenthal Management Corp. with a canvas messenger bag. I'm only dropping off a résumé, that's all, I'd told myself on the way to the office building. I'd been telling myself a bunch of things in the days leading up to my trip to the company office: *Luka already has me drinking coffee in the lobby, fine, whatever, but he hasn't seen Cyrus pooping in the lobby or I'd be gone . . . There's still time . . . relax, Stephen. Go to Charles H. Greenthal, okay? Go there and drop off the resy . . . Wear business casual, not a suit like you're ready to skip the interview and should take an executive's job instead . . . it's just a résumé, after all.*

I didn't know if there was beef between Douglas Elliman and Greenthal, like the beef between Ubers and yellow cabs, but I knew Charles H. Greenthal was a competing management company. I also wasn't really certain that I shouldn't wear a suit to drop off my résumé. I would've worn Speedo shorts and a crop top if it got me a new job before my termination at 905. I'd been feeling certain I was innocent when my only crime had been being young and Latino. Then I saw the footage of me drinking coffee in the lobby and I begrudgingly accepted that I'd broken a rule, however trivial it was. Then Cyrus squatted and pooped all over the lobby's marble floor. I'd taken the entire situation into uncharted waters. How would the union begin to protect a man whose dog took a shit at the job? I didn't plan on finding out. In early March 2010, I took the train downtown to drop off my résumé at Charles H. Greenthal. They had no history on me, no knowledge about minor—or major—lobby infractions. And I prayed the girl at the front desk didn't hate young Latinos, or I was fucked.

I needed a job. I couldn't go through a lapse in paychecks. I was paying tuition. There was rent and car insurance. The bunch of small bills that together pack a punch. I had no plan beyond "be a doorman at another building"—there was a lot riding on my visit to Charles H. Greenthal.

Needless to say, I was certain my bag would fuck me over.

I had recently flipped through one of the catalogs left out for recycling and spotted the tote bags that the residents often asked me to toss into their cars. I scoffed at it, thought, *Pfft, look at this bullshit bag . . . $30! . . . Price is reasonable, actually, for all the use it gets . . . but the shit doesn't even zip or close, so what's the point.*

I ordered a canvas messenger bag.

Fuck outta here with that tote bullshit. I'm a worker. I'm from the Bronx. A messenger bag for me, thank you very much. I'll repurpose it, use it for my schoolbooks.

I paid $65. Listen, my bag closed. Four times, actually, because after the zipper there was a flap and two buckles. Papi had taught me that sometimes it's better to pay more, if you're getting more. That's how I reconciled the purchase of a canvas bag I'd only ever seen on Park Avenue. I had not considered that I was getting so close to the job that I'd begun admiring its nuance. It was unseasonably warm that February day on Thirty-Fourth Street, but warmer for me as I'd become hyper aware of my bared affections.

Sweat beaded on my forehead and ran down my back as I stood on the curb. No matter what I told myself—that the people in the office had no idea I was on my way to drop off my résumé, that they didn't know who I was or that I worked for the competition—I recognized my need for a big break. For the first time in my life, I was thinking things through, trying to get out in front of a burgeoning situation instead of colliding with it head-on. I was growing.

I finally crossed the street and arrived at the Greenthal entrance. It was locked. No doorman, just glass double doors with a brass panel on the side. My eyebrows shrugged as I worked the information through my mind: a management company that staffs buildings with doormen doesn't have a doorman at its own front entrance. It seemed like irony I might appreciate on another day, but not on that day. I was there on a mission.

I pressed the button next to "Charles H. Greenthal Management Company" written in bold type and waited. My confidence was in the basement, not even the cellar. The basement. A cruddy, dank basement like the ones in the Bronx. There are no wine collections down there.

The management's office lobby was as nondescript as the front entrance. A tall counter pressed into the far corner. There was a young lady behind the counter and over her right shoulder, spreading across and away from her like a jug on its side, was the office. It was a mess. Tall stacks of paper sat atop cabinets that loomed higher than the cubicle walls meant to hide them. I couldn't see a window.

"Sir?" the lady behind the counter said. "Is there something I could help you with?" She was young, maybe in her mid-twenties, with the kind of honest smile that activates cynicism or breaks it down, depending on the asshole recipient of the smile.

"Uhhh, yeah," I said, turning away from the office catacombs. I reached into the canvas bag and said, "I just wanted to leave my résumé with you guys."

"Ahh, okay," she said from behind the counter. The girl had a pleasant and expectant look on her face. I took a liking to her. She was doing her best to make sure she didn't look practiced, like she hadn't repeated the résumé transaction a million times before lunchtime.

But I knew the deal. There are few moments more hope killing than the résumé handoff. You spend hours typing a better narrative of yourself—neat lines of facts are more convenient than the muddled story—and then you pull at one of the stash of printouts in your folder in the hopes that this is the one, the one where people see your name and lightbulbs go off—here's a superstar. Your name would catapult the company, they know it, so they called because they had to; they won't lose you to another company.

I've opened the door a hundred times for doorman hopefuls over the years. I could tell when they didn't have experience in a lobby. Some went overboard and bizarre on presentation. A stained, baggy suit that your overweight grandfather bought on Fordham Road won't compel a doorman to pull the super from the plumbing crisis in apartment 5C. *Hey, Mr. Evans, you've gotta see this guy! He's clearly a great candidate for a doorman position here on Park Avenue!* But walking up to the door in a Hawaiian shirt and flip-flops won't comfort him either; it'll make him laugh and choke on his coffee. Instead of calling the super, he'll pick up the receiver and dial the locker room to say, "You guys gotta come see this asshole in a Hawaiian shirt!"

You can walk up to a doorman building wearing a three-piece suit with a taxi whistle hanging from your neck, and it won't boost your odds of getting a doorman job. The doormen already working in the building are trying to get their friends jobs in the building. And the super might be working his own hustle. Some supers hire men on the condition that they sign over their first two checks to them. Point is, doorman jobs never stay open for long. There's a line of guys ready to fill the spot, and they're usually connected to a doorman working there. That's how I got the job, remember?

You've gotta know somebody, man. That's what I used to say to the guys who popped up to 905's front door asking for jobs.

Later, I would say more. I would see the desperation in their eyes, the tension in the bridge of their noses. These men would approach Park Avenue's front doors all day and, standing at my open door, turn their heads one way and the other; their eyes would take them up and down the avenue like there was a door more special than the rest, more special than mine. I'd open the door, and they were ready to walk away in rejection. I knew my next words would carry a lot of weight. They might have camped outside the building if I said something careless like, "I don't know if we're hiring." For some guys, a doorman position was their last shot at a decent job.

The day at the competing management company's office, I placed my résumé on the counter and zipped my bag. Then I swung the flap over its buckles and slipped each one into its corresponding lock. It's the kind of thing I like to take next to no time; I'd paid $65 for an overly contrived canvas bag that made me work for free.

"Well . . . good luck," the girl said thoughtfully. Then came the hope-killing moment. She put my résumé on top of all the other résumés. My name on top of a bunch of other names belonging to doorman hopefuls. I was fucked, bag or no bag.

"Yeah. Thanks." I offered my best smile. Then I swung my bag around my shoulder and pressed the elevator's call button, contemplating my precarious position at 905 Park Avenue. I was a doorman hopeful, while working as a doorman.

I was almost gone.

"Hey, wait!" I heard from behind me. I spun around.

"Yeah?"

The girl had stood up and was leaning across the counter, her forearms holding her up.

"Can you wait a minute? Do you have some time? The vice president would like to talk to you."

How the fuck.

"Yeah . . . uhhh . . ." I slid up to the counter and fixed my bag in a hurry. Then I fixed my composure. The unexpected break I had been looking for? It might have appeared and was poking its head through a door that had suddenly opened, albeit slightly, and was winking at me in the most suggestive manner possible. "SureIhavesometime," I blurted.

I couldn't read the vice president of the management company, and her office's decor wasn't helping. There was a plant with long branches, but that's just a plant with long branches. There was as much metal in her office as there was wood. There was lots of gold. Certificates and gold trim. The rug was gold. Her hair was short. She had a funny name.

"Michael?" I asked, shifting in my chair. I didn't want to bomb the interview, but I tend to fidget when a woman tells me her name is Michael.

She leaned back in her chair and laughed. "Yes, it's Michael, but with an 'e,' so . . ."

"So, not Michelle?"

"No, not Michelle. Michael, with an 'e' . . ."

"So, Michael-y, rhymes with likely?"

"No," she said, still laughing and enjoying my stubborn disbelief. "Nope, it's still Michael. And you have to pronounce it that way. But you spell it with an 'e' at the end."

"Ahh." I nodded. I had nothing else. "Okay. Michaele."

"Yeah, blame my Irish parents. They liked to have fun." Michaele peeled my résumé away from her messy desk and held it to her face. We were finally getting to the interview part of the interview. "So . . ." she said, returning the sheet of paper to her desk. "Do you like jazz?"

My heart rate was following the route of my résumé. Up and down, but the up was killing me. I needed her to ask the right questions so I could give the right answers and figure out if this was it, my big break, a job in another building!

"Um . . ." I cleared my throat. "Yeah, I like jazz. Love it, actually."

"Figures, that's great," Michaele said, nodding her head. She dug an elbow into the seat's arm rest and placed her chin on her fist. She peered at me across her desk and held her stare, never blinking, never moving. I stared back at her and tried to pick up something. I scanned her forehead, the bridge of her nose, her lips. Nothing moved, not even her eyes. They remained trained on me, and offering nothing. How was I doing? What did she think of me? She wasn't saying.

"I love jazz," said Michaele. "Miles Davis. Coltrane. Louis Armstrong."

"Oh, I love Louis Armstrong! He sounds like a grandfather with a hobby."

Michaele laughed. I gave in. She wanted to have fun; I was going to have fun too.

"And Thelonious Monk," I said. "Only the best name in the history of names!" Then I paused, held out my hand, and affected solemnity. "No disrespect."

Laughter blew out of Michaele's lips and her head flew back. Her chair squealed as it violently returned to its recline position. I didn't know if it was my big break, but it was definitely the best impromptu date I'd ever been on.

"These jazz names. They're amazing," I continued. "You think when they're kids and they read their own names out loud—'My name is Billie Holiday'—that they *know* what they're supposed to do, like go fulfill a prophecy and become jazz pioneers? Cuz seriously, Chick Corea, what is that, it's the worst name ever and it still sounds better than mine."

Still reclining in her seat, Michaele smiled and pointed my way. "I could tell you knew your stuff when I first saw you."

I knew I had gone too far. "Well, I love jazz, but I'm not gonna win trivia anytime soon. And actually, I think I've run out of names."

"No, no, no, Stephen." Michaele tapped on the résumé with her finger. Continued tapping. "I could tell you were building material. I was right. Five years. Five years and change," she said as she sized me up. She could tell how much experience I had just by looking at me. The woman was a machine.

"Ohhh," I responded. "How'd you know?"

"I could tell," she said, pleased with herself. Was it the canvas bag? It wasn't even beige, the usual choice for Park Avenue residents buying canvas bags. I'd chosen olive to deviate a little, but as it turns out, the canvas bag may have been what kept me on Park Avenue.

Michaele picked up the phone from somewhere on her desk. "I've got a building for you. It's actually my favorite to work with. Great staff and the superintendent is the nicest man on the planet." It all sounded so good.

Michaele made the call.

15

HIGH STAKES

The impulse to overshare often gets the best of me. If Michaele hadn't found a building for me, the ensuing job search would've led me to HR offices at Starbucks or Best Buy. I would've slid into the seats across from polo shirt–wearing managers and showed them my palm, indicating *Stop, before things continue, you should know I was just fired for being young and not-Albanian.* It's retail, not open-mic night for angry poets. Corporate doesn't want to be moved, it wants to wear a stiff smile while dismissing you and suggest, as you reach for the doorknob, that you pass by the customer service desk: gift cards are a quick and easy option around the holiday season.

If Michaele hadn't made that call, I would've gone on dates, sat across from many hard women, and showed them my palm, indicating *Stop, before we eat, you should know I just lost my doorman job. I'm looking, though.*

A Bronx woman doesn't normally care what you do for work as long as you have a job. Her neighbors enjoy welfare and WIC for their droopy-eyed kids, but she doesn't want that for herself. She's about to graduate with her BA in something or other and will post photo carousels of herself in cap and gown. She's come a long way. She'll like that you've enrolled yourself in a liberal arts program too. It'll prove that your mind has more stretch than the assholes she's dated. Thing is, you'll excel at skills with zero net worth, so have a job. The assholes she's dated had jobs.

She doesn't care what you do as long as you receive a steady paycheck. But drop *that* bomb—you lost your job—and watch her disposition change. It doesn't have to get to that point. Have a job.

Her parents will care a little, if you get to that stage in the game. Her father will ask and you're going to answer, "Yes, I'm in the union," and that's it, you have an ally. The job security and medical benefits means his daughter will remain on steady ground, even if you piss him off one day and he buries you in it. The girl's mother will be curious about the residents. How rich are they? Any famous people in the building? At some point, she'll remember she has her own job to do, which is getting to know the young man sitting next to her daughter on the couch, but, still curious about Park Avenue residents (Park Ave is far from Throggs Neck, after all), she'll ask a powerhouse question, the one that could bring about your demise: Do the residents like you?

There are myriad ways to fumble the answer to this diabolically booby-trapped question. One answer you must avoid is *Yes, of course.* Trust me, it's not the right answer, Doormen. Better to say *I think so . . . I mean, they've kept me around this long* (shrug your shoulders at this point, maybe chuckle in deference to her authority). Why is this answer better? It redirects to an all-important truth: you have a job.

The women at the downtown boxing gyms spend their mornings in boardrooms and meetings with CEOs they've yet to overtake. On weekends, they post selfies in minimalist bedrooms where the only flare comes from a single vine snaking across the white wall in the background. These women don't sympathize with the layoff; they scorn associations with it.

It's hard enough surviving the "What do you do?" portion of the conversation. You say "doorman," and they find the humor in it. "Like in *Home Alone 2*?" they ask, their smiles suppressing the laughter hoping for release. If it gets past that part of the conversation, and also past my overly informative and prolonged response—"Well, Kevin met doormen at a hotel. I work at a residential building, so the people live there and I get to know them. Their family and friends, I get to know them"—then I'm golden; I have a friend. But arriving at "I lost my doorman job" is a juggernaut of a revelation. These women will drink cosmos past happy hour with the ugly fella as long as he has a great portfolio and exposed brick somewhere in his apartment. That's not me. The first time I saw exposed brick I wondered when the wall would be finished. Then I wondered if my friend was paying discounted rent because of the as-is condition of the apartment. And later, selfishly, I thought I could afford the rent.

There's nowhere to go after getting tossed from a job where you stand at a door and open it/close it for forty hours a week. I was earning a BA in English, a degree lacking a job placement component. If Michaele hadn't hired me, I would've been available for more open-mic nights with angry poets.

After my hiring at 411 Park Avenue was official, I walked into Luka's office and placed my two-week notice on his desk. I said nothing as I did. He read the first sentence and said, "You've gotta be kidding me." It was a short letter, a paragraph followed by a sentence expressing gratitude, but I hoped its brevity conveyed another idea to him and, eventually, the staff and residents: that a man could walk away from 905 Park Avenue.

And just in case that message was lost upon Luka, or it never went beyond his office, I squeezed in another, one I knew would make its rounds. "By the way," I told him from his office door. "The letter offers a month's notice because I'm gonna work the next two weeks and then go on vacation. Those two weeks of vacation the building owes me? I'm takin' 'em. That all adds up to a month." The message was *fuck you*. I worked two more weeks at 905, rested another two for which I was paid, and arrived at 411 Park Avenue on a chariot of euphoria.

16

CAST OF CHARACTERS

Ibelieved I was the hottest pick on the 2010 doorman market. I was
in the prime of my youth, three years returned to college, and the
slimmest I'd been in a decade. I had experience as a doorman too, but
not just during the day, on the nightshift as well, a detail that made
Michaele nod lustily behind my raised résumé. I was like one of those
five-tool baseball players that rarely appear in history. They could do
it from all over the field. When *that* kid walks into your room, you
do what it takes to put him in a uniform. Michaele brought me from a
tanking cooperative to the surging one she presided over. George Stein-
brenner would've been pleased. He had a thing for superstars.

Moments before my first training shift at 411 Park Avenue, I stopped
for a talk with the building's super, Mr. Atwell. Sitting across from him
in his office, I marveled at how out of place he seemed in a basement.
While the building's porters strolled around the basement in their
maintenance uniforms, he sat in a cluttered office that looked accidental,
like it was really a storage room with a desk dropped into the middle.
On the wall beside him was a collage of calendars, the ones handed out
for free by plumbing suppliers. On the far wall was an assortment of
appliances I knew he'd collected from residents over the years. That's
what happens: people move or they die, and the items left behind by
their estate stay at the building, where employees take whatever their
two hands can manage on the train ride home.

Supers dress with one foot in the weekend. Some wear chinos and
casual buttoned shirts, like Evans did at 905, or they wear jeans and

sweaters. Other supers I met looked homeless and you had to tell me you weren't kidding, that really *was* the super from across the street.

Not Mr. Atwell. He wore business suits. I could even see the outline of his undershirt, a crewneck, which impressed me. It was an expression of practicality I didn't see much anymore. The undershirt soaks up sweat, so it doesn't show on the buttoned shirt. Makes sense. It also makes the shirt's whiteness more vibrant. He had a letter opener on his desk too. There were lamps and brass items piled together against the far wall beyond Atwell, who sat behind his desk wearing a shirt and tie that made him look more like the curator of an antique collection at Sotheby's.

He pulled a tenants list from a desk drawer and said, "I'm sure you know from experience not to try memorizing names." He said the list was just a reference meant to help me in the next few months, and before I knew it, I wouldn't even need the list, I'd know everyone. "Oh yeah," I assured him, not looking at the list as he passed it into my waiting hand. I folded the pages in half, then in quarters, and shoved the suddenly collapsed list into my pocket.

"I won't try memorizing," I said, and louder than was necessary. I hoped to convince myself too.

The tenants list is like that first page in a stage play, the one with the cast of characters. Whenever I looked over it in middle school, I hoped to get a feel for the names, maybe guess at what my experience with each one would be. Problem was, the tenants list was even more sparse on details than the cast of characters; at least on that page, you could read a name, follow the dots leading to their roles in the play's universe, and have an idea. Shylock . . . moneylender. Hamlet . . . son of King Claudius. Desdemona . . . Othello's wife. And some names were tailed by descriptions like "close friend of Romeo," which told an early story, but the residents list Mr. Atwell gave me was a chart with names and apartment numbers wedged between the lines. I could not glean much from listings like "Jim and Lauren Sullivan, 3D" except that a man and woman living in the apartment shared the same last name.

I agonized over not knowing what to expect from the names and apartment numbers on the list. At 905, each apartment number on the mail slots had a story that was known to me. The slot marked "14A" received Kaplan's mail, most of which asked for his support or his money. Mr. Kaplan had been a high-ranking member of a recent presidential administration. You put in four years for the highest office in the land, it remembers *you*—Kaplan was assigned two bodyguards that stayed with him during business hours, one of them a burly Italian who talked to us in the lobby while waiting for Kaplan to come downstairs every morning. He told me stories about his years as a New York City detective. I once worked up the nerve to ask a question about his job. I asked if being on patrol was mandatory; if I were ever to join the force, I'd want to skip that part and start as a detective. He shot me a look of amused disbelief and snorted. "You kidding me, kid?" he asked. "You can't just walk out of the academy and start at detective on your first day. You'd have to walk the beat a few years first."

The mail slot for "4D" pointed to simmering hostilities. Where Mrs. Godfrey stalked the lobby twitching her head like a hawk hearing a twig break from a mile in the sky, Dr. Godfrey slumbered through it. His limp arms would swing at his sides like out-of-sync pendulums and he'd drag his shoes the length of the lobby's marble floor. He had a clean and even look about him, which is what preppy outfits can afford you, but his flabby torso looked to have been unevenly dropped onto his waist, like he might slide off his legs if not for his polo shirts always being tucked into his chinos.

The only signs of life from Dr. Godfrey came one Sunday evening when he pulled up to the building in one of his many luxury sports cars. The Lamborghini was his favorite. The doors on both sides swung open with a synchronized urgency I'd previously seen only from detectives in TV shows. Mrs. Godfrey emerged from the passenger side comforting her eight-year-old son Robby, whom she'd pulled from the back seat in the middle of an ugly cry. Dr. Godfrey swung around to the trunk, where I met him to receive a canvas bag, then another that he nonchalantly placed in my hands. Holding their bags, I escorted Mrs. Godfrey and a still-ugly-crying Robby into the building, where she bent at his side to comfort him with words like "lovey."

I turned for a final look at the sports car and saw Dr. Godfrey still standing at the open trunk. He'd watched the entire transaction until its end, with Mrs. Godfrey disappearing into the building. He took a deep breath and when his chest swelled forward, his frame shifted so that he actually looked to be stacked upright. It was then, at the end of his ex-hale, that his eyes darkened and looked piercingly at the building's front door, and for a moment, it seemed a primitive impulse coursed through him, like he might claw and snarl in defense of his one last possession. That urge seemed to disappear as quickly as it revealed itself. He closed his eyes and slammed the trunk shut before sighing his way back to the driver's door. The coupe eventually crept away slowly and with some trepidation—which is strange coming from a Lamborghini—and I wondered if Dr. Godfrey was at the wheel deciding whether to make the turn toward the parking garage or blast straight into an alternate life.

I had a beat on all the residents at the previous cooperative. I knew to stay on my toes around board members, like the husbands from 2A or 7C, as friendly as they were, because they were the type to flex their board-member muscles. If a doorman's name gets mentioned at a board meeting, it's usually not complimentary. Members like to keep the board president accountable, and there's no better way to accomplish that than by complaining about a doorman. If they're feeling especially wronged—"My wife had a headache and nobody was in the lobby to call 911" is a claim that comes to mind—demanding suspension or termination makes things right.

17

HEAVY HITTERS

After three training shifts at the building, I couldn't bear it any longer. I had to know. I'd worked with several different doormen and maintenance men during those shifts, and none had come close to casually disclosing the information I needed. Fifteen minutes into my fourth training shift, I slid beside one of the doormen, a short, elderly Puerto Rican man named George, and put him on the spot. "Who are the heavy hitters?" I asked him. Having already worked five and a half years on Park Avenue, I knew the pertinent questions to ask. "I'm guessing we start with the board president?"

"*Heavy hitters,*" I heard from behind me. It was Lorenzo, a middle-aged Puerto Rican, standing underneath the lobby's chandelier. He was assigned to the elevator on that shift and knew how to pick his spots: the chandelier was in the center of the lobby, where he was in the vicinity of any conversation in the lobby and was also a quick pivot away from the mouth of the elevator. Lorenzo nodded in approval of the term. "I like that."

"Heavy hitters" was a term I had come up with at 905 to refer to problematic tenants. Terms like "ball-breakers" or "assholes" worked okay, but if a resident walks in on you calling him an asshole, you're fired. If a resident hears you say "heavy hitter," you can whip a look at your partner and act embarrassed, as if the resident walked in on another meaningless conversation about baseball. You can even invite her to join an impromptu analysis on the 3-4-5 hitters in the Yankees' lineup. You can't do that calling a resident an "asshole" to her face.

Mr. Atwell had assigned me time with both doormen that evening: four hours shadowing George at the door and four hours shadowing Lorenzo on the elevator. The plan was for me to work a mixed bag of shifts for two weeks and slide over into nights at the end of that second week.

"Yeah, the board president," George responded, smiling broadly. I was relieved. He seemed entertained by my question and happy to share. "Ambassador Abrams, 17A. He'd be a heavy hitter for sure." He looked deep in thought, as if measuring severity. "And make sure to call him 'Ambassador' too, not 'Mister,' or he'll remember that."

"That's for sure, he'll remember," Lorenzo said. "Next thing you know, you'll be getting pulled into the office and then Mr. Atwell will stress about *that* too."

The tail end of his comment stood out to me: Mr. Atwell was a chronic worrier. I had sensed that about him already. Maybe it was all the calendars in his office. If I was constantly being reminded of the day, the week, the month, and from every angle, I'd be stressed too.

George shook his head and laughed. "Ohhh, yeah," he said, *"Ambassador* Abrams. Don't screw that up." An old-timer with a lengthy white mustache and rimless, round spectacles, George had been all smiles and handshakes when we met and seemed to celebrate me just for being there.

"So wait," I said. "Ambassador Abrams. Ambassador to which country?"

"He was the American ambassador to . . ." George said, taking a moment to recollect. ". . . to some country out there . . ." George brought his hand by his head and whisked away the country's significance. "Afghanistan, I think . . . or something-stan . . . Kazakhstan?"

"Ahhhh . . . one of those 'stan countries, huh?" I brought my hand to my head and with our patented American indifference to the rest of the world, did the same.

George laughed. "Yeah, one of *those* countries."

Moments later, the three of us waded through the shift's slow spell—George sat near the glass watching people walk by, Lorenzo near the elevator with his hands clasped behind his back like a cyborg in low-energy mode. I gave the chandelier a try and stood underneath it. "So wait up a sec," I said to neither man in particular. "Mr. Atwell . . . he stresses a lot?"

"Oh sure," said Lorenzo from behind me. Flush with excitement, he hurried into the center of the lobby where I stood. "You seen his face?"

During our conversation in his office, I had noticed that one side of Mr. Atwell's face looked dented. From underneath one ear to his neck, a big dent. "Oh yeah, I did," I responded. It had caught my attention, but I was easily distracted by all the different-size calendars.

"Of course you did," Lorenzo said, laughing. "Mr. Atwell looks like he got kicked in the face by a horse."

"What happened to him?" I asked.

The elevator rang. Lorenzo spun to answer the call, leaving me in the lobby alone with George, who had gotten to his feet to lean against the glass. He was engrossed in watching pedestrians walk by. The building's facade was all glass with a front door that led into a sliver of a space that was itself backed by more glass, making it a vestibule with the feel of a fish tank.

It didn't look like George was interested in telling me why Mr. Atwell had a dent in his face.

I would come to learn that this was George's way, that when he wasn't dealing with tenants or taxicabs, he'd sit and watch, or stand and watch, but he'd take moments as easy as he could get them. I'd come to appreciate his way soon enough, but I wasn't there yet. At *that* moment, the one that found me standing in one of the two doorways that spilled into the vestibule from the lobby, I wanted him to feel as burdened as I did, as anxious as I was to know all the tenants' names and faces. I wanted George to share the same sense of urgency I had, the one hoping to have expectations for each resident weighed, packed, and ready to ship. But he didn't; he knew the residents already. George had passed each one over his mind's scales many years ago, and it's the kind of thing you do only once. He was sixty-eight years old, six years over retirement age, and would take it easy. That morning, George kept the side of his small frame pressed against the glass like it was a glue trap for doormen. I spun away from the vestibule and retreated into the lobby. I needed sanctuary.

There was a shiny hardness to the building's lobby. The floor was made of beige marble and the far walls in the vestibule erected of darker, green marble. There was glass in most places and mirrors in the places in between. All the furniture had a sheen to it. The corner cameras looked down on everything, none of it welcoming. It was too pristine, too solemn. I knew a lot about working a building but very little about working 411, and it showed.

"That's the tenant list, right?" George asked, not moving from his position against the front glass. "Don't bother tryna memorize those names, man. There's no point. In your head, try matchin' faces and floors instead."

"Oh, I hadn't thought o' that," I said, releasing a long breath over the list. "Faces and floors."

"Yeah, man," George said. "You'll start remembering faces, start bringin' them to the right floor, and you'll get it soon enough. You'll bring 'em upstairs with luggage, take them to their door, and boom: you'll remember *that* fuckin' door because it belongs to the assholes that made you carry twenty pieces of luggage and couldn't even give you a dollah. You'll remember you took those assholes to 14C." That is what a life preserver hitting the open water sounds like.

"Let me see that fuckin' list," George said, tearing himself away from the glass. A woman outside waved at him as he turned away, and he didn't notice. She walked past the door and seemed disappointed that she hadn't caught his attention. George looked over the paper and grinned. "You've got some fun ones on this list."

"Yeah, I figured."

George ran the tip of his finger over the column of names and settled on one. "This guy," he said. "A real ball-breaker. Always grumpy, always sayin' some shit."

"Right," I said, looking over George's shoulder at the list. I set a mental reminder to write "heavy hitter" next to his name later.

"Mrs. Geller . . . what a bitch," George said, shaking his head. The list was talking to him. "She's actually out right now."

"Oh, I think I met her the other day. Weird-lookin' lady, right? Loves the color orange? Glasses, hair, pants—everything orange? We met. She shook my hand."

"Right, that's her. Yeah, she's out right now, gonna be back soon. Watch out for her. She used to be president of the board but acts like she's still the boss."

"Oh yeah? So what happened, she got tired of it?"

"No, the other board members got tired of *her.*"

I wrote "heavy hitter" next to her name.

Outside, a woman stopped at the door and after not spotting anyone, peered through the glass for a better look. It couldn't be me she was looking for. Lorenzo? It was either George or Lorenzo. I was wearing a former doorman's uniform, just like a summer guy would, and had no friends in the neighborhood.

"Holy fucking shit," George said, his eyes widening over the list. He jabbed his finger into the middle of the list. "Fucking 6F."

"Okaaay," I said, my concern rising. George, with his Depression-era mustache and circle lenses, looked like the morale-boosting fellow from the Monopoly game, and that guy knows more than just Park Avenue, he strolls through the entire neighborhood. Why would he worry?

"Ms. Novak. That's a crazy bitch."

"Well, that's great."

"Yeah, it's not just you that's gotta be careful with her, we're *all* careful around her." He slid the list over the counter and returned it to me. "Definitely write 'heavy hitter' for that bitch. Write it in big letters cuz she's the queen bitch of heavy hitters."

I groaned, then wrote it. It was good advice. Still, I tried encouraging myself. I decided I had a clean slate with those folks. New building, fresh start. I'd try to win them over. The residents and I would share peace.

The elevator's bell rang, signaling its return to the lobby, and the door slid open. Out came a portly woman dressed in black from head to toe. Lorenzo tailed behind her with his head lowered and his hands clasped behind his back like a stumped philosopher.

If Park Avenue ever commissions a museum dedicated to the feral tribes of New Yorkers it converted to doormen, Lorenzo's uniforms will be the ones on display. His were the only uniforms I ever saw that made me wonder about the uniform-making process when I would've preferred to keep it on the list of origin stories to not give a shit about. Tall and slender with a handsome, weathered look, Lorenzo had the posture of a suit stand, as if long ago, an Italian tailor had received the first bulk order of doorman uniforms and thrown a swath of fabric over him, snipped at the excess cloth around his body's outline, and caught sight of an index finger rising from a fold.

On me, doorman uniforms were tight in some spots and loose in others, no matter how many times company reps measured me, but on Lorenzo they were aggravatingly perfect.

"Hello, Mrs. Miller," George said with the slight raise of his palm.

"Hello, George!" the lady crooned cheerfully in her finest Meryl Streep. She stopped short of the vestibule's entrance and somehow, without any perceptible movement from her lower body, pivoted her wide frame in my direction. She had the steady but deliberate motion of a cruise ship. After coming to a full stop, Mrs. Miller stared at me.

With Mrs. Miller's eyes peering my way, I hand-cranked my thoughts through the process of elimination: *George is at the door . . . Lorenzo is behind her . . . I'm the only person on this side of the lobby. It can only be me she's staring at for this long.*

She looked me over with a pleasant, almost playful smile. I continued doing nothing because that's how I normally respond to stares from women dressed in shadows. Around a deliberately all-black outfit, I stand befuddled and misplaced. After what felt like an hour's worth of eerily good-natured silence, she turned to look for answers from Lorenzo instead.

Lorenzo rolled up to Mrs. Miller's side as if on skates. "This is Stephen, ma'am," he said with an easy smile. He raised a palm and gestured my way slowly and with finesse, like he was closing a sale. "He's the new full-time guy replacin' Tony."

"Tony's leaving us?" she asked, turning fully to face Lorenzo. She was wearing dark glasses but had tilted her head forward so her eyes could peer over its frame.

Lorenzo placed a hand on his chest and chuckled as if entertained. "Naaaah, not *thaaaat* Tony," he responded. He showed her both palms and shook them, communicating to her she was in good hands. "Tony Borowski, the night man. *He's* leaving us." I was listening. I was learning. I had gone from a building with two Joses to a building with two Tonys, and I was taking over the night shift for one of them, a Tony Borowski no one described in full.

As far as I could tell, there were two weeknight guys at the building, a Puerto Rican and an Irishman. They were one and two on the seniority list, and the Puerto Rican Tony took all the overtime. There was an Albanian on staff too: Teo, the handyman. He was a nice guy. Maybe too nice, apparently: the guys called him a pushover and described him as aloof and submissive. I tried feeling bad for him, but a rush of relief overcame my attempt at compassion. Too-nice, submissive Albanians are usually not gunning for young Latinos at the workplace. At 411 Park Avenue, I could breathe easier.

When it came to Borowski, however, the guys said little. They described him as a tall and crazy Polish old-timer. He sounded like Bill from 905 to me. Needless to say, I wasn't looking forward to meeting him. *He* sounded like a heavy hitter.

"Ahh, okay . . . well, good luck, Stephen," said Mrs. Miller. She rotated herself to look me over once more and blinked, seemingly shifting into a new gear. Her smile was surrounded by folds that looked like extra, backup smiles. "Welcome to the building."

I thanked her and shook her hand with added zest, allowing myself to glow, which I can confirm is not an imaginary effect exclusive to pregnant women. I felt good. I was glowing.

After sharing a brief, friendly exchange with Mrs. Miller at the entrance, George turned the door's lock with a flip of the wrist and pushed it open with his shoulder, following its swing onto Park Avenue. The sounds of car horns and passing pedestrians sprang into the lobby over a wave of chilly spring air, rejuvenating me.

George checked his watch after locking the door and spun around. "You been on the door long enough. Mr. Atwell is gonna want you on the—"

"I got 'im. I'll take him," Lorenzo said, cutting in as if I was a prize. My cheeks warmed from the embarrassment. Lorenzo turned and sidestepped, gesturing toward the invisible path to the elevator. Grinning, he nodded at the elevator and said, "Let's get you going in there." Lorenzo was one of the smoothest motherfuckers I'd ever met in my life.

I'd be the nighttime doorman at 411 Park Avenue in two weeks. As the only employee working during the late shift, I would be required to remain in the lobby except for supernaturally short trips to the bathroom or the supply room. The elevator would run unmanned during my entire shift. That didn't mean I could avoid training on the elevator. Like a server picking up a host shift, a doorman eventually works other assignments. I'd soon pick up a daytime shift, and I might have to run the elevator; without prior training, I'd be "new" on the elevator despite months working at the building. Mr. Atwell had thought ahead (or, worried ahead). The two weeks of training at 411 included a crash course in the delicate and complex world of the elevator.

The elevator detail is a safe, low-risk assignment for the new guy because the worst he could do is bring a resident to the wrong floor. It's not a good look, but there's room to maneuver. You say, "Sorry, I'm new." Maybe the resident is a heavy hitter, and she sighs and shakes her head and you have to say it again. And maybe she's mumbling something, so you stick your head out of the elevator after she steps out. You say it again, at her back this time—"Sorry, I'm new"—and that's awkward and possibly scary for her, but there are no serious consequences. You're sorry. And you're new. And you can repeat that later when she calls management accusing you of chasing her into the hallway.

Put the new guy at the door instead of the elevator and it's a different ball game. The doorman's number one priority, the one that belies his custom-tailored uniform and shiny shoes and clip-on bow tie, the one that his salt-of-the-earth charm can't deny, is security. It triggers the unforgiving, intolerant protocols inherent to the job. If you're not a resident's friend or a relative he recognizes, you need to arrive at the door with a name, not an apartment number. All buildings have apartment numbers, but the tenants have different names. When doormen hear names, they call the corresponding apartment to request permission to grant entry. The doorman can't be a rook because a rook doesn't know names.

If you come with a name the doorman knows, say, Birkman, and after buzzing 13A, the residents say, "Never heard of him," you're back on the street, and the only way the door ever reopens for you is if you return carrying the hot dogs the doorman sent you to buy after your dismissal.

"So . . . I heard you worked at a building before comin' here," Lorenzo said in the elevator moments later. It was a question. A request. Lorenzo wanted to know how I came to be at the building.

We were on the way back to the lobby after bringing an elderly couple, the Blooms, to the eleventh floor. They had been immediately and incredibly polite, though to varying degrees. The husband seemed to switch to a state of amused patience when his wife began unleashing enthusiasm over meeting the newly hired doorman. She seemed to want the elevator ride to go beyond the eleventh floor just so I could continue telling her about myself. I could tell by her husband's amused smirk that he'd seen it all before, her welcoming new faces with unbridled joy.

I tried applying George's face-to-floor technique in response to Lorenzo's question: as soon as the elevator slid shut on the eleventh floor, I got to committing their faces to memory. It wasn't a difficult task; they had been abundantly kind, she for her welcome and he for not getting in the way of it. I would never forget their faces.

I made room in my mind for Lorenzo's question and the Blooms' faces disappeared.

I had not yet decided how to discuss my experience at 905. How candid should I be? I could rattle off the classics—*I needed a change of scenery; it was a dead-end job that didn't offer opportunities for growth; I felt underappreciated*—but those stories don't fly with doormen. Doormen open doors. They take packages from a delivery boy's hands and bring them to a resident's doorstep. Occasionally, they get the opportunities to point tourists in the wrong direction, and that's fun, but their expectations peak at direct deposit. They know what the job is; it doesn't change. If they work their way up the ladder, it's the one in the supply room. Flowery sentiment doesn't work with doormen.

Full-time doormen don't switch buildings. It just doesn't happen. You don't give up the years of seniority at one building to start at year zero with another. But I had. I had given up five years of seniority at 905 to come to 411 and start at zero like a rookie. Only extenuating circumstances lead to a move like that.

The guy at the bottom picks vacation time last, after everyone has chosen their time and left the hottest weeks in July and August so he can travel to an island where it's even hotter. That's what I had signed up for, to be the last guy booking flights.

It was clear that the guys had been talking and trying to figure things out.

"Yeah, I worked at another building," I said, repeating the obvious.

Lorenzo said nothing. He veered his body toward the elevator's door in anticipation of its opening and said, finally, "Gotcha."

The elevator reached the lobby and released us.

"Okay," I said, walking past him and catching sight of the lobby floor's gloss. I looked into the marble's wavy gloss and lost myself.

Doormen talk. That's their dominant trait, talking. It's the same as a sniper excelling at accuracy or the Mets being proficient at mediocrity. You get a group of doormen together and it's over. The walls blush.

It's your job to talk to your shift mate. Maybe he's the quiet type, but sooner or later, conversation will burst out of him and you'll have to volley it back. It's unavoidable. Banter eats at the time on the clock and that's what you want, for the shift to fly by. If you both commit to a conversation, and I mean *really* commit, like with Italian hand gesturing and Latin temper infusions, forget it, you'll be spraying saliva at each other for eight hours, and before you know it, you'll be on the train ride home.

If you don't talk, your coworkers won't trust you, and if they don't trust you, they stay away from you. You don't want to be doorman non grata. If your shift mate is assigned to the door, he'll stay glued to it to avoid going anywhere near you. If he's on the elevator detail, he'll stand watching the elevator's entrance for eight hours because that's the only mouth he trusts. He certainly won't hang near the door and go near yours. Try calling yourself a superstar when your partner prefers an elevator over you.

18

BILLIE JEAN KING

During my next shift with George and Lorenzo, I opened up completely. I told them about my time at 905 Park Avenue. I told them about Luka. They were astonished. George nodded throughout my telling of the story and shook his head at the crazy parts. I knew Lorenzo was intrigued. Lorenzo used to make it sound like he'd endured every experience ever known to mankind, like he was a human archive of experience. Nothing ever surprised him. "That's why I always tell people . . ." he used to say whenever he heard others tell a story. But not that day. That day he listened to my story with tense eyes, never saying anything.

I assumed I had accumulated some favor.

"So what's with Geller?" I asked, ready to change the subject. I'd been curious about the orange heavy hitter from 2F. The elevator rang, and Lorenzo walked away to answer the call, leaving me in the lobby with George.

"Geller, shit . . . she's the reason why Mr. Atwell looks like someone stepped on his face."

"What? How you mean?"

"She got to complainin' about this and that, demanding all these changes in the building, like with the hallways' carpets and shit, and nothing was ever good enough. And then she spent some of the building's money on fixin' up her apartment."

"Wow."

"Yup. And you see that painting behind you?"

There was a wooden art deco painting of Times Square on the lobby's back wall. It was huge, spanning the entire wall and standing the full height of the lobby. "I would open the door many times in the ensuing years for tourists who thought that shitty painting was a landmark. That's how big it was, so big that tourists' lusty eyes would spot it and knock on the door with requests. I'd snap the photos for them just to avoid another selfie stick extending near my face.

"See that frame?"

"Yeah."

"Why does a painting on wood need a wooden frame?"

I laughed. "Wow, that's a good point!"

"There you go. So when she was president of the board, she had the frame put onto the painting, and guess what happens . . . the value of the painting goes down because the frame was screwed onto the original wood. Bitch had treated it like it was canvas needing a wooden frame. It didn't. It was already wood. Tenants were pissed off."

"So that's when the board gave her the boot."

"Eventually. But not before Mr. Atwell got throat cancer."

"What? From smoking?"

"Nah, man. From stressing."

"About Geller?"

"Yup. Doctors told him too. They said it was stress. He'd been stressin' so much over the job that he got cancer in the throat."

"Wait, how do you get throat cancer from stress?"

"From talking to her so much? Complaining about her so much? Who the fuck knows. But he got throat cancer, and the one stressing him at the time was Geller. Fuckin' crazy shit."

Just then, a young Latina walked by the front door. She wore a loose skirt and a long jacket with a chunky purple scarf falling from her shoulders. It was one of those layered outfits that serves to obscure the figure of the average woman but failed to obscure hers. Undeterred, this girl's curves showed. George walked into the vestibule in the middle of a jitterbug, all shoulders and side lean. Catching sight of him, the girl waved and mouthed "Hiii" enthusiastically. Her entire outfit, flowing behind her like a flag in the wind, seemed to be saying hello to George.

"George, what the hell?" I asked, hurrying into the vestibule, my feelings of inadequacy peaking. You can be as sophisticated and mature as you want to be, but there's no preparing for that first time you're overlooked for an old man. I joined George at the glass facade, hoping she'd see me and maybe, just maybe, look for me the next time she passed by the building. I wasn't that lucky. "What's the deal with all these girls always looking for you?"

He was still waving and wouldn't be interrupted. "Hey, mamita," he slowly muttered through a grin. It registered. She smiled again. But not at me. I was right next to George and grinning like a toothpaste commercial, but nothing, not even a glance from her. Then I saw one of those social nuances that tells me everything: her smile remained on her face as she turned her head. Saying hi to George brought her bliss and a pleasant escape. George kept waving. He kept waving even though she couldn't see him wave. "Look at that ass, huh?" he said, his neck twisting farther as she walked away. George continued waving.

"I mean, yeah, nice ass," I said, annoyed but still glad to see her through the crowded street. Then I turned to him. "But bro, what's the deal?"

"Listen," George said, sniffing like he was bored, like he had answered the question a dozen times that day. Then he flashed a broad, honest smile. He was enjoying my misery. "It's the mustache. I've been standing at this door for years. These women always see me here. They don't know me, they know the mustache, and they love it!"

I made peace with the reality that I'd never get love from passing ladies the way George did. I would work the overnight shift. There's nowhere near as much foot traffic on Park Avenue during the late shift. Maybe a few dozen ladies on their way to nearby Tao or Lavo, but that's about it. And they wouldn't be looking for my mustache. Mine was nowhere near as full as George's. His had character. Mine was blond at the ends. At bad angles, all you saw was a dark patch under my nose. I look like a Brown Hitler in some pictures. The ladies on the way to Tao or Lavo aren't looking for Brown Hitler.

The elevator returned to the lobby and out came a style nightmare. Her hair was wispy and cropped short like a child from the dust bowl. She wore an LL Bean jacket, the entry-level zippered one for crisp breezes and light drizzle, and relaxed-fit jeans of denim too coarse-looking to have been made in my lifetime. To round out the throwback montage, she wore white Keds that evinced practicality, like she could wear them to shoot layups. The most fashionable item she wore was the scowl on her face. We locked eyes as she passed me, and for a moment, she relented. She said hello, and I, heavy-legged from fright, mustered a fingers-only waggle.

She had incorporated a purse into her ensemble. It wasn't chic and leather and sleek, like the purses swinging in the flocks of long-legged models on their way to Tao. Hers was quilted and cylindrical like a pill made of fabric and was covered in elaborate floral patterns. The bag seemed like a deliberate addition to her outfit, as if she knew how unique she looked without it—like an aged manager at a sporting goods store—and hoped to keep you off her scent for a bit longer with a dot of youthful femininity.

George waved and greeted her at the door like a professional. She said "Hi" and called him "Jorge" in a decent Latin accent before turning up the street with a stone-faced determination usually reserved for bank heists or terrorist attacks.

George locked the door behind her and shook his head.

Lorenzo, who had stayed at the mouth of the elevator, sneered. "A real piece of work," he said.

"I didn't see Billie Jean King anywhere on the list," I said.

George laughed. "That was Novak," he said. "Bitch from 6F."

"Oh, wait a sec. Novak. The one you called a crazy bitch."

"Yeah. The one you might call a heavy hitter."

"Damn, man. She came as advertised. Maybe even worse cuz she looks like she works at a hardware store."

"You see Billie Jean King working at a Home Depot?" George asked, laughing.

"No, you're right, but only because I don't see Billie Jean King wearing that apron they wear at Home Depot."

Lorenzo entered the vestibule. "She's actually a teacher."

"What? Her?"

"Yeah, man. She's an English teacher at one of the private schools on the Upper East Side. She tutors kids privately too."

"Parents leave their kids with her in private?"

"Yeah, man. And make sure you don't say things about her in Spanish when she's around—"

"Nah, no way."

"Yeah. She knows Spanish."

"Oh shit."

A wide grin peeled across George's face, causing his long white mustache to stretch. He enjoyed my drummed-up concern. "Don't worry, man," he said. "You'll see her a few more times this weekend and that's it; you'll never see her again cuz o' your shift. She always gets back in right before the overnight shift."

"Dat's a shocker," I said dryly. "She looks like a creature of the night."

Lorenzo sat on the bench across from me. It took some getting used to, the sitting-underneath-cameras-intended-for-security, not-doormen thing. "So you know what happened with Tony, right?" Lorenzo asked, his hands clasped over his crossed knees like a guest on a talk show.

What was it with him not wanting to be more specific about the Tony on his mind? A last name, a nickname, *anything* would've helped. I took a guess. "Umm . . . you talkin' about overnight Tony?"

"Yeah, that's the one," said Lorenzo with a pleased look on his face.

"Mr. Atwell told me he was retiring," I said.

George seemed to awaken at the mention of Tony. He stood up from the small bench in the vestibule and walked into the lobby, leaving the door to talk to me. "Fuck no, he didn't retire," George said. He walked farther into the lobby and sat on a leather chair. There were two chairs in the entire lobby I had been told were forbidden to doormen. I understood why: they faced the door directly and would make the sitting doorman appear too "at home" while at work. George was sitting on one of them. He was one of *those* guys: old enough not to give a fuck but nice enough to be excused for being that way. "Tony got forced out, man," he continued. "One of the tenants called up and complained. Management had enough. They said, 'Hey, you quit and keep your pension, or we fire you and you don't get a pension.' He chose the pension."

"Damn, that's rough," I said, not giving this Tony Borowski guy much thought. "But at least I don't have big shoes to fill."

"Nah, you don't," George said over his shoulder as he rose to his feet again. "Borowski gift wrapped that shift for you." He whirled around to face me and swung a make-believe paddle at a ball. "He's a good man though."

"I'll be alright then," I said and glanced at my watch for the time. Dinnertime soon.

"Hey, one of your training shifts is gonna be with him, right?" Lorenzo asked. Now he wasn't even using names, just pronouns. It was too soon for that.

"You talkin' about Tony Borowski?"

"The one and only."

Mr. Atwell had scheduled me to work a two-week medley of daytime and evening shifts at the building. The last three shifts would be the most interesting. I'd see two overnight shifts with Ramón, who worked on Borowski's nights off. Finally, I'd work one shift with Tony Borowski before taking over for him as the full-time overnight doorman at 411 Park Avenue.

Lorenzo thought my schedule was hilarious. "Mr. Atwell probably scheduled it that way so Ramón could show you how to work the overnight shift—"

"I mean, I worked overnight shifts at 905 . . ."

"—and Borowski could show you how *not* to work the overnight shift."

Lorenzo's head rolled back in self-affirming laughter. I groaned. I realized he'd ignored my comment to have an easier path to his punch line. It was another joke on Borowski, and it had become clear that those were jokes that demanded laughter from its audience. Still, I really wanted to address this idea that I didn't know how to work a building. I wasn't that green. I knew how to work a building. Lorenzo kept laughing, and I let it go.

"You know why he got forced out?" Lorenzo asked me eagerly. George quietly slid past me and returned to the vestibule to watch the door alone. He didn't seem interested in the conversation anymore.

"Nah, not at all. Nobody's given me any details on that," I said. My level of intrigue was at all-time peak levels. I was desperate to know how an old man close to retirement gets shipped out of a Park Avenue building. Cooperatives prefer older men to young men. I was replacing a man in his late fifties, a demographic often tapped into by Park Avenue because men *that* old appreciate full paychecks and even fuller benefits, and they work that way, with an aim on sticking around.

"So 10B's daughter goes out one night in the fall. It was November, come to think of it. I only know that because I remember wondering if the bullshit with Borowski would make them cut our Christmas bonuses even more than they do, those cheap fucks."

"Oh, the Clarkes are cheap?" I'd heard about the Clarkes already, though for different reasons. They drove in from the Hamptons on Fridays at seven p.m. sharp just to grab a parking spot in front of the building, which is the lowest thing you could do if you have doormen at your building. Instead of keeping the car in one of the nearby underground garages like other residents, the Clarkes drove up to the building in their current favorite car (at the time, a Cadillac Escalade) and sat inside the idling vehicle until the clock struck seven. Then the doors opened and out they'd come, often decked out in designer clothes, and leave luggage with the doormen while they went for dinner. The car would sit in the same spot all weekend while the building's doormen looked for parking throughout the neighborhood, sometimes driving around for up to an hour until they gave up and spent more than $20 at the lot. It happened to me a few times when I worked day shifts. I'd drive past the Clarkes' car a dozen times looking for parking until there was no time left and I decided to park in a garage. I'd squeeze the steering wheel tightly as I backed into a spot between a Porsche and a BMW, knowing the Clarkes' Escalade was a better fit.

"Oh yeah. The Clarkes are some cheap motherfuckers," Lorenzo confirmed. "Fithdy dollahs at Christmas.

"So . . . their daughter," he continued. "She liked to party. Comes back home late one night—from a bridal shower, I think—and she's lookin' good," Lorenzo says, coming to a full stop. "Like *real* fuckin' good."

That last detail became an early favorite to win Best Part of the Story. Lorenzo couldn't possibly know how good she looked that night unless Borowski told him and that was unlikely. First off, the nighttime doorman rarely talks to the rest of the staff since he's alone until he gets relieved by one of the morning guys.

Besides, it seemed to me that Borowski was not someone the guys stopped to have chats with. They'd talk *about* Borowski, but they didn't talk *to* him. Maybe George, but not the other guys. As far as I could tell, Tony Borowski was the building's undesirable, and the overnight shift was his dungeon.

It was more likely that Lorenzo's emphasis on Clarke's daughter looking "real good" that night came from impressions she'd left on him from previous encounters at the building. She'd walked through the front entrance and said hello a dozen times. She'd been in the elevator with him and said hello another dozen times, and the many impressions she'd made on Lorenzo had pole danced their way from his fantasies to his memory. He could now describe how she looked on any given night even if he wasn't there.

"Alright, so she's lookin' real good," I noted.

"Yeah, her fine ass comes up to the building, and Borowski opens the door. She steps inside and he says—get this—he says to her, 'That dress really shows off your legs, and let me tell you—they look great.'"

Okay, let's be real. The man deserved to get fired. It's the kind of thing you tell your wife, not a woman at a Park Avenue cooperative. The union doesn't have a section in the handbook for doormen catcalling residents, no *Legal services are available in the event that you comment on a female resident's bountiful anatomy* anywhere in its pages. Everyone involved, from resident to building staff to management, expects a doorman to refrain from hitting on female residents. When it happens, it's a short story, one that goes from the slush pile to the shredder because that man is fired with a vengeance.

It was Tony's audacity, however. It was the *I don't give two shits; I'm just gonna say what I feel right now because look at how that dress shows off your legs!* It was some old world, gunslinger kind of courage, leading me to become concerned that I would underwhelm Borowski when we met.

I composed myself. I'd attended a few literature conferences by then. I knew to look and sound like I was on the right side of every story. It wasn't in the union handbook, but it should've been: after hearing that a doorman catcalled a resident, I was required to contort my face in such a way that it displayed an extra-large portion of outrage. Onlookers had to be convinced I was disgusted. "Unbelievable," I said, my brow stooping and the rest of my face as solemn as a puddle of mud. "That's just so crazy." George was still in the vestibule and not contributing to the discussion, but he wasn't deaf. He heard me echo the company line.

It worked. Lorenzo went for my stunned condemnation of Borowski and grinned slyly. The story's red bow was coming. "Oh yeah, man. And then she tells her dad—fucking Clarke, that cheap fuck—and he calls the office. Management tells Borowski he needs to retire or he gets fired, but if he goes with retirement, he gets a full pension. If he doesn't quit, he'll get fired and get no pension. One month later, you're here."

I said it again, adding only a shake of the head that time. "Unbelievable," I repeated. Sometimes doing too much gives it all away.

"I know!" Laughing, Lorenzo unbuttoned his jacket. "Shit, I'd love to be there to see Borowski train the guy dat's gonna take his job," he said and patted his knee.

I caught sight of a small frame approaching the door. It was an old lady—Mrs. Geller from 2F—and she had cut a straight path from the lip of the sidewalk to the front door. George, his guard lowered because he was looking at his phone, might have spotted her if she'd taken a smooth, diagonal route to the door, like normal humans do, but not Mrs. Geller; she had walked from the sidewalk's curb, which was well outside of his radar and where people are "not for the building." At the last possible moment, she lurched from the curb to the door, like she was doing a surprise inspection. Lorenzo and I watched her rapidly arriving at the door. Lorenzo didn't say anything.

"Yo, George!" I said. He looked up and flew to the door like he would keep it from falling. All that paddleball—the old man could move.

"That's Geller," Lorenzo said quietly from my side, "from 3A." I thought to say, "I know, Lorenzo," but I refrained and sighed instead. Lorenzo turned and walked to the elevator to wait for her.

Geller had a rapport with George. After he took her shopping bags at the door, they exchanged pleasantries and he led her to the lobby. "This is Stephen, Mrs. Geller," he said, tilting his head in my direction. "I think you may have met?"

"Ahh, yes! We did!" she responded.

"Hello, Mrs. Geller," I said, trying my best, like I did the first time I met her, not to convey horror.

So much orange. She wore orange-framed glasses with orange-tinted lenses. I don't know which was more bizarre, the fact that she wore bell-bottoms or that they were orange bell-bottoms. Her jacket appeared to have lived a former life as an orange lampshade. She wore a hairnet but lived on Park Avenue, so she couldn't point to a kitchen job as an excuse for the hairnet. She wore red lipstick, a sharp and shocking departure from her orange esthetic, and squeezed out a voice so nasal it sounded like cats mating.

"How do you like the building so far?" she asked. I thanked God that I didn't sound like her and later prayed He didn't give me her voice as a punishment.

"It's great, Mrs. Geller," I said, smiling and nodding my head. "I'm glad to be here." Lorenzo and Geller headed to the elevator as I stayed with George.

"That bitch is crazy," George said. He had returned to the glass. "I know you saw me talking to her like we're friends. I've had my problems with her, trust me, but I've been lucky. Maybe it's cuz I'm old like her . . ."

"Maybe it's the mustache," I countered. Getting comfortable with George was easy. I sat on the vestibule's bench to celebrate.

"Maybe," he said, laughing. "Bitch is nuts. All nice today; last week, she cursed my dinner."

"What?"

"Yeah. On Saturdays we don't get any dinner relief. So when I left to eat my food, Lorenzo was up here alone. She walked in and found out she'd be riding the elevator by herself. I see her the next day and she goes nuts, starts complaining. I told her, 'Mrs. Geller, I was at dinner,' and she says, 'Fuck your dinner!'"

"Damn, that came outta *that* old lady?"

"Yeah. That was last week. Today she's my best friend."

That's the kind of information about a resident that settles it for me. I'd always be on alert around Geller, the scourge of paintings and doorman dinners.

The lobby died down after Lorenzo returned from taking her to the third floor. No residents coming in or going out. We all sat in silence. George continued waving at ladies walking past the door, and Lorenzo sat with his hands stacked on one knee. I kept it simple too. I quietly wondered how the upcoming shift with Tony Borowski would go.

19

BAWB

Park Avenue residents rarely concern themselves with new door-men. They pay thousands of dollars in monthly maintenance fees and expect to get what they pay for: a property management company working in tandem with a building superintendent to train, supervise, and manage a staff of building workers. They pay good money not to worry about the new doorman and how well he's adapting to the build-ing. These are the residents who streak through the lobby, tossing hel-los and good mornings as they go without looking in your eyes. They mispronounce your name for a few weeks. When you realize what kind of tenant they are, the kind that doesn't care who's in the uniform as long as the uniform opens the door for them, you don't care when the weeks of hearing your name mispronounced turns to years. They're miscellaneous residents, like extras in a scene. They provide scale—there is life in the foreground, life in the background. I don't have a name for these tenants.

Doormen are different. The seasoned doorman wonders how the new doorman will affect the hard-earned harmony at the building. The job is an easy one, after all. You dress well and get paid well to do mindless work that convinces you you're better than the UPS guy, the FedEx guy, and the Chinese delivery guy. I knew all about this. I had dealt with my fair share of new guys at 905 and with each one—Kenny, Ju-lian, and Jose Lopez—wondered which would be the asshole who ruined our culture. I assumed the men at 411 might have similar concerns, so I addressed them immediately, the best way I knew how: by making

solid contributions to their discussions on baseball, women, and Puerto
Rico. They talked about the same things as the doormen at 905. Those
were the top three topics discussed in Park Avenue lobbies, as far as I
could tell. I'd walk past several buildings on the way to the one where I
worked. If I stopped to talk to a doorman from another building, it was
always baseball, women, or Puerto Rico that we discussed. The union
contract is often mentioned. The possibility that we'll go on strike too.
But the conversation eventually rights itself. The Albanian doorman up
the block from 411 wouldn't stop talking about Puerto Rico or the other
Latin American countries he'd visited. I stared at him dumbfounded
when he first rattled off the list. Knowing he had me captivated, he
switched to Spanish to make it official. Then he mentioned the Latinas.
That was all he said—*Latinas*—then he closed his eyes and moaned. It
was awkward, me standing there in plainclothes watching a uniformed
doorman moan on the street. But you see what I mean? It will always be
baseball, women, or Puerto Rico. With Michaele I discussed the items
on my résumé, but she was an account executive at Charles H. Greenthal. With Mr. Atwell I discussed not memorizing the tenants list, but
he was the super. I would never spend eight hours in a lobby with him.
If I wanted to alleviate the staff's concerns about me, I'd have to let
them know I was one of them immediately. My first shift, I initiated a
conversation about baseball, women, and Puerto Rico, the way every
doorman should.

I played softball too. George enjoyed hearing the recaps of my latest
softball games. Sometimes he'd squat into a defensive baseball stance
and simulate throwing a ball the way he did at second base when he
played on Brooklyn's fields during the fifties. Ramón, who came from
the Bronx and sounded like the inspiration for Al Pacino's character
in *Carlito's Way*, was more concerned about my softball equipment—"I
gotta guy . . . works for a company . . . they're about to make a deal with
the Yanks . . . I can getchu some stuff for cheap," he said weeks before he
brought me a shiny softball bat and sold it to me on the cheap.

Sammy was a short and sturdy middle-aged man from the same

Ecuadorian town as my mother. One time, he propped a foot on the heating duct running along the bottom of the lobby facade and offered his assessment on my Ecuadorianess. "Everyone's Puerto Rican, man, but you, you get to be half Ecuadorian. And your dad was born in Brooklyn? *Olvidate*, bro, that makes you more Ecuadorian than Puerto Rican, but you haven't been there so, no, not really. You're not really Puerto Rican *or* Ecuadorian. Bro, you haven't visited your mother's country. What is wrong with you?" Sammy used to walk like a kingpin, all belly and shoulders, like he could make a call, and boom, I was being dipped in concrete mix under work lights somewhere in Jersey. But Sammy lived in Jackson Heights with all the other Ecuadorians. And he ate lunch on the edge of his seat, with his arms flanking his food, as if there were scoundrels nearby during a time of great famine. Sammy was a fucking doorman. Nothing more, nothing less. I was about to start up the engines on a sweeping response when he added, "Look at that big ass walking by."

Most doorman monologues are interrupted or punctuated that way, with the sighting of an attractive, curvy woman. Her big ass takes precedence. The Big Ass Walking By ended our conversation.

Only a doorman of the highest caliber can segue from the Big Ass Walking By to a monologue covering an unrelated topic. "Look at that nice ass" has never been followed by a pinch of the chin and "that gets me thinking." Find the doorman who covers the surging homeless population in the city—"How much blame do we assign to the governor? How much to the mayor? What can we do?"—after finding the big ass in the crowd, and you've got yourself a star doorman. The Big Ass Walking By is an end to things, not a beginning.

20

TONY BOROWSKI

I wasn't just the New Guy in a uniform. The guys made me feel like *Someone* in a uniform. I was a book-smart doorman: I didn't just serve raw feelings, I presented ideas informed by history and more intelligent individuals. I'd say things, then wait for a response, and when none came, I realized they were listening for real, so I kept saying things. We weren't always on the same page though. One evening we discussed the next election and we initially said the same things—"Fuck that guy . . . politicians are all corrupt"—but then I added something about the Electoral College and how our votes don't count the way we think they do. Ramón, who was at his usual position on the bench, lowered his newspaper, nodded self-assuredly, and got to his feet. "You went to a college for voting?" he asked, folding the paper like his next words would count as a whole day's work. "What a waste of money."

My first two weeks at the building, I hovered through the hallways feeling a sense of purpose. I had goals. I resolved to become the best nighttime doorman on Park Avenue. I'd heard that Tony Borowski didn't clean anything. I would clean everything. Twice. I'd put together an imposing lineup of cleaning solutions, whip on the rubber gloves, and make the lobby cry. The lobby would sparkle and shine, and it would speak for me even after I'd gone home, even as I slept. Mr. Atwell and the rest of the staff would huddle together and point to the marble floor and the glass and every other surface in the lobby. They'd marvel. "Wow, this kid is good," George would say as the others nodded behind pursed lips. I would be the staff's ace, the one holding down the fort while everyone slept.

Conflict during the overnight shift? Handled. Cantankerous delivery people? Suppressed. The housekeeper arriving at five a.m. to ask for apartment keys since she forgot her set at home, turned away at the door. The nanny with a trickle-down sense of entitlement? Treated like a housekeeper, something nannies guard against. The wayward resident attempting to do laundry alone in the basement during predawn hours when only the ink on newspapers should be wet? Informed of his stupidity, though not in so many words, with words like "If something happens, if you slip and fall, there's nobody down there to help you; it could be hours before anyone knows you're hurt." You have to use words designed to reprimand the resident for their nonsense without risking termination. Remember Doorman, you will never lose your job for pushing up against the exception to the rule with the rule.

The men were on my side, as far as I could tell. They leaned in when hearing me seesaw from talk of professors to the prior night's game and were impressed by my natural ability to sense when to halt my oratory gallop and join the hushed pondering of the Big Ass Walking By. I was a new breed of doorman.

At the end of my first week, George asked me what my schedule looked like for the second week. I dug inside my jacket for the index card on which Atwell had written my schedule and read, "Two evenings, three overnights." George's brow perked and he smiled. "You'll be workin' with Sean and Tony Rojas on those two evenings," he said, shaking his head, and walking away. George was great at cliffhangers.

Sean was Irish with a bloated face and cheeks that jiggled. His wild, shocked hairstyle begged for gel or pomade or any hair product on the shelf, but he would never listen. It would take too much effort. Sean lumbered around the building's lobby as if he'd never contained energy in his life.

Sean was calling the local diner for a coffee and bagel within minutes of the shift's start. After accepting his delivery, he walked away from the door with the bag, propped the mail room door open, and spread his food across the table like he was showing jewelry. He was a doorman who didn't stand at the door. It was my first and lasting impression of him.

Puerto Rican Tony, the senior man on staff, sat on one of the twin forbidden chairs in the lobby with an amused look on his face. Sean was his protégé, the one who'd learned his world-class incompetence and alcoholism. While Sean ate a standing meal in the mail room, Tony lounged on the plush leather seat with his legs crossed watching the foot traffic outside. When either of them changed position, it was to walk to the garbage bin and toss in another beer can. Mr. Atwell was in his office with the security monitor glaring down at him—I had passed its open door on the way up to the lobby—but Sean and Tony didn't seem to care.

It's not uncommon for doormen to loosen up after the super has gone to his apartment at five p.m. Sometimes the guy at the door tosses his duty cap, and the other doorman gets comfortable on a bench while he reads a paper. That stuff doesn't usually happen while the super is in his office, but it was happening just then, and right in front of me. Tony and Sean were flexing. For them, the weekday shift was like a Sunday morning at one of those slow, side-street buildings. At one of those buildings, you can close your eyes for an hour on Sunday morning before a resident rings for the elevator. Tony Rojas, of course, took it to the next level. Balding and smirking, he sat in the lobby like he was in the front of a bodega slapping dominoes on a small wooden table.

A lady drew close to the door. My legs tightened along with my instincts calling me to the door. No, I couldn't. It wasn't my job; it was Sean's, and I couldn't step on his toes like that.

Sean was still in the mail room. He was completely oblivious to the lady at the door. Tony was watching her stand at the door but hadn't moved in the slightest to cover for Sean. I decided I'd do it. I'd open the door for the lady. I shuffled toward the front door.

"Hey!" Tony said sharply, from behind me. He threw his hand up too, signaling for me to stop moving. "Relax," he said, a wash of calm arriving at his face. I was being given another chance to do the right thing. I stopped, never opening the door for the lady still waiting there.

She wasn't a resident. She was a tourist asking for directions. "I thought it was a tenant," I said, feeling helpless. I turned to look at the mail room. Sean hadn't moved. Maybe the bagels at that diner were so good they made a doorman forget his one job was watching the door. If so, I wanted a menu.

"Yeah, Stephen," Sean said through slow, uneven bites of his bagel. "Relax." Sean was missing several teeth and used liquids to soften the food for the few remaining teeth he had. His eyes clenched and his face contorted as his jaws carefully guided food into the back of his mouth. He took a few bites and, seeming disappointed, brought the cup of coffee to his mouth.

"Alright," I said, feeling dejected. Sean and Tony were not cooperating.

The two continued with their unorthodox training methods: still in the mail room behind me, Sean slurped from his cup while Tony punched a hooked finger into the buttons of a cell phone from the seat. I accepted the reality that I wouldn't learn anything new during that shift. As senior doormen, Tony and Sean felt entitled to do nothing, and they wouldn't let my eagerness to be helpful get in the way. I remained standing, the chandelier over my head more like a thought bubble than a glassy light fixture. Tony and Sean were celebrities at the building. Tony had started in the late seventies, long before Mr. Atwell arrived at the cooperative. He had seen kids at the building become adults who left to have kids who now visited their grandparents at the building. In the following years, I would see children walk through the door and run to Tony, who provided a cheap and easy grandfather fix until they reached their pop-pop's apartment.

Sean had walked into the building's weekday-evening shift on his first day.

There's no chance of this happening for anybody else. You can forget about it. There's no way you're walking into the weekday-evening shift on your first day. You start on the night shift or one of those mixed bag shifts where you sample each time slot.

Sean had a mother working at the union. She made a few calls and that was it; her son was working primetime on Park Avenue alongside the senior top dog at 411 Park Avenue, Tony Rojas.

You've gotta know somebody, man.

I engaged residents when I could during the two shifts with Tony and Sean, but I always felt leashed around those two, like I wasn't meant to go further than a smiling hello. They spent their hours guarding their prestige and nothing more. I sensed that any display of effort or diligence would be viewed as a trespass. The rollout of my new, all-conquering doorman identity would have to wait until after my two-week training shift; that much was clear.

Every Park Avenue cooperative has a set of doormen who achieve a special harmony after hours of reconciling nuances, personalities, and working styles. They never change the game, however. The game stays the same: one man works the door while the other runs the elevator. With few exceptions, that's the way the lobby works at any building on Park Avenue. Tony and Sean had something else going on—Tony was sensei and Sean his fading protégé—and no one else was invited to their dojo.

There were a couple of guys who had their own thing going. The general consensus was that Peter Campbell, the lanky, elderly Irishman who worked the morning elevator, was a fucking weirdo: he ate liverwurst between dry slices of white bread and washed it all down with tap water he poured into a faded Rangers coffee cup. That shit *was* weird— the modern New Yorker eats tastier processed meat and spends money for water—but I found it endearing too, as if his meditative bites into the liverwurst sandwich connected him to the cobblestone streets and steamships his forefathers knew.

Ray was a jolly, old Irishman and just below Tony Rojas on the seniority ladder. He generally arrived to work in the mornings with two six-packs of beer in a brown paper bag and guzzled all twelve by the time his shift on the service elevator ended at three. He didn't drink beer in full view of the cameras; there were storage rooms for that. His basement task list: hiccups through reddened cheeks, belly scratches over untucked maintenance shirts, and a discriminant helping hand, which was understandable since it was often busy holding paper-bagged beers in dark corners of the basement.

Peter and Ray made room for me. During a training shift with Peter, he let me run the elevator alone for fifteen minutes while he took his coffee mug to the lobby's slop sink for a refill. He used his trainee the way I did at 905—as an excuse to take multiple, lengthy breaks. This can only be a compliment to the trainee. You allow yourself a few breaks here and there after you've sensed that your trainee has enough working brain cells to learn the job on his own. You give him a few pointers, something like "Hey, don't be a fuckin' idiot," then you sit and read the paper while he works the elevator by himself. This is the way Peter and Ray trained me.

Ray offered me a beer during one of my training shifts. I wasn't training with him in the basement when he offered; I was training with Sammy in the lobby and wearing a doorman uniform like Sammy too. I wasn't wearing the blue maintenance uniform Ray was wearing, but it didn't matter to him. He wanted to celebrate my having made it to the building, said I looked sharp in the doorman uniform, so he gestured to the storage room and said there was a paper bag on the floor. I declined, but mostly because I was new and didn't want to get in trouble for something as trivial as drinking water-flavored domestic beer. Undeterred, he offered a beer to a contractor, who also declined, leaving Ray nodding in contentment at not having to share.

During the evening shift the following day, Tony Rojas asked, "I'ng guessing ju know about Borowski, eh?"

"Yeah, I heard about—" I began.

There was someone at the building entrance. Sean, who had made the journey into the vestibule by then, noticed and slid over to open it. Tony rose to his feet and straightened his jacket to prepare for a greeting. It was Novak, the lady whose wiry silhouette and light blue LL Bean jacket had reminded me of sporting goods. Her eyes were glued to me from outside the building, and they stayed there as she stepped into the vestibule. She didn't proceed into the lobby. Instead, she waited in the vestibule as Tony dipped into it and came up alongside her. Sean, who had just finished locking the door behind her, stepped up to her other side.

She continued staring at me through the vestibule's glass while they answered her questions, their palms showing as they explained. An impromptu resident-doorman meeting in the lobby? I'd never seen it happen.

I went back to pacing. It was my only play.

"Yeah, he is," I heard Tony say.

From the corner of my eye I saw her nod long and slow, as if embracing a difficult truth. After some time, she made her way into the lobby with Tony following her.

"Hello, ma'am," I said, succumbing to the impulse to defend myself with politeness. My greeting tailed after, but she showed no interest in acknowledging me. She ducked into the elevator with Tony, and I stayed in the lobby with Sean.

"Bro, what the fuck was *that?*" I asked.

"What was what?" Sean asked in return.

"What just happened? You, her, and Tony just had a little meeting and discussed me at one point."

"Oh, right. She hates you. Something about you being new and young and taking an old-timer's job."

That stung. She'd seen me *one* time and decided she'd hate me without ever having a conversation with me. I mean, we're within our rights to hate hipsters, emo kids, and Civil War reenactors, but she had no cause to hate me. Ms. Novak had seen me one time and decided I was inferior to a man who was being cast out of the building. I left it alone, tossing all concerns about her to the wind.

(Years later, her housekeeper would reveal that Novak, in a fit of rage, once told her that she viewed all Latinos as stupid and dirty. When I heard that, I pumped my fist like I'd won a prize. "I knew it!" I shouted. I was ecstatic knowing it wasn't only me, it was *all* of us she hated.)

Tony returned to the lobby with a pleased look on his face. My eyes followed him all the way to the chair where he sat and met my stare with his own. He offered nothing more, and after holding his stare a little longer, he looked toward the building's front entrance. The pleased look returned to his face, and that's when I knew I could barely rely on him for honest conversation, and I shouldn't rely on him for honesty at all. He would not share the particulars of his conversation with Novak because having a private conversation with a resident gave him power I didn't have. Tony Rojas appeared to have enjoyed the conversation. Not wanting to allow him anymore power over me, I stared ahead too.

"So . . . about Borowski," Puerto Rican Tony said. He shifted his weight in his chair and released a lazy sigh. The man behaved like he was on a beach, a cold drink in his hand, watching the skies dim. "One crezy motherfuckah."

"How's that?" I asked.

"Ju know he doesn't do shit here, right?"

I ignored the irony of this job assessment from Tony Rojas and processed his statement instead. It had become clear that any activity from me would justify my hiring. I would spray Windex on glass, and boom, probationary period over. For a decade, Tony'd been coming to work and mailing it in for eight hours at a time. How was I not a better option than Tony Borowski?

"I just started, man; I don't know much," I responded. "I mean, he doesn't clean much, from what I hear."

"Yeah, yeah, okay," Tony Rojas sneered.

"Hey, Tony!" Sean shouted from the mail room behind us. "Tell 'im about that time with the Clarkes!"

Oh shit, I thought. An opportunity to contribute to the conversation and sound like I belonged! "You guys talkin' about the night with their daughter in the miniskirt?" I asked.

"Naw man, everybody knows that story," Sean smirked. I couldn't get a win with those two.

"Dat mothafucka," Puerto Rican Tony began. "The Clarkes cung home and Borowski thakes their bags, passes theng to me. They 'bout to walk into the elevada wit' me when he sehs, 'Hey, Merry Christmas.'"

I didn't get it. "What's wrong with that?"

"It was fuckin' April."

"Whoa."

"Jeah, they fawgot to give hing his Christmas money."

Sean cackled in the mail room, but thankfully, not while gargling baked goods. That would've been a mess.

Puerto Rican Tony continued. "Yeah, they said, 'Don't worry, Tony, we didn't forget your Christmas bonus,' and he says, 'Me neither.'"

Sean yelled, "Hey, Tony! Tell him about that time with the Leavitts!"

"Fuckin' Borowski," he began again. "The Leavitts cung home late one night, and the Leavitts, they had family coming in-en-out, ju know, becuz they from California and wanna enjoy the city, but the Leavitts, they goo' people, so they say, 'Hey, Tony, don't worry, we won't bother you anymore. We're going to sleep.' Mothafucka says, 'Yeah, me too.'"

Puerto Rican Tony laughed from the door and Sean laughed from the mail room to which he'd returned. I joined in from underneath the chandelier. It couldn't be helped. If their reports were true, Tony Borowski wasn't a menace; he was a legend.

"Take it from me, kid," Borowski said at the start of my training shift with him. "If the motherfuckers in this place say you should go one way, it'll be safe to assume you should go the other." It was my tenth and final training shift, the one before the overnight shift became mine. Unfortunately, I had to work that tenth shift with Borowski. He stood at the door examining the darkened avenue. "Then there's a couple o' other motherfuckers that will tell you the other way is safe. At that point, you're fucked both ways."

Well damn, I thought. *Thanks for the pointers.* I stood next to the lobby's counter rigid with apprehension. All doormen offer unsolicited advice, but Borowski's advice sounded glaringly wrong: it was ill-timed, laden with inappropriate words, unwanted. He was like a Times Square hustler forcing a copy of his rap demo into my hands. I wasn't there for that. None of the other doormen had thrown around blanket statements with the same steel-ball delivery, though. I became slightly curious, which I thought was reasonable—all that intensity from Borowski had to mean something, right? I wasn't about to ask the boogeyman to elaborate, however. No way I'd become a character in the next Borowski story in my one and only shift with him. I'd been lucky. He'd only been mildly unpleasant with me to that point.

I had been in the locker room with Borowski in the moments leading up to the start of our shift. We changed into our uniforms at the same time, but at opposite ends of the table and in complete silence. I knew he wasn't the kind of man who engaged in small talk while he and another man changed clothes in the same room, so I left him alone. I don't know how I knew he was like that, but I knew.

Sometimes I crack jokes or make silly observations to break the ice. I considered pointing out that it's all about eye contact in those situations, that you can engage in more than small talk in a locker room, that you can have a full-blown philosophical conversation with another man while both of you change clothes, as long as you maintain eye contact. I've done it before. You keep your eyes glued to another man's eyes in the locker room and somehow, it's not odd at all. Something about Tony Borowski, though. Stone-faced, he buttoned his work shirt while staring directly into his open locker at nothing in particular. I knew he wouldn't be receptive to any new ideas from some young kid he'd never met before. He lowered himself over a chair to tie his shoes and sat in my direction by mistake. I call it a mistake because the moment he realized he was facing me, he spun around on his chair so he could face his locker again. I averted my eyes, but realized he couldn't see me not looking, so I embraced the awkward moment and remained there. He tied the other shoe in front of his locker and rose to his feet to pull his pants up and buckle them. I made sure to be looking at the other end of the locker room when he did that because with guys like Tony, you have to establish your straightness or they assume you're gay just for being slightly unclothed and in the same vicinity as them. There was nothing to see at the other end of the locker room, just a rack with uniforms and a few more lockers, but I didn't want to take any chances. I gazed the fuck out of those uniforms and the lockers.

"Alright, kid," he said after grabbing a Thermos from the table. "Let's get on up there." I was wearing the doorman uniform because Mr. Atwell said the night man was required to wear it for the first hour of the shift. Tony was wearing the porter uniform because he hadn't observed that requirement in years. By the time I said okay, slipped my cell phone into my pocket, and grabbed my messenger bag, Borowski's long strides had taken him halfway through the basement's hallway and steps away from the service elevator that would take us to the lobby. I bolted from the locker room to catch up to Borowski. The man did not fuck around.

The service elevator slid open in the lobby and Borowski blew onto the marble floor like a gust of October. Once underneath the chandelier, he shooed Sean away with his backhand and said, "Alright, get the fuck outta here." He appeared aggravated just seeing Sean, who had been standing quietly at the mail room's door, obviously, and not the front entrance.

Next he rushed Puerto Rican Tony out of the lobby. We're talking about the number one senior guy, Mr. Big Cojones. Borowski didn't ask for updates. There was no, "What do I gotta know?" None of that. There was a dismissive, identity-erasing wave of his hand followed by, "Alright, now *you*. Get the fuck outta here." Puerto Rican Tony pointed at the mail room to try and update him anyway. There were packages in the mail room he should know about. He said, "In the mail room, you got—"

"I got you leaving," Borowski told him. He was standing at the counter and reading through the logbook. I was still in the back of the lobby near the elevators. Sean and Puerto Rican Tony walked by me with their heads down like their souls had just been discharged from their bodies. I stood near the bench, not certain that I should greet them as it might have cost me my life. I nodded at each one and went back to being awestruck: the only other Polish doorman I knew, Bill at 905 Park Avenue, had only hated Blacks; Tony Borowski hated everyone equally.

Only the greats have moments of glory as their careers wane. Kobe scored sixty points in his last game as a Laker. In his final at-bat as a Yankee, Derek Jeter hit the game-winning single in front of a raucous crowd at the stadium. Borowski was in the ninth inning of his doorman life, but he was in rare form and swinging for the fences.

After he dropped that bomb about the motherfuckers at the job, I stood there saying nothing, and he didn't like it. He'd turned around from the front door and was boring a hole in me with his eyes. I didn't know what the fuck to say. It's not like I knew anyone on the staff well enough to say, "Yeah, fuck those guys, if they tell me to go right, I'm going left!" I'd just met Tony Borowski. What did he expect, for me to take his side in an impromptu conversation on his last day at the building? He hadn't warmed me up. You want me to agree that someone is a piece of shit, reference someone everybody hates so I can see the possibilities.

Borowski wasn't the type to warm you up. He was all boom, no countdown.

He peeled away from the door and walked up beside me. "I'm dead serious, kid," he growled, his words tumbling over me. Tony Borowski was a tall and slender old man, but he was built solid. He'd never gone quietly into any night. "The ones with the biggest mouths, those are the ones that will fuck you. They're lickin' their chops soon as you walk away. And watch out for these tenants. There's a few apartments in this building that's wall-to-wall assholes."

Borowski was turning over lines like skip rope, and I didn't even have an "okay" for him. That had to change. You talk to your shift partner—that's the way it works. I had to say something, something good, or he'd blow his top. It didn't matter that it was the first and last time I'd ever talk to him. It felt like a life-and-death situation since it was Borowski I was dealing with.

A few things about Tony Borowski were clear to me right off the bat. He was one of those old-school cats with convictions. You could see it in his erect posture, which made him appear taller than his already above-average height, and in his gaze, which scanned over everything. Borowski was a baby boomer from New York City. When those guys rolled up their sleeves, it wasn't for stylistic purposes, it was for range of motion. They'd put a building up during the day and knock someone out at the pub that night. Though far from flourishing—lots of things have to fall apart, maybe several times, for an elderly man to find himself working the overnight shift at a building—Borowski endured. And he was going to make damned fucking sure you knew he was busy enduring. Everyone heard from him whenever they were in the lobby. It was the toll that had to be paid for passing through his domain. I would become the new overnight doorman, but not yet. Until Borowski walked out of the building one last time in the morning, it was his show.

I didn't know what to say about the motherfuckers at the job, but it was time to say something. I've met enough men with pencil mustaches like his to know one all-important detail: they expect a response. I decided I'd play it safe. Playing it safe is supposed to be good enough, like turning the volume from 0 to 4. "I gotcha, Tony," I said. You put the volume from 0 to 4 and you'll have a pleasant listening experience without bothering the neighbors or hurting your ears.

"*Gotcha?*" Borowski responded, pivoting suddenly. He was no longer facing Park Avenue; he was facing me straight on. "You . . . *got* me? Kid, you got shit."

"Okay . . ." That was a failed first try, absolutely, but I righted myself quickly. Tony wasn't picking a fight, he was passing the torch, and I was ready for it. "What do I gotta know?"

He shared. He told me which doormen I should watch out for. These he called motherfuckers. Sometimes he called them assholes or pieces of shit. Sean and Tony Rojas were motherfuckers, assholes, *and* pieces of shit. Just below them on the list was Lorenzo, but only slightly below. Lorenzo had arrived at the building only a year before I had, but he'd climbed the ranks quickly and become one of the top three mother-fuckers at the job. Borowski said I should keep my eyes open around all these guys.

He told me which doormen I could trust. It was a short list. He called the men on that list "stand-up guys." George was on that list. I'd even-tually understand why George had distanced himself when Lorenzo discussed Borowski in disparaging terms. Borowski and George lived near each other in Queens. They often stopped to chat about life in the old neighborhood. Borowski sometimes called George, and not to curse him out, but to awkwardly ask how his day was going. George would later talk to me about these calls with sadness, like he wished Borowski could reveal more about himself. Still, George never held Borowski's hardness against him, and the day Borowski called to ask for a ride to the hospital for a cancer screening, George didn't hesitate. He said, "Yeah, sure, Tony. I'll take you." Borowski was long retired by then but, to George, still someone who mattered. The day Lorenzo tried telling me about Borowski, George left to lean against the vestibule's glass and quietly watch the pedestrians outside because he was a stand-up guy.

Some time passed and we stood at opposite ends of the front desk in silence. It was just like in the locker room—we made sure we never locked eyes. Instead, we looked through the glass vestibule at the street. Park Avenue is always more subdued than the other avenues and especially late in the day, but that night it was more quiet than usual. There was no traffic from cars or pedestrians. It was all sidewalk, the street's lane markers, and a bushy median. Park Avenue was a desolate

wasteland staring back in solemn observance of my arrival at the building and Tony Borowski's departure.

"Listen, kid," he said.

"Yeah?" There were seven hours left in the shift. Seven hours left for
him to enlist me in a Tony Borowski story. I braced for it.

"It's a building. Steel and bricks, but that's all it is, shit from Home
Depot."

I thought I was smart, but I didn't know where the fuck Borowski
was going with any of that "steel and bricks" bullshit. He must have
picked up on my confusion.

"Kid, it's just . . . a job," he said, beginning to lose his patience. "And
it's a uniform." His eyes passed over my bow tie, then my suit jacket,
and fell on my Oxford shoes. He glared at my uniform with the kind of
scorn usually reserved for the mariachi band that walks into the train
and starts performing just as the song in your headset arrives at the
good part. "You make it something more, make the people here more
than they are, kid, you'll get taken."

I didn't know what the fuck Borowski was trying to say.

"Once in a while, show them who you are"—Borowski tugged at his
belt and pulled at his pants—"outside of that uniform." He took a deep
breath and said, "Let them know it's *you* choosing to say 'Hello, ma'am,
Hello, sir,' it's not *them* choosing. It's not them and their paychecks or
their big fucking building."

I nodded again, but this time with a flicker of understanding.
Borowski wanted me to stay in the lobby with a foot outside the door. I
could do that. I nodded and said okay.

He waved me away. "Go," he said, clenching his eyes like the impromptu mentorship had hurt him. The conversation was over. Sighing,
he said he needed to rest and took a seat in one of the plush, forbidden
chairs. "Go downstairs. There's plenty of places for you to sleep in the
basement."

There really aren't many places to sleep in any basement, you know, because of mice and water bugs (even Park Avenue buildings have them), but I headed downstairs to the locker room, took a seat, and turned off the lights. In the dark, I listened to the fan's whirring and wondered if Mr. Atwell would call Borowski the following morning to ask about me. I'd heard from the rest of the staff that Atwell had been asking them about my performance during training shifts. Would he ask Borowski, though? It seemed unlikely, seeing as how Tony considered Mr. Atwell a gutless puppet, and when someone views you that way, he tends to show it. Tony Borowski was not the kind of person Mr. Atwell would've called, I don't think.

My eyes strained through the darkness and located Tony's locker wedged between George's and Lorenzo's. I would eventually take his locker, but it would be several days before his name plate was removed and mine was glued on. For several days, Tony Borowski's name lived on at the building, if not in open criticism, in passive silence on my locker.

Supers always ask training doormen how the new guy trained. "How'd he do?" they ask. It might happen at the end of the shift or the next day, but they always ask. I like to imagine Mr. Atwell dialing Tony the next day to ask. Mr. Atwell would've called without any concern over waking him because Tony did all his sleeping at the building and everyone knew it. I like to imagine Borowski still swinging for the fences even after being sent to the bench. "How'd *who* do?" he would've roared in response, causing Mr. Atwell to retreat into a stutter. It would've hit Tony all at once, the reality that in the process of being forced into retirement, he'd also been forced to train his replacement, and he would've lowered his head on his side of the call. He'd press his own awkward silence into the conversation as his mind shuffled through a lifetime's worth of gritty memories. I like to think that my face showed through the weeds. "Oh, the Kid," he might have said. I want to believe that he'd be sitting in his Astoria apartment and, while looking mindlessly out of his living room window, he'd suddenly transport beyond the glass and the steel and the bricks of the tall buildings in the distance. I want to believe that while holding the receiver to his face, Tony Borowski said, "The Kid's gonna be alright."

"So how's it feel taking over for a guy that was fired?" Lorenzo asked me one morning after I'd worked the overnight shift. I'd already been working Borowski's old schedule for three weeks. George was in the lobby after relieving me early, and Lorenzo would join him soon. He stood at the table reaching for items—chief among them a bizarre roll of dollar bills befitting a seventies low-level drug dealer—and stuffing them in his pockets. He needed only to slip on the suit jacket. The shirt, bow tie, and vest were already on.

"He wasn't fired; he quit," I responded while tying my sneakers. I was ready for the drive home. I had closed my eyes for a couple of hours during my shift, but I was ready to get some rest at home.

Lorenzo put his arms through the jacket and popped it over his shoulders. He knew the uniform fit him like the envelope around a paycheck: perfectly.

Lorenzo sneered. "Nah, man. He was fired!" He grabbed his cell phone from the table and said, "We told you the story already! What, you weren't listening?" He walked out of the locker room laughing, and I drove home, pleased to know that Tony Borowski had left 411 Park Avenue when he was good and ready to leave.

21

THE MUSEUM AND THE SUPER MONK

I settled into my overnight position at 411 Park Avenue nicely, and with purpose: I knocked out all my shift work—mopped the marble floors, wiped the glass windows, and cleaned the restroom—all in one hour. Everything had to be just right: at midnight, a deliveryman arrived with a large coffee and a muffin, which I walked back to the mail room where the screen on my laptop showed the latest essay I was crafting for a literature class. Mr. Atwell had once mentioned the potential to work on my studies during shifts, and I hadn't just mulled the idea, I had planned on it. The building's lobby became the writing lab where I worked on writing assignments while the city slept.

My academic crusade continued its march into the fall of 2011. It wasn't just the good grades I was earning by then; it was me establishing a presence in my classrooms too. I was exhibiting a confidence I hadn't seen in myself since pagers and JNCO jeans. When I raised my hand in the middle of lectures, I didn't ask questions, I offered fresh perspective, like when I wondered out loud if Shakespeare had gone to the Bible for ideas. I challenged professors too. During a gender studies class, I once asked my professor if she knew how male thinkers had responded to the first and second waves of feminism. What was the social dialogue like? Women had been slamming their fists on tables—didn't the fellas respond? Henry David Thoreau caught the beginning of feminism's first wave—did she know if he ever wrote about the protests over women's voting rights? My professor didn't think male responses mattered, and I said she was covering for not knowing.

Yes, I was older than most of my classmates, but I wasn't interested in being the disassociated classmate who sat in the room like an auditor. Those people treat their age like an intellectual moat. You know you'll never connect with them. Fuck that, I was there to engage. All the adversity I'd seen by then equipped me with a lens on literature that my classmates didn't have. I had been a fallen, hunched figure at one time and a deeply flawed figure *all* the time, allowing me to relate to the protagonists in the stories I read. I'd nod along as I read authors' plots with understanding. The work didn't surprise me or overwhelm me; it gratified me.

Later that semester, I was walking past a bulletin board at school when the words "Essay Contest" grabbed my attention. I turned around and raised my eyes. A white sheet of paper had been raised horizontally with a thumbtack plunged into its center so that the ends peeled toward the crease in the middle. The page looked to be suspended in flight and waiting for someone to release it. I reached up, pulled the thumbtack out of the page's center, and brought the sheet to my face.

Sure enough, the words were there: "Essay Contest." I drew closer to the menagerie of ads and announcements and pressed the page's wings against the board so that I could jot down the relevant information.

The competition, a collaboration between John Jay College and the Rubin Museum, entailed choosing a work of art from the collection and writing an essay that explored how the piece expressed the idea of justice. I was encouraged: I'd won Best 300-Level Essay a year earlier. I could do it again, right? Just by trying hard? There was a slight complication: I belonged in the class for which I wrote the winning essay. It was a 300-level literature course and I wrote a 300-level essay. I didn't belong in *this* contest, however; it was tailored for prelaw students, and I knew that because the entire bulletin board was addressed to students in the law department. I was an English major. Second, and more importantly, there was a cash prize for first place. Three thousand dollars. I resigned myself to the fact that dozens of prelaw students were at their screens at the same moment, each crafting outlines and arguments

designed to win the cash prize. Officials with the college's law department and the Rubin Museum would be ready—they weren't going to
throw $3,000 at a halfway decent essay from a prelaw student. The es-
say would have to stand out. That's what did it for me, when I thought
of standing out. Standing taller. I wanted the challenge of beating an
entire department of prelaw students as an English major. While they
sat at their screens salivating over $3,000, I considered my strategy. I
was a long shot. For me to win, I'd have to write an essay that would
make one judge email another judge with the subject line "Read this
essay." I'd have to write something that made that first judge's eyes go
wide like whoa.

I printed out the contest's details. It was 2011, a full ten years after
I'd held the expulsion letter in my hands. I had another sheet of paper in
my hands then, this one offering me an opportunity to get ahead, a jolt
of money, and some glory for my best efforts. I decided I was the only
student on any campus in America with the intelligence and talent to
write the winning essay. There would be no one else in the entire country who could win, no prelaw student or intellectual. I was being sent
on a great quest to win the first annual Rubin Museum Essay Contest.

I was ready to quit one hour into my visit to the Rubin Museum.
The museum had six floors dedicated to Himalayan art, all showcasing
pieces that dazzled me as much as they bewildered the hell out of me. It
was a barely clothed Buddha one minute, a tapestry of mysterious symbols the next. None of it cried, "Legal themes you wanna write about
here!" It was monsters and dragons and Buddhas with strategically
placed robes. Great material for the horror genre, or trivia night, but
not for an exploration of justice.

(If Martin Luther had been born into Buddhism and its brand of
iconography, he would've written 95,000 Theses, and the resulting document would've been too thick to nail onto a door. He would've been
reduced to a less-dramatic delivery choice: the bike messenger. The
bike messenger would've left the gargantuan folder with the doormonk,
who would've been required to sign his initials, but if no doormonk

answered the door, the belly of the Buddha beside it would've been as good a place as any.)

Sulking, I sighed my way down the staircase to the museum's basement. *Why not?* I wondered. None of the museum's other Himalayan exhibits had inspired a link to justice. Another uncooperative exhibit wouldn't hurt.

It would be the kind of final disappointment that liberated, like the time I reluctantly went on a third date with a girl after quitting on her. At the urging of a homeboy who thought I had ended things too early, I decided to give the girl another chance. Once at her apartment again I took a look at her bookshelf. Nothing had changed: *Twilight* was still the only book on the bookshelf, and that was it. I decided I'd never see her again. There was a twinge of disappointment because I was in my mid-thirties and no closer to settling down, but I had tried. I carried a similar mindset as I reached the Rubin Museum's basement: one last try'll do it. I'll hit the basement real quick, just to know I wasn't a complete asshole today, just a partial one. Then I'll bounce. I can say I tried.

HERO, VILLAIN, YETI: TIBET IN COMICS read the exhibit's sign. *Whoa,* I thought. *Comics, as in comic books?* I had experience with comic books. I had no thoughts about the contest, however. I was only concerned with finding out when DC or Marvel ever mentioned yetis and Tibetans. I didn't remember seeing either of them in any of the comic books I read as a teenager. I was intrigued!

I did a loop through the museum's exhibit, hoping to latch on to something familiar. It didn't take long. Alone in the Rubin Museum's basement exhibit, I marveled at the two comic books before me: the November and December 1973 issues of *The Invincible Iron Man*, published nine years before I was born, which cast practitioners of a Tibetan strain of Buddhism as their chief antagonists.

Raga, already a pariah in his communal family because of his hot temper, explodes into a violent rage after learning that a former student-lover marries another man. He kills both the woman and her husband. The Black Lama, a mystic capable of interdimensional travel, finds Raga and offers to teach him how to channel and control his emotions. Raga knows he needs to lie low for a while, accepts the offer, and after a long period of isolation, learns how to use meditation to harness his fiery soul and becomes very powerful.

What kind of justice was that? Not any I was used to. I knew about prison sentences and needles and electric chairs. I had read in the newspapers about the Rockefeller drug laws, which measure justice in ounces. Someone punches you in the face, you're within your rights to punch *them* in the face; I knew that kind of justice too. Mami had taught me all about it in kindergarten, remember? I was well acquainted with retributive justice.

I thought further: my guy Raga had caught two bodies. You try that in New York, you get a manhunt, front-page notoriety where the *News* and the *Post* finally agree, and multiple life sentences. Not so for Raga, not even the usual comic book justice, where the death of an innocent woman is depicted in its own frame, her eyes staring lifelessly upward, and sets off a war that shakes the cosmos (the death of her husband alone wouldn't have made you turn the page, let's be honest). Raga had somehow evaded the Hammurabi, Moses, and Giuliani codes, and gotten himself adopted by a super monk instead.

I studied the comic book's illustrations of post-rehabilitation Raga. He was a new man. Powerful and self-assured. Things were trending upward for Raga.

It was all there, in the comic book: the basis for an argument. With some work, I might be able to construct a persuasive essay. I knew it would be the only way to set myself apart in a contest geared toward law students. The average informational essay wouldn't cut it.

I certainly had the time and the space: with the winter's cold setting in, few residents were going out at night, allowing me to convert the silenced lobby at 411 Park Avenue into a satellite branch of John Jay College's library. With constant deliveries of coffee and stretches of quiet time wherein not a single tenant exited or entered the building, I had been producing my best academic work for months.

22

O'RANGE MAN

I was sitting in the mail room at work a few weeks later when the gleam of a car's exterior pierced the darkness outside the building. *Shit,* I thought. *I have a customer.*

It was a late-arriving resident pulling up to the building in a shiny SUV. On a Sunday night, it meant they'd driven from outside the city with luggage in tow and possibly fruit and vegetables from their estate, something residents like Mr. Kaufman liked to point out: "That fruit came from the trees on my property! Smell them! Don't they smell fresh?" Mr. Kaufman liked to hear me say yes, but with enthusiasm, which I rarely did. I always said yes as dryly as possible. I didn't want to encourage him because I knew what would happen if I did. I was well versed in his other line of questioning. "How's it hanging?" he often asked. I knew what he meant, and he always found a way to win. I would never say, "Not well," so I said, "Very well," and he'd laugh and heehaw and slap his knee while I stood at the button panel wishing the elevator would plummet to the bottom of the shaft.

"They're called pussy fruit," he often said when showing me the bags of fruit in his trunk. "They taste like pussy. Go ahead, take a few. You'll love them since they taste like pussy."

(I went two years calling the produce in his trunk "pussy fruit." Then I saw them in a crate at Whole Foods. The sign referred to them as pawpaw fruit, and when considering Mr. Kaufman's subscriptions to porn magazines and weekly deliveries of erectile stimulants and the number of times he asked me "How's it hanging?" with a smirk on his face, I can understand why he'd change the name of the fruit: "pawpaw" was not exotic enough.)

I was dealing with more pressing matters. With me in the mail room were my laptop, the only criminal justice book I owned, and pages with my notes; I was at a critical juncture of the Rubin Museum essay and wanted to see it through. I needed to. I had settled into a great seam of writing and couldn't think or feel beyond the endeavor to add words to the screen. I continued typing, a move as risky and foolish as any carried out by a doorman (Day One of Doorman Training: *You see a car pull up, drop everything and see who it is; if it's the president of the board and he doesn't see you at the door, you're fired on the spot.*) I had just finished a sentence when I spotted a long, brown leg extend itself from the passenger door. Fuck. It was Ignacio, which meant Mr. O'Leary was the driver.

O'Leary was a heavy hitter on the way to the building Hall of Fame. During one of my first overnight shifts at 411, I sat in the lobby reading a newspaper when I heard the elevator ring and its doors open. From the elevator's corridor emerged a tall White man in a long bathrobe. On his head was the richest, brightest white hair I'd ever seen. As if his hair wasn't enough of a spectacle, I realized with great horror that his bathrobe was untied. The robe's belt hung at the sides, revealing a sliver of his inner thigh. It was a very orange inner thigh. He settled underneath the lobby's chandelier and shifted all his weight on one leg and bent the other leg forward slightly. There is no training session or advice from a sage doorman that can prepare you for such horrors.

"Well, hello there," said the Great White. "I'm Mr. O'Leary."

"Hello," I said from my seat. I should've stood up. Politeness is part of the job. I simply couldn't. My eyes were glued to the belt. It was the worst first-time ever: I had gone from never facing a man's inner thigh to having a conversation with one. It's not the kind of thing you write in a journal. *I saw Mr. O'Leary's inner thigh today. It was very orange.* Some moments arrive immediately ripe for the forgetting.

"I'm Stephen, the new night man," I continued. I remained seated;

instinct told me if I stood, O'Leary might view it as an escalation. He might step forward and shake my hand, unwittingly (or wittingly) causing the robe to open farther. Or worse. I didn't want that. I had experienced enough trauma by then to sense when a catastrophe is drawing near.

"Ahh, well," he said, shuffling his feet, "if I had known the night man was this handsome, I would've come down sooner." He stopped moving and smiled from underneath his brow.

The robe didn't fall, a cause for my mental health's everlasting celebration. I laughed and looked away, but then realized I might look like I was blushing. I didn't want to encourage.

The episode needed to end.

"How can I help you, sir?" I asked in hopes of finding a quick solution.

O'Leary went blank. The question must have thrown him off. He had probably thought it was playtime. "Well, my cable is out, and I was wondering if the night man could come upstairs and take a look." He smiled again, this time not showing his teeth, but unlike Evans, who intended to hide his teeth, O'Leary smiled like a villain, wild and unabashed. "And you're the night man."

"Right, I am." Getting out of this one would be easy. "But it's a cable box issue, and the staff has nothing to do with that. Even during the day, all we'd do is tell you to call the cable company. Besides, I'm not supposed to leave the lobby." (Remember: you will never lose your doorman job for following the rules. On rare occasions, a doorman benefits from the rules.)

O'Leary was stymied. Would he rally?

"Well, okay," he said and waited. I stared him in the eye and held my gaze, exuding more resolve than I'd shown around women who'd displayed a lot more skin.

"Have a good night, sir," I said.

I didn't feel bad. I've experienced more than my fair share of rejection. A middle-aged wealthy man living on Park Avenue could stand to hear no once in a while.

Weeks later, O'Leary walked up to the building with a tall, dapper young man on his arm. He introduced him as Ignacio, and we all knew he'd stick around for a while. Mr. O'Leary had begun divorcing his wife when I started at the building, and he coped with the separation by keeping a steady flow of young men running into his apartment. This was the first time he'd ever introduced one of them to us, however.

Ignacio. I didn't know him, but something about him was familiar. He was a muscular Dominicano who wore bright slim suits and loafers without socks, but that wasn't it. Sockless Dominicanos in tight pants were a regular sight in the Bronx. It was his face. It was nicked all over, and even his unkept beard couldn't hide the scars behind it. Ignacio's face had seen its fair share of knuckles. And it was his hair. He kept a high 'fro punched in by two receding hairlines. When you have one bald spot, you go completely bald; it's a well-meaning rule—a clean-shaven, stream-lined head looks better than one with missing hair—but he didn't give a shit. It was the kind of self-neglect you notice in the hood where some folks see walls crumbling and let themselves crumble too. Ignacio wore slick, fashionable outfits to navigate a life with O'Leary, and kept a loaded smile on his face when O'Leary introduced him to us, but he hadn't fooled me. Ignacio and I had seen the same streets, but he thought he'd made it because he'd earned some closet space on Park Avenue. Every subsequent time they pulled up to the building, his smirk remained. Never words, just a smile peeking from the side of his mouth, and I hated him for it.

Ignacio knew I hated him and seemed to know why—we were both young, but he was pampered and I was still climbing—but to his credit, he stayed silent every time we saw each other. We'd lock eyes and he'd quietly smile at me, looking away once he seemed satisfied with the contentment he'd displayed. Ignacio had transcended the hood and enlisted me in his daily, silent coronations.

I knew it was time to leave the mail room when I saw Ignacio swing his other leg over the pavement, stand up, and peer inside the lobby in search of me. Daytime doormen are always at the door when residents arrive at the building. The resident's car will pull up to the canopy and the doorman is there with an arm reaching for the handle. Residents expect to see the arm reaching for them every time they pull up to the canopy. The night man has some flexibility since he's the only staff on duty and must occasionally step away from the door to clean something in the lobby, but the camera told a different tale on my shifts: I knocked the cleaning out early and quickly, then spent the rest of my shift in the mail room writing. Mr. O'Leary and Ignacio had pulled up to the canopy, opened their own doors, and had begun pulling their own luggage and groceries from the truck.

I quickly fetched the lobby's brass luggage cart and brought it to the car as they lowered a few bags onto the sidewalk. It was an indicator of my job performance that night: when you're on your toes, the resident doesn't reach the trunk before you do and certainly won't bring a bag to the sidewalk. That was all *my* job.

"Oh hello, Stephen," a no-longer enamored O'Leary said before bending over the back seat to retrieve bags on the other side of the car.

"Hello"—I started, realizing I was talking to his ass—"Mr. O'Leary. Welcome back." Ignacio must have caught me looking, then caught some feelings, because he slid up beside me, snorted, and began peering down at O'Leary's ass like it had done something to him. The depths of absurdity look like Ignacio attempting to outstare my unintentional stare of O'Leary's ass. It was a quandary: either I kept my eyes on O'Leary's butt cheeks and engaged in a vicious battle of gazes, or I joined in one of the most unexpected team efforts on record. Don't think for one second that I didn't consider the former. The thought of engaging him in a contest of wills enticed me. I would've had the upper hand: a doorman stares through the lobby door for most of his shift; that's a lot of staring, enough to make a man a champion.

Alas, I bowed out and let Ignacio win by looking away slightly—at the door well, then the tire, and finally the curb—before repeating the cycle again. I made it look like I was the kind of madman that glances

at every object in his view, even the ones not doing anything signifi-
cant. I even shot a look at the fire hydrant, fuck it. I didn't need Ignacio
thinking I was going to compete for O'Leary. I surrendered like a motherfucker.

"Thanks. Just finishing up here," O'Leary said over his shoulder. He
reached back, handing Ignacio a duffel bag. Ignacio seemed disgusted
by it, holding it out in front of him like it was a freshly decapitated head.
He shoved it into my hands.

I shoved the bag into Ignacio's chest and scowled at him. O'Leary
was still reaching over the truck's back seat, but his ass no longer had
me in the audience.

"*You* put it in the cart," I told Ignacio. "You're closer."

I had leaned on reality—Ignacio's proximity to the luggage cart—as
my excuse in case O'Leary heard me from inside the truck and pro-
tested. It's a trick I used many times as a doorman. Ignacio's proximity
to the luggage cart couldn't be denied. On paper, it would read like common sense. Only my tone could have been questioned, and I'd simply
claim a misinterpretation. Thankfully, O'Leary didn't hear anything,
and Ignacio said nothing.

Later, I caught sight of O'Leary and Ignacio staring at me from the
elevator. I'd helped them to the elevator door with the luggage rack and
left them there. "Anything I could help you with, gentlemen?" I asked.

"You're not going to help us upstairs?" O'Leary asked. Ignacio
glared at me with a look of satisfaction on his face, as if he knew what
was coming next.

"No, I'm not, Mr. O'Leary. I need to watch the lobby," I responded.
Again, you can't get fired for pushing up against a rule with a rule, in
this case the one about bringing residents' bags to their apartments—
unless you had to man the lobby alone during late-night hours. The
night man doesn't do deliveries or help with luggage. He stays in the
lobby to keep it secure and that's it.

Mr. Atwell called me the day after my run-in with O'Leary and

Ignacio. He asked me why, why, why I hadn't taken Mr. O'Leary upstairs. "You have to take care of Mr. O'Leary, Stephen!" he whined.
"Some residents need a little extra care, and he's one of them."

I told him I wouldn't treat Mr. O'Leary any different than any
other resident, that if women and children didn't receive elevator service during the late-night hours, why should *he*? Mr. Atwell pulled his
breath. I was throwing building rules at him, and there's never been a
day when the rule enforcer liked to hear the rules thrown back at him. I
made it worse when I asked him if he realized that O'Leary had his own
bagman. His name was Ignacio.

To his credit, Ignacio hadn't been the one to complain. I knew that
because O'Leary never mentioned me shoving a bag into Ignacio's chest.
It's the kind of complaint that gets you fired, no questions asked, and
I'd made Ignacio an honorary doorman for ten minutes. The union
wouldn't have sent a delegate to represent me; they would've sent their
regards. O'Leary's complaint regarded my lackluster service, not the
escalation of the cold war between me and his bellhop. No snitching, it's
code on the streets. Ignacio wasn't fully reformed, after all.

Mr. Atwell and I didn't talk for weeks. I wasn't initially concerned
because a night man can go long stretches without seeing a super since
he's left the building before the super starts working. But then I noticed
when I hadn't received a call from him in a while. He had been calling
me routinely to ask how I was doing or to share building updates. He
was always worried that I'd fuck something up. He must have needed
a break from hearing my voice after the O'Leary incident because he
never checked in on me again.

I took first prize in the Rubin Museum essay contest on justice. As a
requirement, I was to discuss the essay during the awards ceremony. As
I stood at the podium with my fingers clamped around a stack of index
cards, knowing the notes were all bullshit. None of them had the names

"Rosado" or "Papi" written on them, the two driving forces behind my essay's thoughts on justice. There were thoughts on justice evaded and justice mishandled.

They gave me ten minutes at the mic. Scribbled on my index cards were thoughts on the essay's intro, body, and conclusion. Sure, this was John Jay College of Criminal Justice and not Cambridge University, but I had to believe that most of these students knew how to write an essay. I considered musing on my research and its findings. Here was the extent of my research: I used the only criminal justice book in my bookshelf; it was the only one I hadn't sold or thrown away. My findings? Two pages of notes comparing retributive and restorative justice. What was I going to do, tell them I read a couple of paragraphs from an entry-level book on justice, banged out an essay on the strength of my resentment toward my father and Pastor Rosado, and boom, I received a $3,000 prize?

There were six hundred eyeballs staring at me in wait for my lips to move. My mouth opened.

"Wow, I'm really nervous," I blurted out.

I don't remember exactly what I said—it was related to my process, but I couldn't discuss how I'd pulled the two most influential men in my life into it. Every sentence had been another strong, aggressive charge addressed to each man.

23

REVOLUSHONG!

Eight years after Mr. Evans offered me a full-time shift at 905 Park Avenue, another lucky break came my way: Ray and Peter retired within months of each other, taking their beer cans and liverwurst sandwiches with them, respectively, and allowing me to shoot up in seniority at the building. In two years at the building cooperative, I went from the graveyard shift to the day shift in the lobby. George had waited ten years, working weeks of staggered shifts along the way, to get a steady daytime shift. I'd done it in two years without working any staggered shifts. Doormen call such unplanned, unforeseen fortune "stepping in shit"—I'd landed in the right building at the right time.

My shift was nearing a close one afternoon when Ramón, who had become an evening doorman after Puerto Rican Tony retired, appeared in the lobby. "Okaaaaay," he said, sighing. Ramón was there to relieve Sammy, the first doorman on duty that morning. Sammy had started at six thirty a.m., and I'd started twenty minutes later, at six fifty. The first doorman to start a shift is the first one to leave when relief arrives. I assumed Sammy, after hearing the service elevator open and Ramón walk onto the lobby floor and say his usual "Okaaaay," would gather his things and bolt from the lobby. I'd then wait another fifteen to twenty minutes for the evening shift's second doorman, Sean, before going home. You know, the usual. Sammy didn't make a move though. He kept his short, boxy frame leaning up against the building's glass facade, a cell phone up to his ear, as if going home wasn't a concern for him.

Ramón must have taken it personal. It must have been the first time his sometimes cranky, always-opinionated presence didn't register. He took a deep breath. "Okay, who's going home?" he bellowed as he walked through the lobby. It was a rhetorical question. He was waiting for Sammy to leave. We were both waiting, and we were both confused. Sammy didn't move at all. He remained at the door, a phone up to his ear, and I didn't know why. He'd enthusiastically scrambled away from the door at the sight of Ramón many times before. Not that day. He was on the phone having a conversation. He must have sensed I was waiting on him to do something because after a few moments, he turned and said, "Hey, Stephen, you go first."

It was unexpected generosity from Sammy, someone who wouldn't share the flu if he had it. Homeboy used to accept entire cakes from tenants with instructions to share it with the staff, and later he'd walk out of the job holding a bag shaped like a cake. When residents threw out furniture, he took all of it. Didn't matter if he had a couch already, you saw a couch in the basement waiting to be picked up by Sammy on his day off.

"You sure?" I asked only half earnestly. There was never a day when I wanted to stay at work longer than absolutely necessary. All he had to do was give me one more push and I'd jet, no questions asked.

Sammy wasn't playing around. The man pressed his lips into the receiver and told his mistress, "Hold on, hold on," and stepped into the vestibule's doorway. Motherfucker said, "Go, go, go!" and shooed me away with both hands. Say no more, Sammy, you asshole. I was gone.

The next day, I was changing into my regular clothes at the end of my maintenance shift when Ramón walked in. He had been the one who'd arrived early to relieve Sammy the day prior. He, too, had expected nothing but the ordinary, for the earlier doorman to leave once he appeared. He'd expected Sammy to grab his bag and walk past him on the way to the basement.

"Hey, why didn't you work the overtime yesterday?" Ramón asked with a baffled look on his face. "You left money on the table. It was an easy shift. Barely anyone came in or out."

I was confused. "What the fuck are you talking about?" I asked. "Sammy let me go and then Sean—" Shit. I had never actually seen Sean in the locker room.

Sean was the second doorman scheduled for the evening. Sean was also the guy nobody on staff could find a reason to respect, the one with missing teeth, remember? He was in his mid-forties and lived with his mother, the one who got him the doorman job in the first place. He left his volatile brand of body odor in the locker room everyday. Sean would also wear our uniforms. It didn't matter if our pants were too big or too small, he'd still wear them; each of us had caught him wearing our uniform at one point or another, and we'd call him out, but he'd swear the uniform was his despite the rolls of extra fabric piled at his shoes and the jacket not closing around his stomach.

Much could be said about Sean, but he was reliable. He could be counted on to be in the locker room up to forty-five minutes before his shift. He'd be walking around in briefs in search of the yellowed shirt he'd been wearing for two weeks, filling the room with his stink along the way, but he could be counted on to be in the locker room much earlier than the beginning of his shift. He had his own process: search for his own never-cleaned uniform or, if it couldn't be found, search for another doorman's uniform to wear. He went through his process methodically and with no concern for our opinions, but he could be trusted to relieve the second man on time.

Ramón was the "half hour early guy" and Sean was the "ten minutes early guy." That's how it was for many years. I should've seen Sean scavenging for a uniform in the locker room that day. I hadn't. I changed without his stench choking the life out of me and didn't even notice.

I was running the elevator when Sean called out. Sammy took the call and didn't tell me about it. He was supposed to. The senior men had worked extra hours that week, including Sammy, and I had been next in line for overtime. Sammy didn't care. He took the call and steered the overtime to himself despite knowing it was my turn. And he knew I'd give in to the allure of leaving the job early. Who doesn't want to get home sooner than they should? It was a brazen maneuver—getting me to leave early allowed him to begin working the next shift while avoiding detection—and Sammy executed it with a master's touch.

Sammy stole overtime from me at the worst possible time. I was paying tuition out of pocket, no financial assistance; I had refused to take loans at John Jay. I had one revenue stream, my weekly doorman paycheck, and it barely covered everything. Rent, car insurance, and tuition all came out of one check. During the 2008 financial crisis, I bought watered-down gas just to afford the drives to school, work, and back home. Things got so bad that my tax lady once suggested I have kids to alleviate the financial strain. "Stephen, things would be easier if you had a few dependents," she said casually. Overtime hours, at one and a half times the hourly rate, were an easier, less-sensational way to lighten the load. Just one overtime shift added two hundred dollars to a weekly check. It was the way to go, but the senior men usually snatched it before it got to me. Sammy stole hours from me at a time when I would've gladly stayed at the building for the overtime. I'd been robbed.

What did 400-level courses or literary conferences have to say about Sammy stealing my overtime shift or my inability to pay tuition? Or about the fact that senior doormen had been stealing overtime from the younger, less-tenured doormen for decades? Nothing at all. Winning an essay contest was a victory recognized in academia, a castle piercing the clouds, and nowhere else. I ached for my coworkers at the building to see my quality.

The call of duty was loud: I had the talent, the conviction, but most importantly, the vision; holding Sammy accountable could lead to the installation of new overtime protocols at the building. It was real-world change, and I'd be spurring it on. I wanted this.

Conditions were favorable. Mr. Atwell was on vacation, and Michaele wasn't responding to emails. Additionally, we didn't have a shop steward at the building to consult with in delicate matters. I had flown into the Bermuda Triangle of accountability: there was no one around to tell me *Stop this, and now*. I imagined a headline: "Doorman Revolution Springs

Out of Park Avenue Co-op." And the subheading: "Summer Shakeup at Building May Change Doorman Industry Forever."

I began writing a petition that demanded an overhaul of the overtime system at the building. It would be nothing like the petition of 2009. This petition would be different: I was going for an absolute victory this time. The overtime dilemma deserved as much: it had been plaguing the entire staff for decades, especially the ones on the lower half of the roster who rarely got called for additional hours. The fight wouldn't be about uniforms and comfort; it would be about a man's livelihood and justice for the decades it had been handicapped.

The battle would yield an incredible victory. Songs would be sung for ages and ages hence, and hey, if someone wanted to erect a statue of my likeness inside the vestibule, who was I to stop them? I was so sure of all of it. The statue would wear a robe to cover my crotch despite evolving attitudes toward public nudity, but if the guys wanted to hang their doorman hats from its head, that was okay. As long as it wasn't on their heads on hot days, I was fine with it.

When I passed the petition to George, he held it up to his face with the utmost reverence, and read out loud: "The current overtime policy at 411 Park Avenue . . . flawed . . . unfair in practice . . ." and zipped through the entire paragraph until his chin dropped into his chest. "This is good," he said, one hand burrowing into his pocket. George whipped out a pen and slashed his signature onto the page like Zorro leaving his mark. "This . . . is . . . good," he said over his slow-churning pen. Once finished, he passed the petition to me and added, "And I don't give a fuck." He caught me somewhere between being taken aback by his sudden display of intensity and the admiration of a man I hoped to emulate to have a chance of liking myself in the future.

As one of the older, tenured men at the building, George was repeatedly called for OT. Signing the petition meant he was willing to forgo the benefits of the system for another that benefited the entire staff. It would entail waiting longer for overtime hours, possibly up to two weeks, but that's the kind of man George was. He managed to hold everyone's affections even as they knew he operated at a constant simmer. I admired him greatly.

In the comments section, George wrote, "I feel this is right," just to reassure me. George was no Jose Ruiz, who'd waited for the entire staff at 905 to sign their names before joining the club. With George's name at the top of the petition, I was off to a good start.

The next one to sign was a shocker.

Teo, the Muslim Albanian handyman, was mocked for many things, most notably by Lorenzo for tying a white rag on the workshop's doorknob during one of his many scheduled prayers. And by George, who mockingly called Teo "the engineer" after fielding calls from tenants who needed Teo to return to fix the same leaky faucet a second and third time. Teo didn't do himself any favors. I'd constantly crack jokes about how high he wore his pants, often wondering out loud if his belly button was between his nipples (a good sport, Teo always laughed). Most importantly, he was Mr. Atwell's second-in-command and unabashedly loyal to him. It was embarrassing. He'd watch Mr. Atwell as he spoke, nod his head to agree with any points Mr. Atwell made, and say, "Yeah, it's true." But not on the day I brought the petition to work. That day, he looked down at the petition a few moments, signed it, and wrote "I feel this is right," just like George had. I should've been alarmed when he copied George's statement in the comment section. I wasn't at all. I moved on to the next coworker.

Frank didn't sign the petition. The current overtime system worked for him too much to oppose it. "It used to be *me* missing out on OT. Those fucking old-timers used to take it all," he said from the stool in the service elevator. "Now it's my turn. I'm not signing anything."

It was a fair point. I wanted to say, "You could've done something about it then, when you were in my position, but you didn't." I swapped those words for these: "Listen, man, we can change things *now* and you can be part of that change! You'd be like our hero! Imagine your name on the petition! *Frank Fernandez, senior man, signed the petition that changed everything.* You'd be a hero for us!"

"Nah, I'm not signing that thing," he said. *Fuck it, we don't need Frank,* I thought, and continued to the next guy.

I knew Sean wasn't going to sign the petition. He grunted at the page when it was in his hands. I thought to snatch it away in case his alcoholic ass mistook it for a beverage napkin. "Can't sign that," he said and scampered back to the front door. I examined his uniform as he walked away, and nodded along to my discovery: I had three inches of height on Sean and they were all there, bunched up in the cuff of the pants he was wearing—a pair of my doorman pants had gone missing and he was likely wearing them. I didn't say anything. What was I going to do, yell, "Take my pants off," in the middle of the lobby? That's doing too much. I wouldn't chase after his signature either.

Lorenzo's refusal to sign the petition was a huge setback. He had arrived at the building only a year ahead of me and hadn't seen much overtime either. I thought he'd be an easy get. He was a huge kiss ass, sure, and tailed Mr. Atwell whenever he saw him, but he grumbled for hours when he didn't get called for OT: he once scribbled his name off the call sheet to protest being passed over; another time, he took the protest pettiness to another level by using Wite-Out to cover his name on the call sheet; he did such a good job with the Wite-Out that he wasn't called for OT for weeks until Mr. Atwell convinced him to write his name and number over the Wite-Out. Lorenzo's handwriting was not much better than Teo's, whose words looked like hieroglyphs, so I figured he'd write his name in huge block letters and say, "It's about fuckin' time!" Then I'd go about my way. That's not what happened.

Lorenzo's thoughts were with Mr. Atwell. "You're gonna do this while he's on vacation? The man is out there resting, and he's gonna come back to *this*? Nah, I'm not signing it."

I would've agreed with Lorenzo's rationale under normal circumstances. Yes, I was essentially setting up Mr. Atwell for an ambush. He'd go from mai tais and tanning lotion to a smack in the face casting him as a failed administrator. He wouldn't be allowed to treat the petition like he did every other sheet of paper—there would be no tossing this correspondence to the side with the intent of forgetting. He'd probably hold it so he could read it again later, so he could decide how to handle the person who wrote it.

Here's the thing: Lorenzo was an asshole, the worst of the worst. In the past, he'd talked shit about Mr. Atwell's kids—how they shouldn't waste their time in college when they were going to be doormen anyway. And how he wanted to fuck Mr. Atwell's wife—how he and Mr. Atwell were the same age but he would do a better job with Mrs. Atwell. Lorenzo noticed that the majority of the staff had signed the petition and knew he wouldn't get in any more trouble than the rest of us. So why did he *really* refuse to sign the petition? Because he wasn't going to lose another doorman job. He'd been fired from his last job—he never went into the reasons why (though after working with him a few years, we surmised he was fired for being a piece of shit; there's really no other reason why you fire a middle-aged doorman with years of seniority and get away with it, unless he's a piece of shit with no defense). He confessed to George that he was paranoid about losing his job. He'd started at the building a year before I had but was in his late fifties and looking to stack his chips for his retirement. If he got fired again, he'd be bagging groceries in his seventies. Lorenzo didn't give a shit about Mr. Atwell. He'd simply lost every line of credit and didn't want to risk relying on his own honor. You fake it till you make it, and in this case, Lorenzo was attempting to sound concerned for Mr. Atwell's feelings.

I had gone rogue at 411 Park Avenue, the second time I'd done so at a building cooperative. I'd soon hand Mr. Atwell a document asserting he'd been running the building improperly for two decades and demanding he overhaul his system. I know a lot about sins. If it failed, my ambush petition would be an unpardonable sin at the building.

After three more men signed the petition, I slipped it inside a manila folder. I had written, "We, the undersigned . . ." on the petition. When you find "We, the undersigned" on a document, you know it means business.

Upon his return from vacation, I stood at Mr. Atwell's desk as I offered a quick recap of the Sammy incident. "It's not the first time it's happened, Mr. Atwell," I said, passing the folder into his hands. "We need a new overtime system."

As far as any of the guys knew, the building had never seen a petition before, not one written or submitted or even suggested. I was convinced it would be the spark of a revolution that would lead to self-discovery among the men—they'd realize that once together, they were powerful. The assholes who hadn't signed the petition would realize they'd be on the wrong side of building history.

I believed I'd done the hardest part already. I'd written the petition. Mr. Atwell could do the rest: he'd completely overhaul the overtime system so that it was fair and allowed every employee an opportunity to work extra hours.

Mr. Atwell sighed. "Well, you sure knew what you were writing," he said as he leaned back in his chair with the petition over his stomach. His calmness was disconcerting. He treated the petition like a slight inconvenience, like a restaurant had delivered the wrong food and he was annoyed to have to wait for another delivery. That was not the Mr. Atwell I knew.

Early in my time at 411 Park Avenue, I learned to read Mr. Atwell's demeanor in the morning to guess how the rest of the day at the job would go. If he appeared agitated, it was going to be a long, tense day. And not because he yelled or slammed doors. That wasn't his style. He brooded and simmered and made you feel helpless, and when you're a doorman who cannot help, you're as close to being an obsolete human being as is possible. Mr. Atwell was always one complication away from a full meltdown.

As Mr. Atwell continued reading the petition, I sensed something else too. It was in the way he read. He read at a steady pace, no bursts or sudden pauses. His eyes scanned over the sheet; they didn't consume it like someone who had just been ambushed by a mutiny. It was like he was prepared. But there was no way he could be prepared for a petition at his desk on his first day back from vacation.

Right?

Mr. Atwell had to have been blindsided, right? I figured half the damage would come from the surprise.

It was Tuesday, the last day of my workweek. When I walked out of the building at the end of my shift, I treated it like a goodbye. I truly believed it was the last day the building would be the same. From that day on, there'd be no more backstabbing among the doormen, only a collective voice that raged against the building's tired, failed traditions. A glorious, new epoch of doorman life. There would be joy and celebrations, and all my fretting over classes and school and overtime would've meant so much more. I'd be a hero, unequivocally and without equal. When I swiped my MetroCard that day, it wasn't a train that took me home, it was a chariot of hope.

When I returned on Friday, the first day of my workweek, I treated it like the first day of my reign. It was seven in the morning and quiet. Perfect conditions for the beginning of a new era. Two hours before Mr. Atwell was due in the lobby to read the logbook's updates for the last two shifts. I savored my bagel, knowing that if I wanted it to, chives cream cheese would taste like strawberries. Victory was only two hours away.

Mr. Atwell eventually appeared in the lobby to read the logbook. Nothing of note, not in the logbook or in his demeanor. He didn't ask any questions. After sliding the ledger into the drawer, he turned and quietly made his way into my elevator. It was the usual. I always brought him to the basement after he came to the lobby to read the logbook. That day, however, I figured we'd reach the basement and he'd say, "Come with me to my office." That meant I'd flip the elevator to automatic and leave it without a man inside. Guess we're having a *talk*-talk, I'd think on the way to his office. I'd lower myself into a seat, thinking, *I hope he's handling everything okay.* And I'd smile with empathy because that's what you do when you've crushed someone. I had everything lined up.

When we reached the basement, he said thank you and nothing else. Then he stepped out of the elevator and calmly walked to his office. It was our routine every morning, and *that* was the problem: it wasn't supposed to be our routine on *that* morning. It was, after all, the dawn of a new era at 411 Park Avenue. I waited inside the open elevator for a few seconds in case Mr. Atwell remembered the role he played in my glorious revolution and made a U-turn. That didn't happen. I heard nothing but the hum of the boiler at the other end of the basement. I took the elevator back to the lobby and stepped out, completely stunned by the ordinariness of the day at 411 Park Avenue.

I stayed in the lobby for a half hour that felt like a week. I couldn't stand the idleness any longer. I swooped into my elevator and dropped into the basement. I needed to know what the fuck was up.

The elevator opened, revealing a huddle of men squeezed tightly into the basement's buttery yellow hallway. They were all there: Mr. Atwell; Teo; Frank on his stool; and Gary, the shift's maintenance man, leaning against the wall. The petition's manila folder was clamped in Mr. Atwell's hand while his other hand was in the middle of a pointing gesture. It looked like a staff meeting I hadn't been invited to.

First, I played it cool. "Mr. Atwell, I want to talk to you about—"

He handed me the folder.

I stood in the middle of their huddle looking down at the petition in horror. The name of every doorman had been scribbled off the list save for two, mine and George's. Teo had even scribbled out his "This is right" comment.

"You've *gotta* be kidding me," I groaned.

I shot a look at Teo. He knew I was demanding an answer. He shook his head no, no, no and tried speaking it too. He managed, "Mmmm-nnnn."

I eventually discovered that Teo was borderline illiterate. He hadn't understood that he was signing a petition that effectively made him a participant in a revolt against Mr. Atwell, his patron. Teo didn't have the stomach for such drama and like the other men, had removed his name. With only two names remaining on the list, the petition was dead.

"The guys don't want to take part in that," Mr. Atwell said. He hadn't even buttoned his suit yet. He was comfortable, in control, the way seasoned politicians are. It wasn't the Mr. Atwell I knew. He'd been prepared.

I found out later that Lorenzo had tipped him off during his vacation. How? Lorenzo had Mr. Atwell's cell-phone number. He was the only one on the staff who'd landed Mr. Atwell's cell-phone number. The rest of us didn't have it because we never cared to work for it.

I wonder what Lorenzo's text looked like. He wasn't good at conjunctions, so it probably read like a telegram: "Stephen circulating petition. Danger eminent. Beware."

The threat had been neutralized by the building, but I remained, and though left without my usual weapon of choice, the written word, I knew I could inflict damage. Standing amid the building's guardians, I felt dangerous. My brow furrowing, I hurled my conviction at them like a sword.

"Fuck these old-ass prewar buildings and their rules and traditions! We don't *have* to continue abiding by everything in the books just because it's what's always been done, especially when it doesn't work! You guys just keep saying, 'Yeah, that's fine by me, since that's how it's always been.' Well, you know what? The overtime system doesn't work, okay? It doesn't work, and it just finished screwing me out of money I needed for tuition! I was robbed, fucking *robbed*, just like you guys have been getting robbed for years." I turned to Frank, turned to Teo, turned to the porter, and with my eyes marked each one as conspirators in a crime worse than mine, that of compromise. "And it looks to me like you guys would rather watch us getting robbed than keep the system out of our pockets!"

"Calm down, Stephen," Mr. Atwell said, the cool disappearing from his face. He was unsettled. I drew satisfaction from seeing him that way. Then I gave it all back.

"What . . . what did you do during my two days off?" I shouted. The men replied with silence.

I never found out exactly what happened on my days off, but I got the sense that Mr. Atwell had used his power and influence to convince the men to remove their names from the petition. In the past, he'd pulled me off to the side whenever his Nice Man image was threatened. He'd whined about other doormen making him look bad and cautioned me against making the same mistake, adding that whenever the chips fell, I didn't want to get caught dealing with the same consequences, right? That was his way. He'd enlist the staff in characterizing him as an always-benign figure and placing any man threatening his image on an island all by himself. He'd almost certainly done the same in this case, and I had made it easy. I was the most hostile aggressor the building had ever seen.

Mr. Atwell didn't answer my question. None of the other men answered my question. They remained quiet as I stood looking into their eyes. They didn't look away either; they each looked at me from their place in the ring. They wore blank, disinterested stares, and though not threatening, there wasn't the slightest hint of the shame I would've felt if I was one of them. I understood. They had won—they knew it—and were stretching their moment of dominance. Just beyond the buttery yellow hallway, the boiler rumbled along.

I tried regaining momentum.

"Guys, we can decide to do new things even though we work in this old building! What's stopping us from doing things differently? Nothing!" I glared at Mr. Atwell and pumped my fist again. "We don't have to keep marching in quicksand. We can change things!" I spread my arms and flared my fingers. I was snarling.

"Stephen, please calm down!" Mr. Atwell said, raising his palms in panic. "You're behaving like a gladiator!"

I looked into the eyes of the four men surrounding me in the basement hallway, hoping I transmitted what my words hadn't. Mr. Atwell . . . the nice man. Frank . . . the opportunist. Teo . . . the Caliban. Gary . . . the bystander. They had all been complicit in the plot to betray and exile me. I remained in their circle a moment longer so they might catch on fire.

"We had this, fellas. We had this!" I shouted at my coworkers' chests, refusing to look them directly in the eyes. It was more respect than they deserved. I told them that they were making a big mistake and that it would come back to bite them on their asses—that they'd lose a shift to the system again, it was bound to happen, and they'd remember the day they spurned our petition.

I looked at Mr. Atwell. "You're not a good man," I said. You might think I was fizzling out, that I had nothing left to say, so I said whatever I could. I knew Mr. Atwell. He maintained his nice-guy image with a potter's touch. He spoke softly to match it. He used little pressure when shaking hands to assure you. Mr. Atwell was convinced of his own goodness, and I had confronted him with a startling contradiction.

The basement floor at 411 Park Avenue was battleship gray, just like 905's had been, and its yellow walls as unyielding as its color guard, whose darkened eyes had thinned with contempt. "Man, fuck this," I said and thundered into the passenger elevator. The door closed slowly, showing me the basement's lifeless colors until it was just the door's opaque metal and my blurred reflection. I pressed the appropriate button, the one with the L on it.

24

CLIMATE CHANGE

I was iced at work after the petition crashed. The fellas slid past me every day, muttering quick hellos as they went and leaving me scrambling to decide whether I should wave—I desperately wanted to be one of them again, after all—or disregard them to protect my ego. I usually nodded and grunted my way into the middle ground. It was a miracle: my coworkers abandoned all our previous topics of conversation, the ones that had kept shifts moving—women, sports, and places to visit in Puerto Rico. They avoided all eye contact and the appearance of fraternization with me. I'd pointed a condemning finger at their century-old workplace and exposed its inadequacies, none of which could be easily forgotten. I was sitting in Pastor Rosado's back pew again and was more invisible than ever.

There was something off about George too. He did the usual thing, spend chunks of time looking through the front entrance's glass panel at nothing in particular. I assumed we'd eventually touch base and talk shit about heavy hitters like Geller, or Lorenzo the doorman, whom we both disliked, and we did, but not for a long time. For many weeks, George remained locked in a silent stare at the sidewalk outside the door.

George was in his mid-seventies. I understood that living more than seven decades came with its share of self-assessment and regrets, but I didn't want supporting my petition to be one of them. That possibility, that he wished he'd never signed the petition, horrified me. I tried to snap him out of his trance during one of our shifts. I shouted, "How are the grandkids, George?" He turned to look at me in the mail room. "Love those kids so much," he said, smiling. I breathed the biggest sigh of relief; you have no idea. *George doesn't hate me!* I thought. He went back to his near-catatonic stare at the sidewalk outside the door, leaving me alone again to reflect on his life.

Lorenzo started walking around the building and got the men talking again. Ladies, baseball, and Puerto Rico. He became something of a doorman pope, beckoning each man to come back home. He was qualified for the position: he'd never signed the petition. Putting an arm around each man to initiate conversations was his way of separating them from me. I stayed on the outside of their ring, all the while fascinated by their sudden willingness to upend the social contract between doormen—you talk to make the hours go by faster—just to alienate me.

It's a discovery that dampens the spirit: you're just a doorman, a man who opens doors. You're still mulling it over when Mr. Atwell scrambles into the lobby to inform you that 5A is hosting another dinner for her DNC friends tomorrow and she's hiring a black-tie catering service and Hillary may show up so make sure to be on your p's and q's. You wonder exactly what the fuck that means since your p's and q's are limited to wearing a suit and opening a door for eight hours. How do you improve on that? And that's the point, isn't it? It could be Hillary or whoever, but you're the one who never changes, never evolves, never grows, because you're a doorman, a man who opens doors. You're like a fish meant to stay the size of your tank; problem is, there's another fish in the tank, your shift mate, and having a shift mate is part of the job. You see how the building works? Even growing to the size of your tank is curtailed by the job and the system of checks and balances it executes through your partner, the building's agent and watchdog. Trust me, he's thinking the same about you.

The men knew what they'd done. It was in their silent, almost mournful dispositions in the locker room. For weeks, few words were shared between us. They lowered their heads or averted their gazes when I was around. I countered by lowering my spirit. I began the process by taking senior man liberties: I repeatedly sat in the lobby in complete disregard of the unspoken *Don't sit in the forbidden chairs* rule. I knew Atwell was watching the security feed. I just didn't care. At school, I wrote like a machine incapable of injecting a warm voice into any writing assignments. I completed my assignments and sat in classes, unwilling to share my ideas during discussions. From me, it was the kind of bare minimum output that I had always correlated with the average student. I made allowances for myself. Too many.

A strange sensation cast over me like a web. It was neither cold nor hot. It did not pain or pleasure me. I felt like a stone on the sidewalk—present but not participating, not viable, unconcerned with the amphitheater of feelings and needs in my life. My mother called; I didn't answer. Didn't return the call either. I was cold to every deliveryman, postman, and UPS driver when they approached the building's door. Pregnant women riding trains would stand in front of me while I sat, and I'd close my eyes and drift away into the sweetest nap. There was no joy in eating food; there was only chewing. I entertained women's hearts just so they could entertain my body later. I cared for no one, for nothing. A shrug was my posture and *no* my baseline answer for everything.

Once you're sliding, it's difficult to stop your descent. You're a prisoner of the ride for however long it lasts. All the effort and good thoughts and kind gestures—it's all inconsequential. Then you tumble forward.

25

THE GOOD NEWS

My little brothers are better at delivering good news to Mami than I am. When they call, they talk about promotions and raises, the kinds of things a working-class mother wants to hear. A few times, they've called to announce the launches of their new careers. Mami's face lights up—you don't even know. She smiles while holding the phone to her ear and says, "Praise the Lord!" Then she lowers her head, closes her eyes, and whispers a prayer of thanks under her breath. "Don't forget to thank God," she says into the receiver.

My brothers have been calling about new houses; those are Mami's favorite. She gets really excited about home ownership. I've scratched my head while listening to them talk and thought, *Well, I own a decent laptop. It's not a MacBook, but it does the job.* The laptop isn't much when compared to a house, and that's what it's all about: worth. If you call Mami with news, it's got to be about something big; it better make a splash. One time, Mami picked up the phone, listened for a second, and ran to the window with her phone at her head. Behold! Outside on the street was my brother Jason, his wife, and my niece, showcasing a shiny new car. It was the ultimate lineup of good news: a son, his family, and the family car.

When I call with news, it's about Ajax, my Siamese cat. He's cross-eyed with two short front legs so he doesn't run, he hops; he's all I can talk about. I could've talked about my day at work, but who wants to hear about my third argument with the little Colombian housekeeper who gets upset when I send her to the service entrance instead of letting her enter through the front door.

Point is, I realized that all my stories from work sounded petty or inadequate. I'd already used the I-have-a-new-job announcement back in 2005, when I came back from Minnesota and took over for Carlos and his knives. And Mami had been instrumental in me getting the job—it was her idea, remember? There's been nothing new since then, at least nothing that registered with my family.

I don't just mention Ajax in conversations, I lean on him heavily. He's the only thing keeping me in a conversation with Mami. "How's my grandson?" she always asks soon after we begin talking. Old age has made Ajax blind and temperamental, leading him to slam head-on into walls and cry in confusion.

During a recent visit to Mami's apartment, I shared the latest Ajax news. "Ajax slammed into something the other day," I said matter-of-factly. "I don't think it was a wall, it must have been something sharper because there was a hole in his head. It got infected and half his face got swollen." Mami gasped and said, "Oh no." Then I realized I was ruining the format—she asks about Ajax; I offer the update. Mami hangs on every word I say about Ajax, whose sentimental value is as high as the listing price on any house or car.

Why don't I talk to my mom about my romantic life? Sure, I'm old enough to be married, and with teenage kids. I'm a handsome guy. Strong and sturdy. Naturally tanned, with fantastic hair. But generating even an ounce of optimism in that department has been challenging.

I recently asked Mami to pray. I had started seeing a girl. I asked her to pray because when it comes to me, her firstborn, seeing a girl for any length of time is good news. With some prayer, maybe the good news turns into waves of good news, then more, and before you know it, Mami's telling my brothers about *my* good tidings. She was sitting in the front passenger seat of my father's van when I asked her to pray. She'd just passed Ajax over to me in his carrier. He had stayed with them while I was away on another trip to Puerto Rico. With Ajax whining inside the carrier at my feet, I said, coyly, "So, Ma, I met a girl. She's really pretty. She's really nice. Please pray for me. And *us*, actually." Mami asked if I'd met her in Puerto Rico, and I said no, she's from here. I met her before my trip. She nodded and said Amen, she'd pray anyway.

I should've met the girl in Puerto Rico. Or said I had. Mami would've prayed more, and then maybe things wouldn't have fallen apart. Homegirl was gorgeous, a former stripper converted into a church girl, but still damaged from her pole days when she had a boyfriend-manager; she couldn't handle seeing me express myself with the slightest enthusiasm. She'd wince, then watch me with her eyes wide, like she was bracing for a left hook or an uppercut. Maybe it was my hand gestures—I can be demonstrative with my hands. Or maybe I resembled her ex? Who knows.

There was a Russian girl. Yulia. She was nervous on our first date, something I found endearing. A former fitness instructor, she was lithe, athletic, and exuded elegance well beyond her years.

Once, while sitting with Yulia on a bench near the East River, I encouraged her to show her teeth when smiling. She had a thing for hiding them. I let the words hang in the air between us. I knew she was self-conscious about the one tooth that, though not appalling enough to be categorized as a snaggletooth, protruded enough to look like a lump behind her upper lip. I waited a few ticks and smiled broadly, exposing my one canine tooth that's perched so high it looks like a fang. It inspires vampire jokes. Yulia laughed and, for many weeks afterward, smiled without cares or concerns.

I was a doorman, and Yulia was on another scale of unfortunate. She was in her late twenties and broke because she was an undocumented immigrant with integrity—she refused to buy a fake ID—and didn't have the support system to accommodate her convictions. Her mother lived in Russia, and her brother lived in the Bronx with a Dominicana who didn't love him, so he had his share of problems. Bedeviled by high standards, Yulia spent much of her time trying to convince restaurants to pay her under the table. Yulia was in a tough spot.

I turned away from her after she offered to pay me to marry her. Sitting beside her on the edge of a flower bed at a Park Avenue median, I realized that she knew what I knew: our relationship had ended a while ago, and she was trying to squeeze some good out of it. "I need to ask you. I need to cross you off my list," she said dejectedly.

I tried imagining what folks in the fraudulent marriage business charge and went as far as ringing up a figure in my head: $20,000 felt right. I figured it's a one-shot deal; I should get it right the first time. She said she knew I wouldn't take the money and run. "I wouldn't," I said gravely. "I know," she said, but she knew where things were headed. I put my head in my hands. The situation was too real for me, too cold, like waking up on a bathroom floor.

It was over. I didn't know which she wanted more, a lover or a green card. I need things to be simpler than that. I want a lover. And I want to clear the mountain of debt showing up on my credit report, but lumped together in a business deal like that? Nah. I want my love unsullied.

I thought about Yulia's proposition a week later. I had tossed away a shot at calling my mother with big news, the news that would've sent ripples through the family and maybe the world: Stephen is getting married! His fiancée is a newly minted citizen! His account is $20,000 in the plus!

Yulia's proposal wasn't right for me.

So we're back where we started. I'm 0 and 2 in the romance department again. It's whatever. I've come to accept that I won't be bringing Mami any exciting relationship updates, not anytime soon, so I have to try matching my brothers' news from another department: academia.

News about academic accomplishments don't usually translate in the hood, especially as they pertain to the arts. I get it. People in the hood are trying to pay bills, make the extra cash for car repairs, or get relatives out of a jam. Some of them are looking to buy houses. You don't get to interrupt their flow with news about writing a bomb-ass thesis.

A few months earlier, one of my literature professors, Richard Perez, had asked me about my postgraduate plans. I was stumped. I hadn't thought that far. The fact was, my academic aspirations ended at earning a bachelor's degree at John Jay College. In my mind, finishing at John Jay would correct my Nyack College experience, but I hadn't finished at Nyack; I left with nothing but school loan debt and an expulsion letter. I'd been held captive for twelve years, stunted and stuck in cold, abrupt endings. So when Perez asked me about my postgraduate plans, I was close to punctuating a conclusion I'd written myself.

That wasn't enough for Perez. He said, "You're the best writer I've encountered in my entire career as a professor. You should go to school for writing." I was floored. I like to hear kind words as much as the next person, but he'd been around some impressive writers. He'd talked about them often, mentioned the incredible graduate schools they attended, and though he'd always called me a brilliant student, I never thought I'd join their ranks as a writer. Here he was saying I was not just as good a writer as them, I was *better*.

I was the best. Knowing that did something to me. Until then, I'd been defined by my job. To my family, I was Stephen, who works as a doorman. To my friends, I was Stephen, who's fun and works as a doorman. To women, I was Stephen, who can't hang out late on the weekends because he works doorman shifts in the mornings. Perez had signaled a new epoch in my life, a time when I could reference something other than a job I'd gotten because I knew someone. I was a writer, and the best one a professor had ever encountered. It was like God had slammed a closed fist on a crowded chessboard, catapulting the combating pieces and clearing the board, save for one: me. I remained, a writer garbed in potential and promise and a crown. Perez had signaled that I was ready to conquer the next space.

Perez and I had this conversation in late 2012. I had already missed several application deadlines to notable writing programs in the city and was within days of missing a few more. One program gave me until January to put something together and, holy shit, it was in the Top 5 in the country for creative nonfiction: Hunter College's MFA. That's where I wanted to go. I wanted to be able to say that I went to a Top 5 writing program in the country, and that I'd earned my degrees in New York City, *from* New York City, as a child of the city.

In December, I applied to Hunter's MFA for Creative Writing and decided that if they didn't accept me, I'd spend all of 2013 acquainting myself with memoir so that I would be a lock when I applied again in the fall. But first, I'd take a shot at the 2013 application.

I had no writing sample. The program wanted twenty pages of memoir. I had never written in the genre. I looked up a description on the genre and confirmed that, nope, I had never sat down and written with the thought *I'm writing a memoir* in my head.

I'd written in the first person before. On Facebook. When things happened at work, or on the train, or at the grocery story, I'd write about them and turn them into status updates. Most of my status updates were long, obligating my friends to click "Continue reading" several times to finish them.

I'd gone to Hunter's open house and remembered a prospective student asking, "Does it have to be twenty pages of one story or could it be twenty pages of multiple stories?" One of the professors said it could be twenty pages' worth of stand-alone stories, and so I spent an evening copying and pasting my favorite Facebook status updates into a Word document in the hopes I'd hit twenty pages.

I had *more* than enough. I had *thirty* pages worth of short memoir stories. The program wanted a double-spaced document—I one-and-a-half-spaced it. What were they going to do, fine me? Toss my application? I'd just apply again the following year, fuck it. I set the document to 1.5 spacing and the miraculous occurred: I fit thirty pages' worth of stories onto twenty pages.

I received a call early in the spring of 2013 while walking with two friends through John Jay's newly constructed building, the one they cleverly named New Building. It was Louise DeSalvo from Hunter's creative writing program on the other end.

"Is our program really the only one you're applying to?" she asked. I remembered that question on the application.

"Yes, I am," I responded. "And if you don't accept me for the upcoming class, you'll accept me for the next one."

She laughed and said, "That's remarkable. Well, we'd like to offer you one of the six spots in our nonfiction program's class of 2015." And just like that, I went from having no postgraduate plans to getting accepted into one of the top writing programs in the country.

"So that's what happened," I said after telling Mami about my call with Louise at Hunter. My mother's eyes lingered over me as if she was trying to figure out how to show excitement and in what quantity. She said, "Oh wow, that's great," but it was unsteady and uncertain. More steady and assured was the severe look she gave me while walking to the kitchen. She said, "Don't forget to thank God." I was so frustrated. I knew God did the impossible, but I'd done the close to impossible—getting into a writing program on the strength of my Facebook posts—and she wouldn't even let me take credit for *that*. How was none of that really great news?

There were congratulatory phone calls and text messages from my siblings too; I was happy to receive them. My father reacted as well. He said, "Oh wow, that's great." He nodded his head sheepishly. "You're going to be a famous writer and write many books now."

"Thanks, Papi," I said. I smiled, but not because I believed it. I didn't think I had the necessary Facebook updates to pull off becoming a famous writer. I smiled because I recognized freedom at first glance; at some point, I had been freed of my desperate need for my father to care about and approve of me. I wasn't angry anymore and felt no bitterness toward him. I was free, and with that freedom, I forgave him and recognized that he'd done the best he could, and it was enough. There is no lighter feeling.

26

SEEING DOLLAR SIGNS

I struggled at the MFA program right out of the gate. I couldn't believe it. Only months earlier, I had shaken my undergraduate professors' hands with pity, knowing they'd soon wither away as I went on to create art from Day One of graduate school. I thought of my first week at Hunter College like the "education" section of my Wikipedia page, as if it was the dawn of a new age. Listen, I was in despair one month into the semester.

There were stark differences between me and my classmates, and I'd noticed them immediately, on the first day of class. I'd initially thought they were reasons to celebrate. Now I wasn't so sure.

One of my classmates worked at a publishing house. She fluttered about, telling delightful jokes that pulled laughs from our classmates. It fascinated me. I didn't share the same experience. Then I realized they were jokes meant for readings and book launches—safe and palatable and affirming of our positions in her orbit. Another girl spent a lot of time at farmers markets and wrote about farmers markets. She dressed modestly but with style, so there were lots of textures and layers to her outfits. During class, she'd look in my eyes one moment, then look away; I didn't know if it was because she hated when my Brown, Bronx-sounding ass looked at her or if it was because she was uncomfortable about her wealth; I didn't know how to interrupt a writing workshop just to say, *I'm around wealthier people than you are—please don't feel so bad for me and please show me the respect of maintaining eye contact when we chat!* Another girl went on writers' retreats in Providence, where she walked barefoot and ate Oreos only when she wasn't plucking berries right off the branch. She admitted being more interested in poetry than prose and laughed at trying narrative, but I didn't laugh because I'd somehow won a seat in the same class and was feverishly trying to glean form from my classmates' writings, and she wasn't helping. Another girl had multiple subscriptions to literary magazines and pulled her books out of the canvas tote bag the *New Yorker* sent her with her first issue. My subscription to *Men's Health* was no match. They didn't send me a gym bag, not even a protein bar, so I didn't mention it, fuck out of here.

One of the ladies in the class had the kind of background in writing that begs to be parceled out in conversation. I'm sure I'll sell her short, but here are the highlights: she had graduated from Northwestern with a BA in creative writing, worked as an editor at a publishing house, and lived with a writer twenty years her senior. She showed us a picture of them together, and I have to say—she didn't lie: he definitely looked older and she definitely looked younger.

"Northwestern," as I called her, was the student expert on writing; we didn't argue her credentials. With a sleepy look on her face, she offered feedback in a tone that said, *You bore me. This entire class bores me. I've let you guys offer your feedback, but now Mama Bear's gotta do her thing, okay? Feel free to hang on every one of my lazily uttered words. You may never get this opportunity ever again.*

Me? I had been an English major at John Jay College of Criminal Justice. It's a mouthful. It's also not the kind of information that wows people. I know because I shared it during the first day's round of introductions. My classmates stared at me with dumbfounded looks that said, "Isn't that a cop school?" And they kept looking at me like there was more to it, like I'd reveal that I came from a family of Latin American writers and artists, and that's why I was there. Instead, I said, "I'm a doorman not too far from here and like to read during my shifts." It was so quiet I heard their eyelids blink.

Northwestern had a thing for writing dollar signs in the margins of our writing assignments. It was her way of saying, "Hey, this section is good, even to me, Northwestern alum currently working in publishing." Let me be clear: I knew about the dollar signs because I'd spotted them on my classmates pages, not because she ever wrote one on any of *my* pages. She had a scaling system too. You could earn one $ or four of them if you referenced Mary Carr in the breadth of your work, or if you wrote thinking about your work's breadth. One time, I saw $$$ on a classmate's first page, $$$$ on the next, and $$ on . . . fuck . . . it was the Poet, next to me, whose pages were littered with dollar signs. I was doomed.

I tried earning a dollar sign from Northwestern at a workshop in early October. At the beginning of class, my classmates passed by my seat and dropped their copies of my submission in front of me, each of them saying what you're supposed to say to maintain a fragile harmony, stuff like *So good . . . Just* [dramatic pause] *wonderful work . . . Beautiful,* always with a pained look in their eyes. Then I spotted the copy with her name on it. I grabbed at it like it was a treasure map. It was there, on the first page, can you believe it? There were a few editorial suggestions, sure, and one paragraph crossed out, okay, but it was there, hovering in white space like a mythical being, a lone $. The leaves in Central Park had begun fluttering to the pavement as autumn crept into the year, but the hope of seeing one of Northwestern's dollar signs on my page was the spring of my heart.

I sat captivated by the cash symbol even as she went on to slam the section I'd written on my dog Mack. It came a few pages after she'd made her mark, but by then it was too late. She'd already written the $ in the margin next to my impressive writing. She certainly made it clear she hated reading about dogs.

(Mack was a clump of fur when my father pulled up to my school with him in the back seat. I was in the fourth grade. By the time I was in middle school, Mack had become a neighborhood legend—the white, mastiff-bulldog mix who terrified pit bulls, but endured the tightest hugs from each child in our family. It was a family tragedy when he died after eating poison during a walk. My father would later speculate that a homeowner who didn't like dogs peeing on the tree outside his house had planted the poison. Mack came home, collapsed, and never stood on his paws again. Papi drove me and my brothers to Van Cortlandt Park late that night with Mack's body in the trunk; there were streetlamps and laws that say you can't use a park as a cemetery, but we were dressed in black like ninjas, so we didn't worry; after clearing a short gate with Mack's body, we walked into the park's thicket until light from the street shimmered through the leaves and branches. Then we dug a hole and slipped Mack into it, and gently, because we loved him. Papi asked each of us to share words and we did and Papi cried. Tears crawled down his cheeks and his voice creaked and I was in awe because Papi never cried. I cried too, for Papi, for Mack, and for myself.)

I was also the only man in my class. No, seriously. There were twelve students and one professor in every writing class, and I was the only male in Memoir. I made note of that on the first day and smiled. I thought, *Wait until the fellas hear about this*. What guy doesn't want to be surrounded by women? I soon realized it was me, I was that guy. Except for one awkward Jewish lady the others didn't talk to, the women in my class made me a pariah. I don't know if it was my musky cologne, or the number of times I said yo, but I didn't feel welcome.

I was the only Latino in the class too. I was also the only one who spoke of uniforms at work, who belonged to a union, who worked with men who looked and sounded like me. None of these details had ever mattered to me before sitting at that conference table during class.

The ladies were spinning yarns in the moments before class one evening. I hadn't learned how to read the room yet—hadn't learned that their soft, airy chuckles were code that translated to *conspicuous Brown man, please don't eat us*—so I took a shot at telling one of my stories. I started: "Crazy thing: I gotta keep my boots on top of my locker at work now. Well, I'm screwed no matter what I do cuz when I leave them on the floor, centipedes and water bugs crawl into them—you don't know how many times somethin' with legs has come running outta my boots when I pulled at them—but then I leave them on top of my locker and my coworker Frank puts dead water bugs in the boots. I mean, it's just pieces of them, like the body and no legs, since it's difficult to catch a live one and then make it stay in a boot. Kinda makes me laugh: when you don't want a bug to camp out in your boot, that's exactly what he does. But when a coworker wants a bug to camp out in my boots, the bug doesn't accept the invitation, he has to catch the bug and dissect it to make it happen. Frank deals with issues like these, can you believe it? Anyway, if I walk around and feel crunching in my boot, I know Frank got me again."

I had never had that many women's eyes on me at the same time.

I had somehow managed to become Tony Borowski at work *and* school, where I was a classroom deformity, a greasy Brown nob, conspicuous even to myself. For the first time in my life, I felt worse for who I'd been at birth than for any mistake I'd committed in the years notched afterward. I was in New York City, my birthplace, where these things shouldn't happen to a native, but the MFA classroom was another dimension anchored in its own customs and hierarchy, and I'd been noble long enough.

27

PARK AVENUE REPS

One afternoon, Gary the porter came up to the lobby and joined me in the vestibule, where I was working the door. His silence during my basement crucible had stung me; we'd previously had honest conversations and shared many laughs—I thought I'd earned some loyalty from him. A few days after the petition fiasco, however, Gary talked to me in full view of the other men, and I remembered that he was the Switzerland type. He didn't like picking sides. Gary had always been one of the most reserved, emotionally disciplined people I'd ever met, and he was fair. Forgiving him was easy.

It was a slow day. No traffic from tenants or deliveries. With George in the restroom, the lobby was as silent as a mausoleum. I'd been pressed up against the building's glass facade, mindlessly watching pedestrians walk by, when Gary entered the vestibule. The intrusion was welcome.

"Wassup, Gary," I said and stepped away from the glass.

"Wassup, Steph," he said too nonchalantly. I could tell Gary had something to say. The vestibule had always been our confessional booth with the roles of priest and penitent changing as needed. Thousands of pedestrians walk by Park Avenue's front doors every day without the slightest idea about the stories swirling around behind the glass.

Gary joined me at the glass and said, "Ayo, I was on the line at Bergdorf Goodman the other day, and I'm ready to pay. Fuckin' nobody's talking to me, it's like I'm not even there. I was getting no service, then I realize it's cuz I'm wearing my porter uniform."

I laughed. "You went shopping in Bergdorf Goodman wearing your maintenance uniform?"

"Well, what was I gonna do, change into my regular clothes and then change back into my uniform for suntin' that's gonna take twenty minutes?"

I saw an opening. "Good point. And it's not like your regular clothes are an improvement—you would've gone in there wearing sweatpants, a T-shirt, and a pair of Jordans and gotten ignored anyways!"

"You fuckin' asshole," Gary said and laughed. Gary was from the Bronx like me but, unlike me, was blissfully entrenched in hip-hop culture. He dressed the part. I was thirty by then and enjoying fitted clothes and parted hair too much to continue dressing like I was in a rap video. For years, I'd been joking on Gary for being Albanian and looking more ethnic and urban than I did.

"So they see me standing there, and instead of ringing me up, they start running to these rich, White ladies who are talkin' about, 'Oh, I'm just window shopping.' But I'm actually on the line holding something I'm ready to pay for!"

I could see Gary standing on a line wearing our building's stiff, boxy maintenance uniform and getting passed over, but I wanted to envision the item in his hands. "What were you paying for?" I asked. I needed to see it.

"Shoes for Yesenia," he said, somehow achieving a facial expression that exuded both dejection and pride. "Louis Vuittons."

How does a doorman afford a pair of Louis Vuittons? Gary owned a successful Bronx pizzeria with his brother (it seems to be an Albanian tradition to buy a pizzeria as much as it's an Italian tradition to sell one). He routinely went over his allotment of sick days to work at the pizzeria, especially when one of the obligatorily hired Mexicans couldn't make it to work. Between the two jobs, he could afford to lose hours at the building, but he made sure he never lost the building job—pizza doesn't come with medical benefits, and buildings do.

Gary never talked long about his finances, but he enjoyed dotting our conversations with hints. I always enjoyed his playful humility.

"This fucking wedding we're going to, man. Little nineteen-year-old that just learned how to play with herself and she's trying to get married."

"Nineteen years old and getting married? Hold on," I said. He'd been dropping clues about more than his finances. "She's Albanian, ain't she?"

The Old Country is the same for everyone. Latinos call it *el campo*. If you're a young campesino, your life is worth nothing if you're not married with kids to work the land before your twentieth birthday.

"Yeah, bro!" Gary responded, laughing. "And since my mom invited Yesenia, I gotta buy her shoes."

"Well, you don't *gotta* buy her shoes."

"I mean . . ." Gary looked searchingly at the floor.

It was a second try for Gary and his girlfriend, Yesenia. They had dated once years ago but split up after Gary left her for a White girl. That last detail, a White man dating a White woman, may not set off alarms in your head, but it did for me. Yesenia was a Dominicana. I imagine that being passed over for a White woman, with the world-class inferiority complex some Latinos still wrestle with, hadn't done much for Yesenia's pride or her standing with her family. When Gary returned to her, Yesenia went on a tirade of Oscar-winning proportions. He'd been paying the price ever since.

After some thought, I said, "Yeah, you gotta buy her the shoes."

We had just begun talking about Albanian weddings when some unusual activity on the street caught my attention. I became ecstatic. "Gary, it's the big fella doing pull-ups again!" I shouted, tapping on the glass in the man's direction.

It was the same street cleaner again. His day, like those of the other street cleaners, was normally spent walking around the neighborhood removing garbage from the ground. Four Eleven Park Avenue was one of the buildings on his route. The building had ordered a brick-cleaning project, scaffolding had gone up, and the street cleaner had taken to doing pull-ups on a scaffolding crossbar outside. It was a classic inner-city workout, the kind the neighborhood guys do in the early mornings.

Thing is, we weren't in the hood, we were on Park Avenue. The big fella was doing a hood workout a block away from Tiffany's blue lace and the Four Seasons' white gloves. All around him were shiny leather brief-cases, private cars, and poodles, but he didn't seem to care. The man wanted to do pull-ups.

A tumble of impulses. As subversive as I was at the job, I took his impromptu workout personally. It felt like a trespassing, as if I was a Park Avenue stakeholder and the large man doing pull-ups outside was intruding on my property. It was *my* crossbar, *my* scaffolding, *my* build-ing. And he worked for the Doe Fund's East Midtown Partnership, so he was an ex-con working himself back into good standing with society. I was a doorman, and he was a street cleaner. I belonged there. I was higher; he was lower. *Doesn't he know this is Park Avenue?* I thought to myself. *You can't do pull-ups on Park Avenue! Go do that shit in the Bronx!*

"This dude again," Gary said, sucking his teeth. "My man got noth-ing better to do." He shook his head and ducked into the lobby to text Yesenia.

I watched the street cleaner land on his feet. First set done. His chest heaved out, then pulled back in. It was a rest between sets. Another one would begin soon.

I reached for the front door's handle. "Watch this," I said from some-where deep in my chest. I turned the lock.

"Huh?" Gary said, quickly returning to the vestibule as he lowered his phone. He knew the drill: once one of the two doormen step outside, the other takes his place at the door. "What are you gonna do now?" he asked, dismay loosening his arms. I pushed the door open and galloped onto Park Avenue. "Let's find out!" I said over my shoulder.

Big Fella chose a perfect day for a workout. It was early in the fall when days are still sunny and warm, but leaves crisp and tighten at the stems as winter looms like a cold whisper. His feet were firmly planted on the ground, his hands were at his waist, and his eyes were raised as he looked at the crossbar. He was completely oblivious to my presence as I closed in.

Lines of sweat ran down the sides of his face as he stared up at the crossbar. His cheeks ballooned, then emptied as he shot out several heavy breaths. Blowing out unnecessarily like that, hard and fast the way he was doing, is a precursor to a set. His fourth set was about to begin. It's like the green light to continue, and there's no way another set begins before shooting out a series of quick breaths.

I slid into the flow of pedestrians and sauntered into the area behind him, as if heading to the corner. Big Fella's eyes narrowed under the bar, and his hands dropped from his waist. He catapulted himself at the crossbar.

He held on. That's all he did. Big Fella couldn't do a rep. His arms trembled as his big hands strained to keep their grip. He was tired. The last set of any exercise is usually the most demanding.

I looked over my shoulder at the building's entrance. Gary had moved so close to the glass he could've kissed it. Watching me anxiously, he pinched the lock with his free hand as if guarding against invaders. That was it right there, the first time I saw Gary lose his composure. He was perplexed and mystified, and I was in command. I let the corner of my lips perk into a smile. Gary didn't smile back. He couldn't.

I ran to the spot beside Big Fella and lunged at the bar, latching on to it with both hands. Wearing a bow tie, a bright white shirt, and a doorman uniform, I began my own set of impromptu Park Avenue pull-ups right next to him.

Big Fella was a gargantuan Black man exercising on Park Avenue, at lunchtime, with no one looking, not the men in suits or the nannies pushing strollers. Not even dogs took a peep! I'd been observing his routine for weeks. No one ever looked or ventured a word his way. I had been similarly disregarded by my coworkers for weeks. The difference was that he'd made it work for him: while everyone ignored him on their way to the office desks and conference rooms, Big Fella did whatever he wanted to do. Watching him exercise his freedom outside the building had made me feel inadequate and small standing inside the building. I leaped at the crossbar to join him.

I completed one repetition. It was a long, torturous rep that was more neck stretch than pull-up. Then a hard flick in the crossbar, causing it to wobble as I held on. The Big Fella had released his grip and left me swinging from it alone. I had neglected to think that far, but I knew better: you never interrupt someone's workout in the middle of a set.

Just as my grip began to loosen, I shifted the placement of my hands and tightened my hold on the bar. I needed a second to think. I could see the perfectly manicured bushes wedged into Park Avenue's median. They crowded together, silent and unmoving, like New Yorkers glazed by disinterest at a helpless bedsheet hanging from a city clothesline. I was strong, but my weight was stronger.

I spun around and spotted Gary at the door. His lips had parted, and his bottom jaw had dropped. He seemed gripped by the fear that he'd soon witness my murder.

The Big Fella bent at the waist and laughter spilled out of his mouth. "Man, you crazy!" he bellowed. "You gon' get in trouble!"

What? I was confused; instead of being outraged by my disruption of his Park Avenue workout, he was worried about *me*. That's not the way these things are supposed to work. *I* was supposed to be worried about me, about my job, and my overall health after goading an ex-con who resembled a rhinoceros.

Then I felt humility unfurl itself over me. There was no malice in Big Fella's eyes. No resentment. I wanted it to be there, in the corners of his eyes somewhere, the same resentment I saw in my coworkers' eyes. He seemed in awe of *me*.

"Dude, what's your name?" I asked, smiling and retreating to the building's door.

"It's Bam Bam," he responded, a proud smile spreading across his face. I stopped moving.

"Nah, no way," I said, throwing my hands up and shaking my head in amused resistance. "I'm not calling another man 'Bam Bam.' Hell no. What's the name on your birth certificate?"

Still smiling, he sighed and nodded. "You can call me Isaac." First he'd allowed me to take room on his crossbar and now he was letting me use his government name, which he obviously didn't prefer over Bam Bam. He was generous and unassuming, like a child. "What's *your* name?"

"Bruno." I'd taken to offering my last name when I thought it might be easier for someone to remember.

"Ohhhh, shit. Check that out. *Bruno and Bam Bam. Bruno and Bam Bam!*"

"I'm not calling you that!" I shouted. I had attached some conviction to the statement, but after a look at Isaac's luminous face, I knew it hadn't registered. I had to be okay with it. Pulling the door open, I turned back to him. "I'll see you, okay, Isaac? Next time you pass by the door, stop and say wassup, *then* do your pull-ups."

His smile was easy and his eyes soft. "Aight, Bruno. You got it."

As I ducked through the building's waiting door, I turned in time to see Isaac walking away, the trash bin rolling beside him like a sidekick.

28

THE BLOOMS

One day, the elevator door slides open at the eleventh floor, revealing a diminutive elderly couple standing on the carpet. It's Ina and Al Bloom, residents of 11A. "Helloooo, Stephen!" Mrs. Bloom says, her eyes lighting up as she steps inside. Mr. Bloom, the more reserved of the two, trudges in after her and takes his customary position behind her arm. "Hello, Stephen," he says. A soft smile raises his lips. His eyes don't meet mine. They tail off to the elevator's buttons, then the analog screen above them showing 11. This is typical of Mr. Bloom. I've learned not to make anything of his noncommittal eye contact. It's his way. And Mrs. Bloom has hers. She starts inquiring about my classes, my professors, and my writing. Mr. Bloom smilingly watches the analog screen tick away numbers as we descend to the lobby. He's listening.

The Blooms, like most residents, have a good feel for the staff members' schedules. Ms. Novak routinely comes home around nine p.m. on weekdays and knows that she can tap into Sean for building gossip. She knows that he works on weekdays only and that there's little traffic at the door at that time. She can sap Sean dry of all the gossip he knows with little interruption. Mrs. Edelman knows that George will be at the door every day and that he'll cheerfully watch her shopping cart while she runs a quick errand around the corner. "George, can you please . . ." she says, but he reaches for the cart's handle even before she begins talking. Even housekeepers know to expect men at their usual positions throughout the building. Jan Hastings's housekeeper expects Frank to run the service elevator every morning. And every morning he places garbage bags by her service door. I picked up Frank's shift one day and didn't place the bags at her door. Jan Hastings's housekeeper called the lobby and asked, "Where's Frank?" She knew Frank had called out because the bags weren't folded neatly at her service door. It wasn't the building's responsibility to supply garbage bags, mind you, but Frank had aways done the poor millionaire's housekeeper that favor, so I went running up there with garbage bags. After years of seeing the same men at the same positions inside the building, people have expectations.

The Blooms are eager to see me. I've been running the passenger elevator for several months and they've taken a liking to seeing me there. They always say hello and I say hello, the usual stuff, but then we talk. We've talked from the eleventh floor to the lobby and taken our conversations across the lobby's marble floor to the vestibule and beyond the man at the door. We've talked past the door and onto the pavement underneath the building canopy, where we share smiles and laughs and where I abandon my post yet again. It's also where Mrs. Bloom places a gentle hand on my forearm and where Mr. Bloom makes eye contact. The Blooms are Jewish, kind, and wealthy, like many Park Avenue couples, but they're distinct from the rest in a very special way: they have my love.

One time, I brought Mrs. Bloom to the eleventh floor, and instead of saying goodbye, I took a step backward in the elevator and sat on the cushioned stool behind me. By then, I knew I could make demands of Mrs. Bloom's time as I would that of any other friend. She smiled and took a step backward too, lowering herself over the stool in the opposite corner. We talked for ten minutes while the overhead camera observed resident and doorman sitting across from the eleventh floor's bright hallway and plush carpet. Those corner stools were decorative and creaky and didn't facilitate long conversations, but we logged another ten minutes of use into them anyway.

Those conversations happened often during my last semesters at John Jay College. Mrs. Bloom asked me "How are things going?" every day, but not like people who ask and don't mean it. She would ask and look in my eyes, searchingly, until I offered an update on my academic and personal life. It was always disarming for me because I was a doorman and that's it. I had never allowed myself to feel like a promising student—not even a person—inside the building. I'd been trained well. Mr. Bloom stood inside the elevator in a state of amused patience whenever she unleashed enthusiasm over one of my recent triumphs. It wasn't just my academics they were interested in, they wanted to hear about my family life too. We shared a connection: they were also originally from the Bronx and had lived on the Grand Concourse when it was meant to become the Bronx's Park Avenue. It never lived up to the billing, so they moved to the real thing. It didn't matter because they loved hearing about my family in the Bronx. As she listened, Mrs. Bloom often clasped her hands under her face, which was always flush with enthusiasm. She seemed to want the elevator ride to go beyond the eleventh floor and into the clouds, just so I could share details. Giving her school updates was my favorite thing, though. She'd smile and pump her fists like the victories were hers too. I could tell by Mr. Bloom's easy smirk that he'd seen it all before. He'd seen her shower others with her unbridled joy countless times, and his contentment radiated every time.

One day in May 2013, Mr. and Mrs. Bloom stepped inside my elevator with anxious smiles, like children on Christmas morning. I smiled too. I would graduate from John Jay the following week, but the Blooms couldn't wait that long. Mrs. Bloom didn't even let me press the Down button. She pulled in for a hug and said, "Ohhh, Stephen, we're so proud of you!" Mr. Bloom walked around Mrs. Bloom, a loaded smile raising his glasses, and said, "Here you go, Stephen." "We got this for you." A gift bag dangled from his fingers. "We're *very* proud of you," he said. I had to be careful: I was still being hugged by the cooing Mrs. Bloom. I gently extended one arm, keeping the other around her, and reached for the bag. Inside was Roger Ebert's formidable *Book of Film*. Mr. Bloom had been the one to choose it as my gift; no one had to tell me: he'd been skeptical about me until I'd told him I majored in English with Honors. It was the "with Honors" part that did it for him—he'd just wanted to know I was serious. Then I'd won him over completely when I told him I minored in Film Studies. Inside the movie book's jacket was a hand-written note and a tassel. Inside the elevator were more hugs too.

Mrs. Bloom seemed to sense something was wrong during my first month at Hunter College. I'd been strangely quiet in the elevator for weeks, even avoiding her eyes. Her voice started rolling over *going* ominously in the elevator: "How are things *going*," she asked, as if pressing a stamp on an envelope. I'd press "11," then say goodbye when the elevator arrived, and watch the Blooms step onto the eleventh floor's carpet. I couldn't bring myself to tell them that my well had run dry. I'd been bringing the Blooms good news about my studies at John Jay for many months, one semester proving more triumphant than the last. There had been no reason to think the trend wouldn't continue at the MFA level. There would be reports of compelling writing daily. More hugs and smiles. More conversations stretching from the eleventh floor to the sidewalk underneath the building's canopy. More of Mrs. Bloom's small hand over my forearm. None of that had been happening.

I became increasingly disoriented as my first graduate semester crept forward. Anguished at my inability to offer the Blooms any good news, I avoided their eyes and instead focused on the elevator's control panel during our rides. I didn't even allow for small talk. Nothing, only hellos and goodbyes like with other residents. The analog numbers changed with every passing floor, and I felt the distance between us grow until, after many weeks, our friendship bent under the weight of convention and politeness. I'd greet them, take them to the eleventh floor or the lobby, then wave goodbye as they walked out of the elevator. There may have been a smile on Mrs. Bloom's face during this time. I don't know; I wasn't looking at her face. I couldn't.

Instead of waiting for good news, the Blooms made it happen. One morning, Mrs. Bloom stepped in front of Mr. Bloom and, with the conviction of someone knowing she had to carry the load for everyone else, said, "We'd love to have you over for dinner to watch a documentary on August Wilson. We think you would get so much from his story." I felt low and undeserving, like I'd betrayed an arrangement, but I said "Yes, thank you so much" anyway. I was not used to being saved and didn't like the feeling of it, but I was in need of it—a rescue—and I wouldn't turn it down.

The night of the screening, I exited Hunter College and walked along Park Avenue to the building. Sean greeted me at the door like he'd expected to see me. "I'll let them know you're here, Stephen," he said after opening the front door. Ramón didn't say anything all the way to the eleventh floor and grunted something like a goodbye when the door opened. The Blooms met me at the door with the happiest look on their faces. It was almost like we hadn't scheduled the night, like my standing at their front door was a great surprise.

There was a plate piled with sandwiches, a dozen chilled Amstel Lights, and a room just for reading and meaningful television viewing. I could feel Mrs. Bloom's eyes on my face as I watched clips of actors embodying Wilson's vision. I loved her for that. I knew she was trying to discern my thoughts on the documentary as they happened.

"Wow, August Wilson sure does smoke a lot," I said. Mr. Bloom laughed and held his chest as if trying to keep from hurting himself. Mrs. Bloom laughed too, but also shook her fist in a mock threat. "But what do you think?" she asked, edging forward in the love seat she shared with Mr. Bloom.

I turned to her and smiled. "I love it, Mrs. Bloom. He's this guy, not tryna be more than average or bigger than his old neighborhood, while creating art *about* the neighborhood." I watched the action on-screen, at the clips of Pittsburgh and the staging of Wilson's plays. "It's all pretty inspiring." She just wanted to hear it, the good news, so I shared it with her.

Mrs. Bloom clasped her hands in front of her face and said, "Yaaay!" She had wanted me to glean something, anything, from the documentary, and if it hadn't been a film on August Wilson, the Blooms would've found some other means to cultivate my blossoming love for the arts. I'm sure of it. Maybe they saw themselves in me, having walked the

same Bronx streets I'd walked. Or maybe they seeded the paths they
walked.

Mr. Bloom spent most of the night sitting in the far corner of the
room with a beer in hand and contentment written into his face. He
knew Mrs. Bloom would articulate the sentiments they shared.

At the end of the night, the Blooms will walk with me the length
of their apartment to their front door, and there we'll chat and say our
goodbyes. I'll tell Mr. and Mrs. Bloom that watching the August Wilson documentary was great, and I'll thank them so much. I won't be so
sure that it made me a better graduate student, but I'll be sure about
everything else: spending time in their home in my own clothes has
outfitted me in agency and freedom; I was not a doorman in their apartment, I was someone they believe me to be, a student, a writer, an artist.
We got close and that's not supposed to happen between resident and
doorman. *Don't get close*, remember? I'll speak delicately because that's
how you share hard truths with those you love.

I'll go to class tomorrow and be completely lost listening to Poet
muse about Oreos and her bare feet while Northwestern slaps everyone with dollar signs except for me, but I won't tell the Blooms about
it tomorrow. They won't press me about it either. Soon they'll invite
me to dinner, but this time at an Italian restaurant several blocks from
the building. We'll eat and laugh. Mr. Bloom will call me Ernest Hem-
ingway, and I'll laugh uncomfortably. Mrs. Bloom will ask if I want
dessert. I'll say no because I've taken so much already from them and
given them nothing. She will ignore my "No, thank you." A cart with
two levels of desserts will get wheeled out, and I won't know what to
say because I've only seen stuff like that happen to people in movies.
The Blooms won't want dessert, apparently, because they won't even
look at the cart; they'll smile, waiting on me to choose. Okay, let's see. I
know two Italian desserts, the cannoli and tiramisu, but from the looks
of the rolling shrine to the Italian sweet tooth, there are more than just
two desserts. More like two dozen Italian desserts. I'm dying here! The
waiter will save me. He'll see me surveying the first level, then the

second, as if I know what I'm looking for, and gently say, "We have a great tiramisu." I want to hug this man. I'll say, "Oh yes, that sounds great," and he'll wheel away the dessert shrine. I'll soon tell the Blooms to give me some time, I'm working hard, and it's the truth—I want desperately to show them good grades and celebrated pieces of writing, any success I could find because they've championed me. They've lifted me up. The Blooms will not want to hear any of that. "Oh, stop that, Stephen," Mrs. Bloom will say. They'll both tell me they are proud of me *already*. They'll tell me how lucky my future wife will be, how proud she'll be. Mrs. Bloom's hand will be on my forearm as she speaks the words, and I'll smile, wondering how we made the leap to science fiction. In later years, Mr. Bloom will pass away, and Mrs. Bloom will move to San Francisco, allowing another friendly couple to move into apartment 11A, but through a moment of grace and kindness to a doorman with dreams, the Blooms will continue giving.

29

THE BLUES

Another Tuesday porter shift today, this one with complications. The last of the leaves on the building's trees fell overnight, and it made the job of hosing the sidewalk take longer than usual. I couldn't let the leaves stick to the wet sidewalk because that's unacceptable. Nobody wants to see wet leaves stuck to the pavement: not the residents, not the super, not Lorenzo. Lorenzo least of all. When he sees leaves stuck to the sidewalk, he warns the super of the impending risk that they'll dry on the sidewalk and leave the imprint of, outrageously, leaves. You and I might laugh about it, but you should see Mr. Atwell after Lorenzo has delivered his wet leaf report. Mr. Atwell sputters around looking for maintenance men who will handle the leaf situation. Mr. Atwell only sees the work, not the man, so Lorenzo is the apple of his eye. Take a poll at the job: Who's the biggest piece of shit human you know? Ten times out of ten, the answer will be Lorenzo. And mostly because he covers by being such a great doorman. If he was a terrible doorman, or at least a mediocre one like Sean, Mr. Atwell might see him clearly then. A few lies told, a few intentionally misplaced items, and boom, Mr. Atwell might think the same as we do, like *Damn, this guy really is a terrible person*. It's wishful thinking, however, because Mr. Atwell treats Lorenzo like he's the standard-bearer of doormen. You've never seen a doorman occupy a vestibule the way he does. Lorenzo stands there with his hands clasped behind his back like he regrets turning down the job at Buckingham Palace.

This morning, I made sure not one leaf remained stuck to the sidewalk when I hosed, not with Lorenzo getting Mr. Atwell on speed dial. I wasn't about to let a wayward leaf sabotage my efforts. I even went two lanes into the street to hose a few stragglers around the corner where they couldn't be seen. I disrupted the flow of cars on the street and got cursed out in so many different languages simultaneously, and let me tell you: all that vitriol, delivered as it was, in fleeting bursts, was exhilarating.

That's when I fucked up, when I started having fun while working. Hosing took longer than it should have and cut into my lunch hour, leaving me only forty-five minutes.

I've got to hustle my ass to the deli if I'm going to make up for lost time. I forgot this week's *New Yorker*—shit, just realized that. Oh well, it's not like I go to Juan Valdez to read. I'm there for La Colombiana, the beautiful married woman behind the counter. She's become my weekly escape, my big-booty Tuesday fix. Once a week, we dance around the burning bush of innuendo and suggestion and, too cowardly to leap in with her, I walk away satisfied that I felt anything at all. I don't care about her, I care only for myself, and seeing her relieves me of my obligations to myself. It makes me feel lighter and wanted, even.

Fuck. I just opened my wallet and saw nothing but creases and folds. I forgot to get cash last night. It's a punch in the gut. I prefer using cash for small purchases like coffee and lunch; that way, I don't have to use a bank app to sort through thirty-seven debit card transactions from the last two days. I can accept this loss, a small one, and pay for my salad with my card, but I've done enough losing. I decide to add the ATM to my route, complicating matters further: the deli is across the street from the building on East Fifty-Eighth; the bank is across the street from Juan Valdez on East Fifty-Seventh; I'll have to go to the bank, then return to the deli, then turn back toward Juan Valdez. Fine, I'll do it. Entertaining possibilities with a married woman is totally worth the trouble.

I walk out of the building's service entrance and spot Isaac down the block. There's no way to miss him. He's wearing the Doe Fund T-shirt that every street cleaner wears. He's also wearing his knit cap at an angle, a shot of flair that I appreciate, but that's not how I distinguish him from everyone else on the street. Isaac is built like a trolley; he's stocky and wide and meanders around with very little sense of urgency. It's like when he nonchalantly goes through pull-up workouts by himself on Park Avenue, only now he's standing by himself on Fifty-Eighth and Lex. It's something you see in the Bronx, where a guy can stand on a corner for hours and it somehow makes sense. Isaac stands slumbering in the middle of the sidewalk like a buoy in a writhing sea of pedestrians. The wheeled trash bin and its yellow utility belt are there too, but he's not moving, not even slowly. I get closer and realize he's staring intently at something across the street.

The pedestrians across the street are walking past Victoria's Secret's display windows. They're in Isaac's line of sight, but he doesn't seem to notice. Isaac is doing the George thing: he's not watching people; he's staring through them.

I have to get my food and eat and enjoy what's left of my lunch hour. Forty minutes. Not too shabby considering it's a stolen gift to myself: each man at the building is allowed twenty minutes for lunch, which I always thought was criminal. I don't have time to wash my Tupperware before getting back to work. I don't have time to brush my teeth. Ridiculous. I never did anything about it until I realized that on Tuesdays, I move around the building completing my tasks unsupervised. I hose the sidewalk, mop the landings on each floor, and finish by polishing all the brass. It's the same every Tuesday, and I've been doing it so long Mr. Atwell stopped checking on me, so I simply complete my tasks early and steal away for an hour break. Today, it's not an hour, sure, it's forty minutes, but hey, that's still twice as long as the guys at the job will enjoy for lunch, and I'm fine with that.

Nearing Isaac, I coach myself: *Say hey and dassit.* I have to keep things short and sweet if I'm going to save my lunch break with La Colombiana.

The pulsing deep red of the Don't Walk signal at the corner goes

static, and a herd of cars roll onto Lexington Avenue. Isaac doesn't
notice any of it. I follow his line of sight but see nothing noteworthy.
It's just a stretch of buildings on Lex. Tall swaths of glass and steel.
Buildings on top of buildings. Nothing out of the ordinary as far as I
can tell. Isaac is simply spaced out.

"Isaac, wassup, man?" I ask, arriving at his side. He whirls around
and his face says it all: droopy eyelids, a lazy bottom lip, and sagging
cheeks. It's the same vacant look I've seen on him when he walks past
the building's front door with his garbage can. It's the face he wears
when his system is in energy-saver mode. He just needs some stimula-
tion to get him going.

I suddenly see the spark of recognition in his eyes. "Brunoooo!" he
cries out in joy. "Waddup, man?" Isaac is fine.

"I'm good, buddy—thanks. Jus' on my way to the ATM." I respond.
"I'm guessing you caught the Jets game last night."

"Yeah, you know I did! They didn't look good, though. They need
a quarterback bad!" His eyes suddenly grow wide with excitement.
"Bruno, you want a piece of my cheesesteak sandwich?"

"I—I . . ." I stammered, warming up to speak.

It doesn't take much for me to fail at dieting, and a cheesesteak sandwich can certainly compel my white flag. The problem is Isaac's pitch:
it's not even remotely tempting. He's offered me food while empty-
handed and standing totally still. He's not gesturing in the direction
of a restaurant or reaching for a plate of food. Instead, his hands hang
at his sides as he stands there, familiar as ever in his navy-blue sweater,
smiling. No sandwich anywhere. Isaac is offering imaginary food. I
can't do playtime today; there's no time.

"Nah, I'm good, Isaac," I say, shaking my head. I pat my belly. "Trying to lose some weight. Gonna buy a salad today."

"Oh, come on, man! You not gonna break bread with me?"

I'm surprised that *he's* surprised. He's offering food that I can't see!
There's still not the slightest motion to a nearby deli or the presentation of a plate with a sandwich atop. I cannot reconsider. I pat him on

the mountain range he calls a back and say, "Nah, but you enjoy your sandwich, okay?" I don't know if I mean it or if I'm being an asshole. I guess since I didn't call it a "pretend sandwich" I'm in the clear. I try rebounding, nonetheless. "See ya later, buddy." I have to get to the ATM!

One last look at Isaac. His arms hang limp at his sides and his head slumps over his chest like a saddlebag. Isaac's heart is broken.

I've gone to the ATM. With cash in my wallet, I'm going over the last stretch of my route in my head: I'll return to East Fifty-Eighth, hit the gourmet deli on the Victoria's Secret side of the street and—yeah, that sounds right—I'll retrace my steps right back to Fifty-Seventh and bring the salad to Juan Valdez! I'll eat lunch and order a cappuccino. I'll be happy to see La Colombiana, and she'll be happy to see me and steam the milk for my next latte. Yeah, that's what I'll do.

I turn onto East Fifty-Eighth Street and spot Isaac again. I'd forgotten about him. His wheeled garbage bin is where I saw it last, in the middle of the sidewalk, but he's standing on the curb, his back turned to me, and in great distress. He's sniffling and wiping his nose on the sleeve of his dark blue sweater. Why is he crying? He pulls something out of his hand and tosses it into the street. Is that bread? It is. Scattered across the street are more pieces of bread. Traffic has flattened them and now they look like white lily pads over the blacktop.

I've never seen Isaac in distress and much less like this, where he's adding to litter instead of sweeping it away. His stoic demeanor, in great contrast to my stormy personality, had always grounded me and brought me comfort, but not today. His vulnerability is not okay with me today. He's forcing me to choose: Will I stay or will I go? I've seen people cry on the street—the city will pull you into its gears and crank away despite your feelings—and I haven't felt much lately.

Isaac isn't a stranger, sure, but it's not like he's ever crashed on my couch. He doesn't even have my phone number. Still, I feel for him, and doing so irritates me. I could walk by him, and he'd never know. He's on the curb with his back to me. The way he's crying—I think it's safe to call it "weeping" at this point.

Fucking Isaac. The pangs of obligation to him keep me anchored to that spot on the sidewalk. Of all the spots to pull a friend emergency, he picks the corner down the block from the job; residents know the blue uniform and know it belongs in the building, not loitering next to a shoe store. Right now, I'm standing idle in my blues a few yards from the building and staring at a distraught giant ex-con with an uncomfortable nickname. I don't belong here.

I glance at the intersection teeming with pedestrians waiting for the Walk signal. This shit don't look right, I think to myself. It's just like when he's doing pull-ups on Park Avenue and nobody notices! Isaac, who's built like a cinder block, is crying while tossing bread at the street. How am I the only one seeing this?

I don't know what Isaac is crying about, but here's my chance at a clean exit. Sooner or later, his display of affliction will attract someone who cares about people, someone similar to who I used to be, and I'll be cast as his caretaker. Even if he's one of the sweetest souls on this side of heaven, I'd prefer to avoid that task. It would eat up my lunch hour. I have to go.

A hand grabs my forearm. I track the length of the arm to the face. It belongs to a small, middle-aged lady. She shrinks into my side as if looking for cover. From Isaac? "Is he going to clean that up?" she whispers, pointing at the street. The entire city is conspiring against me and my lunch break with La Colombiana.

I bristle. Her tone is familiar. It's perky but expectant. She's looking for a specific answer, and it's built into her question, like when you shake your hands *No, I'm just passing through*, but the ball is tossed into your chest anyway because, tough luck, you're in the game now.

The lady lives on Park Avenue. She's not a resident at 411, but she doesn't have to be. I know she gets mail on Park Avenue. The silk naval-themed Hermès scarf. The quilted waist-length jacket. The hem of her slacks falling flat and uninterrupted over patent leather Prada sneakers. Her hair is telling stories too. She's got that Jackie O hairdo, and it's fresh—lots of volume with every strand in place.

"Clean *what* up, ma'am?" I ask, staring into the side of her head. She's still looking at the street, not at me.

The lady assumes I know the reason behind Isaac's crying. She assumes I know Isaac and that I'm responsible for him. I don't know why. "Take a look," she says, pointing at the street. "See for yourself." I walk away from her and step up to the edge of the sidewalk next to Isaac.

About a foot from the curb lies a pigeon pancaked into the street. The feathers are matted together in a wispy mass. I don't see any blood. No beak or feet. The wings are spread though. Fully extended. The pigeon must have caught sight of a tire surging in like a rubber tsunami and spread its wings to fly away. It wasn't fast enough. Now it's a time stamp, a dried mass of ashen feathers on a no-name street in Midtown East.

"Bruno," Isaac moans over my shoulder as he drags his feet to the curb. "I was feedin' the birds and then a car drove ova this one." He runs his nose over his sweater's sleeve and with a long drag clears his nostrils.

"Maybe he should pick up the poor thing," the lady whispers from behind my other arm.

"What the f . . ." I say, startled by the lady's sudden return to my side.

The three of us stand on the curb staring at the flattened pigeon: Isaac, myself, and Lady Avenue of the House of Park.

Lady Avenue ties me to Isaac because we're both wearing blues. I'm wearing the building's blue maintenance uniform and Isaac's wearing the Doe Fund's blue uniform. I don't know who she is, but I recognize the presumptive power she holds over me, and I bristle.

"Hey, Isaac, how are you?" I ask. It's a seemingly pointless question because I know exactly how he is: Isaac is mourning a dead pigeon. I ask the question anyway because I want Lady Avenue to know that checking on Isaac matters more to me than paying mind to her concerns.

"I'm okay, Bruno," he moans. "Just . . . the bird . . ."

"I know, Isaac," I say while tapping Lady Avenue's forearm. "Mind stepping over here?" I ask her. *Here* is just a few paces farther away from

Isaac. She nods eagerly. I turn away from the curb, and Lady Avenue follows me to our original spot behind Isaac. It's just me and Lady Avenue again. I don't want Isaac to see or hear anything. I want to shield Isaac.

"Listen . . ." An unusual poise overtakes me. My voice chills as I, like one of my wild ancestors, struggle to make peace with decorum. "You can go now," I tell Lady Avenue.

"Excuse me?" she says incredulously.

"Leave."

"But the bird!"

"The bird is dead."

"Right, so he should—"

"So . . . it's not going to be anything *but* dead from now on. And since there's always so much traffic on this street, in a few minutes it'll be little crumbs of dead. In an hour, a few flakes of dead. Tomorrow you won't see any more dead. But you see the big guy there?" I ask and gesture to the gargantuan man whose shoulders look like a painted horizon. "*He's* alive."

"I know, but—"

"But nothing. He's alive, and he's not okay right now. I want him to be okay, and you're not helping, so you need to leave. I'll take it from here."

"You'll make sure the pigeon—"

"Fuck . . . the pigeon."

Lady Avenue of the House of Park departs, her perfectly tailored pants barely creasing at the knee with each step. My lunch hour is down to just thirty minutes now. I take my derailed ass to the curb and stand with Isaac.

It feels like church, like when I bow my head and close my eyes in prayer, only I'm on East Fifty-Eighth bowing my head over a bird's remains. Slowly, I turn my head and peek at Isaac. He's in the last stages of a good cry.

Then it hits me. The flattened bread. The dead pigeon. Isaac crying over that dead pigeon. It's all my fault. I pat Isaac on his shoulder in the hopes of consoling him. While he mourns, I have time to lather myself with guilt. All that bread Isaac was flipping at the birds on the street? It was bread from the sandwich he'd offered me when I was on my way to the bank. There *had* been a cheesesteak sandwich. He had been so distraught by my rejection of his offer that, in his grief, he began feeding pigeons with it and one of them didn't see the car coming.

I'll eventually tug at Isaac's arm and point out the obvious, that you can't feed pigeons in traffic, but that'll come later. Right now, Isaac is crying over a pigeon's death—crying *over* a pancaked pigeon—and it's all my fault. Making things right with my friend Isaac is all that matters. The building isn't going anywhere.

I know a sure-fire way to get the job done.

"Hey, um," I say, tapping him on the forearm. "Bam . . . Bam." I don't look him in the face as I say it, though. It's my first time, and it's uncomfortable as fuck. It's the kind of thing you have to work up to. I'm looking at the pigeon again. A few of its feathers remain intact. There are quill feathers and a few fuzzy down feathers too.

"Hey!" Bam Bam says. "You called me . . ." The glint has returned to his eyes. "Take half of my cheesesteak sandwich, bro!"

I stare at him, dumbfounded. I'm still gung-ho about cheering him up, sure, but now I *have* to know: Where is Isaac hiding cheesesteak sandwiches?

"Come on, Bruno!" he pleads. "Break bread with me!"

"Alright, Bam Bam. Let's see this sandwich."

Bam Bam's eyes grow wide with excitement. He pumps a fist. "Alriiight, my man Bruno!" he shouts. Bam Bam seems to soften and shrink under the weight of an immense joy.

He turns from the curb and walks to his garbage bin. *You gotta be kidding me,* I think to myself. "You'll love it," he says. His meaty arm extends past my head as he gestures behind us. "I bought it from the falafel guy up there on Third," he says.

"The falafel guy on Third," I repeat. A falafel guy making Philly cheesesteak sandwiches on Third Avenue? I look up the block to Third and don't see a guy fitting that description. Isaac tugs at the garbage liner and pulls it over the opposite side. "You shoulda seen him make it, Bruno!" he said. "The guy is legit! He put the cheese and it melted, and it looked so good!"

Bam Bam bends at the waist and dunks his entire torso into the mouth of the garbage can as if performing a self-baptism. I glance at the intersection. The people at the corners. The riders in the cars. No one has noticed. He straightens back out. "Hey, Bruno?" he asks. "You okay with hot sauce? You like spicy?"

"Yeah, Bam Bam. I'm okay with spicy." He dives back in.

I hear him shuffle a few items out of the way. Then a break in the action. A hand grabs the lip of the garbage can and he pulls himself up. You should see the smile on his face as he stands cradling an aluminum-foiled hero.

They were always there, in his rolling garbage bin. Bam Bam stores cheesesteak sandwiches in the garbage.

"Here you go," he says, offering me a sandwich with his other arm extended at his side like a magician after a magic trick. I have no answers. I shake my head and smile. I never saw Bam Bam coming.

I can't bring myself to reach for the sandwich. Taking a step closer, Bam Bam says, "Don't be scared, Bruno. Watch." With his free hand he unwraps the aluminum foil and begins the delicate process of pulling the wax paper away from the sandwich. It is the most horrifying glop of sauce, meat, and bread I have ever seen. The careful arrangement of ingredients, if it ever existed, is gone. "Go ahead, Bruno! Tear off a piece! But just a piece. We're down to one sandwich, and I gotta eat too." Philly cheesesteak sandwiches *a la basura*.

The sandwich is cold. There are chunks of meat and cheese on the pavement. I've pulled at the sandwich and come away with only a handful of soggy bread, exposing a flap of hanging cheesesteak. Bam Bam laughs. I laugh too. There's a tumble of bread, meat, and cheese on the ground, but Bam Bam is happy, and if Novak or Geller catches me out here, it's worth my job because I'm happy too.

Bam Bam and Bruno, Bruno and Bam Bam. We're on the corner
of Fifty-Eighth and Lex with our backs against Steve Madden's glass
exterior. Bam Bam has a foot against the glass, so I lean back and put a
foot against the glass too. It's really the only way to eat a cheesesteak
sandwich with your ex-con maintenance buddy.

This is the last time I'll ever see Bam Bam. I'll become agitated
weeks later when I see another street cleaner walk past 411's front entrance for a third consecutive day. I'll think, Shit, maybe Bam Bam has
a new route. On the fourth day, the new guy, a dwarf by comparison,
will stop in front of the building and do his job. He'll sweep up garbage
and dump it into the bin and spray the base of the streetlamps and tidy
things up, and it'll piss me the fuck off because he's not Bam Bam doing
pull-ups. So I'll walk out of the building, this time without a word to
my coworkers, and I'll ask the street cleaner, "Hey, what happened to
Bam Bam?"

"Bam Bam got his third strike, bro," he'll say, and I'll grow sad, not
understanding how the purest soul I ever met had any strikes against
him at all.

It's our last day together. A slew of cars pass over the dead pigeon.
A dump truck too. They don't stop for anyone. It's a quarter to one, but
with the clouds and the light breeze it feels much later, like a cluster of
lit windows at dusk. I'm done with my half of the sandwich, but not Bam
Bam, not even close. He's taking his time with it. He breaks off pieces of
the cheesesteak sandwich, lifts each chunk over his head, and gazes at
it longingly before dropping it into his waiting mouth like a child with
his heart on full display.

He eventually finishes the sandwich and says, "Mmm, that was
yummy," and slaps at his fingers.

Bam Bam and I stand there watching the intersection for thirty
minutes.

"Hey, Bam," I say.

"Wassup, Bruno."

"You thinkin' about scooping up that pigeon, though?"

Cars stop at the red light, releasing a torrent of pedestrians onto the crosswalk. The construction crew mills about their work site, laughing. A mailman stands tucked away in a building's shadow and smokes. The city crackles through its lunch break while Bam Bam and I lean against a corner store, reveling in our own.

ACKNOWLEDGMENTS

To my mentor Kathryn Harrison, thank you. I almost walked away from the graduation ceremony thinking I'd done enough. Thanks for pulling me to the side, then pulling again after six months passed without a peep from me. I'll never, ever stop being grateful for your stubborn belief in me. You are my hero.

To my agent, Molly Atlas, with the best name in the business. Few memories shine as bright as our first meeting when you pressed your finger into my thirty-five pages and asked for more. That was seven years ago. Give Ali Ehrlich in publicity a high five for me. Thanks for being in my corner.

Adenike Olanrewaju. Your care and compassion—the way you treated my story like an infant placed in your hands has affected me deeply. I am in awe of your instincts, which should be studied. You have been a perfect steward. Let's do this again sometime.

I'm grateful to the team at HarperCollins for their kindness and enthusiasm. Olivia McGiff for the bomb-ass front cover. Kate D'Esmond and Katie O'Callaghan for paving the road to launch. Zaynah Ahmed for her perseverance. Liz Velez for being the glue. It's not every day you meet a family that gives you unlimited access to their snacks.

A special word of thanks to Richard Perez, who told me over and over, "Write yourself into existence." I hope this works. Take a moment to pat yourself on the back, Richard. You're golden.

Thank you, Allison Pease, for being there when I came running.

"Fuck beauty," is what you said. You made me feel like an absolute bitch, so I made sure my second year at graduate school was different. Thanks for the kick in the ass. I'm still feeling it.

I wish to honor the memory of the late Louise DeSalvo. I was walking through the cleverly named New Building at John Jay College when she called, inviting me to the Hunter College MFA. It was my first time speaking with royalty.

My brother, Hansel Castillo. You have believed in me and spoken life over me since you scooped me up at that strip mall in Puerto Rico twelve years ago. *Mi hermano del alma, te amo.* Steak and spaghetti— soon.

A word for my childhood friend Timothy Lopez. I pray this book is a small measure of justice for you. I thought of her and you often while writing it. Love you, bro.

Enrique Rivera, I'm glad you're back. You're an inspiration even if your picks are faulty. Love you, man.

Rest in peace, Dan Wanless. Thank you for always smiling with your eyes.

Team Handsome is Caleb Jordan Lee, Caren Khachatrian, Picasso Aponte. George U. Won. These gentlemen kept me grounded during many storms. They are my brothers.

I took a break from editing in late 2023 to crash an awards ceremony with Jeffrey Reale and Carlton Moore. Thanks for your friendship, boys. Let's do it again.

To my sister Gracie Marie Bruno: I am grateful for your enthusiasm and support. It means the world to me. I'm so very proud of who you are and what you've accomplished. I love you.

Rachel Isabel Bruno. *Atelita.* My baby sister. My description of your drawing notwithstanding, you have the heart of an artist. Find your method and your medium. Quickly. The world needs you. I love you, Little Punk Face.

Gamaliel Marrero and Gino Caropreso displayed blind faith, support, and trust in me when I was at my lowest. I'll never forget.

I am indebted to the New York City educators who poured themselves empty to bring me a classical education in the Bronx. Marlene Losak of P.S 246; Anne Piotrowski, Lenny Plastino, and the other PACE Academy teachers at M.S. 118. Bread and circuses abound while I carry what they bestowed upon me.

Ayo, John Jay College. Did you ever give the new building a name? Who knows. Who cares. I hope I've made you proud.

People talk a whole lotta shit about the creative writing MFA. I needed it, and badly. Was it easy or fun? Hell, no. But that's where I found my voice. That's where I met Kathryn. Thank you, Hunter College.

Robin Kemper and Jonathan Rizzo were my only friends at Hunter College. It's their turn next.

To the men at The Buildings: Nick Kolgjeraj, Mike Martinez, Noel Kane, Paul Pacelko, Anthony Manfredi, George Lisojo, Andrew Trinceri, Manny Aguilar, Isa Idrizi, Kenny Burdier, and Ricardo Sofiste. You watched me grow up. I'm proud to have called you my coworkers the last twenty years. I like to think some of us are friends.

A white-gloved word of thanks to the residents at both Park Avenue buildings. I had a job because you could afford doormen, and with that job, I paid my tuition at John Jay College. I'm grateful to all of you, even the heavy hitters. I'll try to stay on at The Building for as long as I can.

To the Konigsbergs—Harvey, Marilyn, and Eric—and Margaret Stohl. Your warmth and support is humbling. Thank you for setting a table for me. Thank you for celebrating with me.

Mrs. Green, your kindness, joy, and generosity has left a mark on my heart that cannot be undone. I honor and cherish Mr. Green's memory. I hope I've made you proud.

The NYC salsa community has been a blessing. I'm so happy all of you came around when you did. ¡La salsa vive!

Whenever I needed a break (a drink), I went to the Milton on the Upper East Side. Mark and Tommy, thanks for taking my money!

Kingsbridge Heights and the rest of the Bronx, I love you. Will you love you, too? If you do, the bookstores will come.

New York City taught me everything I know. Ayo NYC: you're a landscape and a timeline, and I'm still here trying to rep you like a native son should.

The United States of America. I don't know of any other place that could've offered me the opportunities I needed to make things right. To quote the masterpiece *Wedding Crashers*, "I'm not perfect, but who are we kidding, neither are you, and you wanna know what? I dig it." What a country.

Dear Grace Isabel Bruno, I've worked hard to bring you this bit of good news. I will rest for a moment, then bring you some more. I love you, Mami.

Papi, you passed along your toughness and your love of stories and animals. I'm forever grateful. I never meant to cause you any pain or distress through the publication of this book. I've forgiven you. Now you forgive you. Love you, Pa.

ABOUT THE AUTHOR

STEPHEN BRUNO is a native New Yorker who grew up scribbling words in marble notebooks and playing sports on the streets of the Bronx. He's a graduate of CUNY Hunter College's MFA program. *Building Material* is his first book. Stephen resides in New York City where he can still be found engaged in poetry and movement in the form of salsa dancing, which he loves.